*W*orldwide websites of

 ## The New Life Mission

Please find your vernacular websites below.
You can download Christian e-books and request Christian books for free.
Feel free to visit our websites below right now!

A
www.nlmafghanistan.com
www.nlmafrikaans.com
www.nlmalbania.com
www.nlmamharic.com
www.nlmangola.com
www.nlmarabemirates.com
www.nlmarabic.com
www.nlmargentina.com
www.nlmarmenia.com
www.nlmaruba.com
www.nlmaustralia.com
www.nlmaustria.com

B
www.nlmbahamas.com
www.nlmbahrain.com
www.nlmbangladesh.com
www.nlmbelarus.com
www.nlmbelgium.com
www.nlmbengali.com
www.nlmbenin.com
www.nlmbhutan.com
www.nlmbolivia.com
www.nlmbotswana.com
www.nlmbrasil.com
www.nlmbriton.com
www.nlmbrunei.com
www.nlmbulgalia.com
www.nlmburkinafaso.com
www.nlmburundi.com

C
www.nlmcameroon.com
www.nlmcanada.com
www.nlmcebuano.com
www.nlmchichewa.com
www.nlmchile.com
www.nlmchin.com

www.nlmchina.com
www.nlmcolombia.com
www.nlmcongo.com
www.nlmcostarica.com
www.nlmcotedivoire.com
www.nlmcroatia.com
www.nlmczech.com

D
www.nlmdenmark.com
www.nlmdioula.com
www.nlmdominica.com
www.nlmdrcongo.com
www.nlmdutch.com

E
www.nlmecuador.com
www.nlmegypt.com
www.nlmelsalvador.com
www.nlmequatorialguinea.com
www.nlmethiopia.com

F
www.nlmfinland.com
www.nlmfrance.com
www.nlmfrench.com

G
www.nlmgabon.com
www.nlmgeorgian.com
www.nlmgerman.com
www.nlmgermany.com
www.nlmghana.com
www.nlmgreek.com
www.nlmgrenada.com
www.nlmguatemala.com
www.nlmgujarati.com

H
www.nlmhaiti.com
www.nlmhindi.com
www.nlmholland.com
www.nlmhonduras.com
www.nlmhungary.com

Turn over

Worldwide websites of

The New Life Mission

I
www.nlm-india.com
www.nlmindonesia.com
www.nlmiran.com
www.nlmiraq.com
www.nlmisrael.com
www.nlmitaly.com

J
www.nlmjamaica.com
www.nlmjapan.com
www.nlmjavanese.com

K
www.nlmkannada.com
www.nlmkazakhstan.com
www.nlmkenya.com
www.nlmkhmer.com
www.nlmkinyarwanda.com
www.nlmkirghiz.com
www.nlmkirundi.com
www.nlmkorea.com

L
www.nlmlatvia.com
www.nlmluganda.com
www.nlmluo.com

M
www.nlmmadi.com
www.nlmmalagasy.com
www.nlmmalayalam.com
www.nlmmalaysia.com
www.nlmmarathi.com
www.nlmmauritius.com
www.nlmmexico.com
www.nlmmindat.com
www.nlmmizo.com
www.nlmmoldova.com
www.nlmmongolia.com
www.nlmmyanmar.com

N
www.nlmnepal.com
www.nlmnewzealand.com
www.nlmnigeria.com
www.nlmnorthkorea.com
www.nlmnorway.com

P
www.nlmpakistan.com
www.nlmpanama.com
www.nlmperu.com
www.nlmphilippines.com
www.nlmpoland.com

www.nlmportugal.com
www.nlmportuguese.com
www.nlmprcongo.com

Q
www.nlmqatar.com

R
www.nlmromania.com
www.nlmrussia.com
www.nlmrwanda.com

S
www.nlmsaudiarabia.com
www.nlmserbian.com
www.nlmshona.com
www.nlmsingapore.com
www.nlmslovakia.com
www.nlmslovene.com
www.nlmsolomon.com
www.nlmsouthafrica.com
www.nlmspain.com
www.nlmspanish.com
www.nlmsrilanka.com
www.nlmsuriname.com
www.nlmswahili.com
www.nlmswaziland.com
www.nlmsweden.com
www.nlmswiss.com

T
www.nlmtagalog.com
www.nlmtaiwan.com
www.nlmtamil.com
www.nlmtanzania.com
www.nlmtelugu.com
www.nlmthailand.com
www.nlmtogo.com
www.nlmtonga.com
www.nlmturkey.com

U
www.nlmuganda.com
www.nlmukraine.com
www.nlmurdu.com
www.nlmusa.com

V
www.nlmvenezuela.com
www.nlmvietnam.com

Z
www.nlmzambia.com
www.nlmzimbabwe.com
www.nlmzou.com

GOD HAS *S*OLVED *A*WAY *A*LL *Y*OUR *T*RANSGRESSIONS

Dear Readers of This Book:

The New Life Mission has been sending out Free Christian Books of Rev. Paul C. Jong through the homepage (www.nlmission.com or www.bjnewlife.org) in order to preach the gospel of the water and the Spirit throughout the entire world. We have been advertising our website on well known web search engines, such as, Google and Yahoo, which is on a cost-per-click pricing basis so that many more people can come to know the gospel of the water and the Spirit. However, this method of advertising has resulted in an increase of costs for us in order to preach this genuine gospel to more souls. Moreover, the current global economic crisis has become an obstacle for our gospel ministry.

Therefore, we, the staff members of The New Life Mission, are requesting you to give our homepage address (www.nlmission.com or www.bjnewlife.org) to many people around you and bookmark our homepage on your computer so that you can access it easily while allowing us to save on these high advertising costs and still be able to preach the genuine gospel to many more souls. Your immediate cooperation will be highly appreciated as this will enable us to send out many more Free Christian Books to thirsty souls. This will be your first step in participating in this beautiful gospel ministry.

GOD HAS SOLVED AWAY ALL YOUR TRANSGRESSIONS

PAUL C. JONG

Hephzibah Publishing House

A Ministry of THE NEW LIFE MISSION
SEOUL, KOREA

God Has Solved Away All Your Transgressions
Copyright © 2013 by Hephzibah Publishing House
All rights reserved. No part of this book may be reproduced, stored in a retrieval system, or transmitted by any means without the written permission of the author.
Scripture quotations are from *the New King James Version.*

ISBN 978-89-282-3090-7
Cover Art by Min-soo Kim
Illustration by Young-ae Kim
Printed in Korea

Hephzibah Publishing House

A Ministry of THE NEW LIFE MISSION
P.O. Box 18 Yang-Cheon Post Office
Yang-Cheon Gu, Seoul, Korea

♠ Website: http://www.nlmission.com
　　　　　http://www.bjnewlife.org
　　　　　http://www.nlmbookcafe.com
♠ E-mail: newlife@bjnewlife.org

CONTENTS

Foreward

People today are struggling more than ever before because of the transgressions they commit out of their weaknesses.

It has become a common occurrence to see many pastors ruining their ministries due to the sins they commit out of their weaknesses. Although they repent and ask God for forgiveness, oftentimes they end up falling into the same sin repeatedly. Such a phenomenon is not a problem that's unique to just church leaders. It is also a problem faced by all congregations and including every church member. As a result, the Christian faith has become a laughing stock to the world and an object of their ridicule. Such a trend is confronting all church members throughout the whole wide world today. Because they were all born as a brood of evildoers from the beginning, they commit sinful acts habitually and are suffering spiritually in God's sight as a result.

Today's out of control sexual culture is throwing the whole world into a great deal of pain and confusion. Christian families are facing severe crisis due to such rampant permissive sexual culture, and religious people around the world are desperately seeking for some spiritual leader to guide them to the right way. In the United States, it's estimated that girls have their first sexual experience at the age of 16 or younger while boys have their first sexual encounter at the age of 15, and not even speaking about the rise of homosexuality. This troubling trend is not limited to the United States, but it is widespread around the world, including Korea. By the time Korean children reach their teens, most of them put in a great deal of effort into making themselves sexually attractive. Yet, their parents have no idea how to deal with their children's sexuality, to say nothing about the very disturbing rise of sexual crimes committed by teenagers.

Although many Christian parents today are trying to educate their children with the Law of God, it's not having any effect. This is true for mature, adult Christians also. Nowadays, even adult Christians are finding it next to impossible to control themselves due to their latent sinful desires, and they are sinning constantly as a result. Consequently, Christians are also being tormented by their sins and lamenting over them constantly. However, the sad reality is that this age's Christian leaders are incapable of addressing such problems of sins and transgressions satisfactorily with the gospel of the water and the Spirit.

Nevertheless, it is imperative for us to realize that there is a living God who can solve away all the problems of sins that are tormenting us. Knowing that human beings would sin against God and man alike, God has prepared the gospel of the water and the Spirit to solve this problem perfectly. By addressing all the problems of sins, God has made it possible for everyone to come into His holy presence. In particular, the Book of Leviticus in the Old Testament, in describing the sacrificial system established by God, and explains how human beings can address their transgressions when they commit them and points out the remission of sins to every human being. Truly, we cannot help but thank our merciful God.

The Book of Leviticus explains the sacrificial system through which the people of Israel received the remission of their sins when they sinned against God or man. Addressing the problem of sin for every human being, God is pointing out in detail how we can all obtain the remission of our sins by giving a specific sacrificial offering according to the requirements of the God-established sacrificial system. From both the Old and New Testaments, you can now find the Truth that has solved away the problem of your sins There is therefore only one thing remaining for you to do now, and it is receiving the remission of all your sins by believing in the justice of God and the merciful and righteous love He has fulfilled for you. ✉

Rev. Paul C. Jong

SERMON

1

You can download Rev. Paul C. Jong's Christian Books on
iPhone, iPad, or Blackberry by going to Amazon's Kindle
e-bookstore (www.amazon.com).

What Is the True Gospel?

< Leviticus 1:1-9 >

"Now the LORD called to Moses, and spoke to him from the tabernacle of meeting, saying, 'Speak to the children of Israel, and say to them: 'When any one of you brings an offering to the LORD, you shall bring your offering of the livestock—of the herd and of the flock. If his offering is a burnt sacrifice of the herd, let him offer a male without blemish; he shall offer it of his own free will at the door of the tabernacle of meeting before the LORD. Then he shall put his hand on the head of the burnt offering, and it will be accepted on his behalf to make atonement for him. He shall kill the bull before the LORD; and the priests, Aaron's sons, shall bring the blood and sprinkle the blood all around on the altar that is by the door of the tabernacle of meeting. And he shall skin the burnt offering and cut it into its pieces. The sons of Aaron the priest shall put fire on the altar, and lay the wood in order on the fire. Then the priests, Aaron's sons, shall lay the parts, the head, and the fat in order on the wood that is on the fire upon the altar; but he shall wash its entrails and its legs with water. And the priest shall burn all on the altar as a burnt sacrifice, an offering made by fire, a sweet aroma to the LORD.'"

This evening, I would like to answer the following question, "What is the gospel?" It has been three days since I came to Seoul, and today I spent some time window shopping. Perhaps that's why my sight is a bit blurry now seeing all that stuff.

When I was a little kid, I heard that you had to pay to look at the skyscrapers in Seoul, so I didn't stand in front of any tall buildings. Of course, someone was just pulling my legs, but as a clueless kid I took it seriously. So I didn't look up at any tall buildings. I was afraid that if I did, someone would come and demand money from me, saying, "Up to what floor did you look? Do you have any idea how much it costs to look at just one floor?" Soon, I found out that you didn't actually have to pay any money to look at the skyscrapers. So I looked up at what was then the tallest building in Seoul, known back then as the Building 63 for the number of floors it had, and I counted every floor all the way to the top. I got dizzy trying to count all the floors. But nevertheless, in my heart, it was clear that the Lord had blotted out all my sins. This evening I would like us to focus our minds and hearts on God, and consider together what the true gospel really is.

In these end times we find many people who believe in Jesus as their Savior. And we also know that many of them preach only the way of the Cross of Jesus for salvation. As a result, countless people claim they have become sinless with this faith. The problem, however, is that their sins still remain intact in their hearts despite believing in Jesus as their Savior. Many Christians are of the belief that although they have passed their original sin to Jesus by just believing in Him as their Savior, their personal sins still remain intact in their hearts. The greatest problem facing today's Christians is that even though they all believe in Jesus, their hearts still remain sinful. So the question, 'Is it right and proper for Christians to have a sinful heart even as they believe in Jesus? No, of course not. If anyone of them still has sin remaining in their hearts even after believing in Jesus, then it is clear evidence that this person's faith in Jesus is very wrong. I can testify about this serious situation based solely on the Scripture. Today at this hour, I would like to address the issue of why all these people misunderstand and believe in Jesus incorrectly. So, to this end, I will also explain what the true gospel is all about.

I'm sure you all know that there are also other catch phrases used by Christians as much as the word, the gospel. There probably isn't anyone among you who does not know the meaning of this word, the gospel. So then, what is the gospel? Many churches and pastors in this world regularly hold revival meetings and advertise them with free abandon. The Lord indeed commanded us to spread the gospel to the ends of the earth. So, at times Christian leaders hold revival meetings with the stated goal of transforming their respective cities into holiness.

They call for the sanctification of the city, urging their followers to evangelize all its citizens. I once saw a banner advertising such a revival meeting that read, "Let's Usher in the Season of Christ to This City!" Practically all Christian leaders nowadays are urging their followers to preach the gospel of Christ, and to expand the Kingdom of Christ to the ends of the world, and to bring about the green season of Christ, etc. all to convert non-believers into believers. The big question, however, is whether or not those who are saying these things really know what it means to preach 'the gospel' as the servants of God had preached it before. Unfortunately, there are only a handful of people that are preaching the gospel with a clear understanding of its true meaning. Although there are many Christians today, few of them actually know the meaning of the word 'the gospel' when they use it.

When we turn to Matthew 7:21, we see Jesus saying, *"Not everyone who says to Me, 'Lord, Lord,' shall enter the kingdom of heaven, but he who does the will of My Father in heaven."* What did Jesus mean here by saying, "he who does the will of My Father"? There is something that God the Father did by sending His Son to this earth, and none other than this is 'the gospel.' The work the Lord did to save mankind from their sins is - the gospel, but few people actually know and believe in this work properly. Who, then, are those who do the will of God the Father? They are the ones who believe with their hearts that God the Father has blotted out all the sins of everyone in this world once and for all by sending His Son to this earth, and who in turn, preach this gospel. Having planned His will, God the Father has saved mankind from their sins by sending His Son along with the Holy Spirit. He has through this given our hearts the conviction of our salvation. Whoever believes in and spreads 'this salvation' is the one who does the will of God the Father. The will of the Father is for human beings to believe in Jesus as their Savior - and for their hearts to become sinless. Sadly, many people are totally oblivious to this fact. It is therefore extremely important for us to first understand the etymological origin of the true gospel.

The Word "Gospel" Is "Euangelion" in Greek

This word means "good news." It is also closely related to the word *"dunamis,"* which means dynamite. When we turn to the Old Testament, we see people of Israel waging many wars. Israel was repeatedly invaded by its neighboring countries. In one of those instances, Syria invaded Samaria with its massive army and besieged the city. Because the invading Syrian army was so powerful, the Israelites couldn't dare to open the city gate to meet the Syrian army in an open field. Instead, they were held up in the city, began running out of food and trembling in fear. The situation inside the city was getting desperate day by day, and eventually a great famine broke out. Surrounded by the Syrian army, they cut off all their supplies, and unless this army withdrew, there was no way for the people in the city to replenish their dwindling supplies.

When we turn to 2 Kings 6:24-33 and 7:1-20 in the Old Testament, we read about the four lepers at the entrance of the gate of Samaria at the time. Even as war broke out in their homeland, these lepers couldn't get into the city for protection. They were beggars, shut out from the city and surviving on scraps.

These four lepers being isolated from the rest of their countrymen and through this war, were also visited by this famine. Having run out of food completely, they thought it was pointless for them to stay where they were, since they would all starve to death anyways. So, thinking that they were going to die either by starvation or by the hands of the Syrians, they decided to surrender to the Syrian army and take their chances. They gingerly went to camp of the Syrians, hoping that their lives would be spared and they would at least get some food. However, when they arrived at the enemy camp, they saw that the Syrians had all fled and no one was there. So the lepers went into the camp and filled their hungry stomachs first, but it soon dawned on them that if they did not take this wonderful news back to Samaria quickly, they would be punished. So they went back and brought the good news to Samaria.

The people inside the city, starving and trembling in fear being surrounded by the enemy and not knowing when they would die, were overjoyed to hear the good news brought by these lepers; and upon hearing this news went out and took into their hands everything the Syrians had left behind when they fled, and the famine was over. This is 'the gospel', the good news and the dynamite the Bible speaks of.

All the people living on this earth have sins in their hearts, and they are facing certain death for these sins. Yet, by sending His Son to this earth, God has blotted out all the sins of the people with the gospel of the water and the Spirit. So how could this be anything but good news? That is why the gospel is called Good News. The gospel power is like dynamite. As human beings, all of us were sinful in God's sight, and therefore all of us had to be cast into hell as the condemnation for our sins; however, God the Father has blotted out all our iniquities, each and every one of them, by sending His Son to this earth. None other than that this is 'the gospel' and the Good News.

With the massive Syrian army besieging Samaria, everyone in that city was starving to death, but God brought the noise of a great heavenly army to the Syrians, and upon hearing this, they became extremely afraid, submitted to this fear, and fled. This was all God's work, for the Bible says, *With men this is impossible, but with God all things are possible"* *(Matthew 19:26).* God had brought the ear-deafening noise of the heavenly army over the battlefield. He had made the Syrians hear the noise of a great army with chariots and horses, provoking such a great fear in them that they fled on their own, leaving everything behind. When the Syrians heard the noise of many chariots and horses nearing them, it was so great that they thought to themselves, "Israel must have formed an alliance with other countries to attack us!" So they scrambled and fled for their lives, abandoning all their belongings behind in the camp.

At that time, the people of Samaria were facing certain death from starvation, but thanks to the special work of God, they put on His grace of new life to live again. How did this come about? It came about by God's amazing noise. God had caused the Syrians to become so fearful upon hearing this noise that they abandoned their siege and fled to their country. Thanks to God, the people of Samaria had won the war without fighting even a single battle. This was all God's work, and the victory in this war was a blessing for the people living in Samaria. They had all been saved from their certain deaths, from the famine, the misery, and the curses that were ravaging them. None other than this is - the gospel.

What is the gospel? It is *"euangelion"* in Greek, and its meaning is "dynamite." The gospel has explosive power, like a dynamite that can implode a whole building leaving a pile of rubble. That is how powerful the gospel is. "Some of you might be thinking, "Who doesn't know about dynamites actual use? What's so new here? You are not the only one who knows this. I know it too." But, there is a purpose behind my discussion of dynamite.

My point is this, although there are countless people in this world committing innumerable sins, when Jesus came to this earth, He blew away all these sins of the world by being baptized by John the Baptist and shedding His blood on the Cross. The problem is, despite this fact, many people still have sins in their hearts even as they believe in Jesus. What does this problem suggest? It shows that many Christians do now know the gospel power of the water and the Spirit even as they profess to believe in Jesus as their Savior. What is so tragic about this is that even though the word "the gospel" is heard often enough these days, few people actually know the meaning of it.

Today's sermon is focused on explaining what the gospel actually is. If there is any sin left in your heart even as you profess to believe in Jesus as your Savior, then this can only mean that the gospel you believe in now is not the God-given gospel of the water and the Spirit. The Scripture includes both New and Old Testaments and is the measuring rod of salvation. It is the basis for our remission of sins. In other words, what the Scripture says God has done to save us from our sins is the basis of our salvation. The work of salvation God has done to deliver us from our sins is all written in His Word, that is, the Scripture, and therefore we can find out how our salvation has been fulfilled by turning to the Bible. Let's then look at the Scripture carefully step by step.

I have a funny story to tell you, so before delving in, allow me to spend just a few minutes to tell you about it.

A Parable about Knowledge

A young man from the countryside went to a big city to pursue his education, and upon getting a doctoral degree in philosophy, he returned triumphantly to his hometown. He had left his hometown as a young man, but by the time he was done with his graduate studies, he was already in his mid-30s. Not surprisingly, many of the people whom he knew back in the days when he was a young adult had aged also, with some of them even showing gray hair. To get to his hometown, there was a river that had to be crossed by using a boat. The boat owner was an elderly man whom this man knew from his childhood. So he greeted him warmly, and when asked about what he had been up to all these years, he told the elderly man that he had gone out to a city to study, and that he was on his way back home after completing his studies and getting a PhD in philosophy. The elderly man congratulated him, and then offered to take him across the river in his boat.

The young PhD got in the boat, and the elderly man began to row. While rowing, the elderly man thought to himself, "It's wonderful that a young man from our village went out to a big city and is now returning with a PhD. This should be celebrated by the whole town." Then the newly minted PhD said to him, "Do you know about philosophy?" "No, I don't know anything about philosophy," said the elderly man. The young PhD then said, "If you don't know philosophy, your life is one-quarter dead." Hearing this, the elderly man was taken aback and became somewhat offended. So he thought to himself, "What nonsense is this? So this guy has a PhD in philosophy, but that doesn't give him the right to insult me like this." Despite feeling slighted, however, the elderly man kept his cool and didn't show his displeasure.

After a while, the young PhD asked again, "Are you knowledgeable about literature?" The elderly man had done nothing else but rowed a boat all his life, so of course he wouldn't know a thing about literature. The young man then said, "It's really sad to live in such a wonderful environment and not know anything about literature. If you are not knowledgeable of literature, your life is as good as half dead." Hearing this, the elderly man got really upset and thought to himself, "What a jerk! I saw you when you were just a kid peeing and pooping in your pants. Now are you telling me that I am as good as half dead if I don't know anything about literature? Such an arrogant little one!" The young man was full of himself, acting very arrogantly just because he had a PhD. But, the elderly man still put up with the insults, even though by now he had no more good will towards the young man.

Swallowing the insults silently by himself, the elderly

man kept on rowing the boat. The young man then asked another question, saying, "What about astronomy? Are you knowledgeable of astronomy?" The elderly man said, "No, I don't know anything about astronomy. Since you are well-educated, you seem to enjoy boasting about your knowledge. But I know nothing about literature, nothing about philosophy, and nothing about astronomy either. I know nothing, so stop asking me these questions." "What a pity that you don't know anything about astronomy. Your life is as good as three-quarters dead," said the young PhD. 'This time, the elderly man got really upset, and began rowing erratically in anger, thinking, "That's it! I should just beat him up with my paddle. I can't stand it anymore! This guy is taking me for a fool."

Suddenly, there was a loud noise and the boat stopped dead. It had hit a shoal, and water was gushing in through a crack. At that point, the elderly man asked the young PhD, "Do you know how to swim?" "No, I don't know how to swim," answered the young man. "Oh yeah? Well, then your life might as well be completely over. You are on you own. I am out of here!"

There is a lesson in this story. What use is it for us to know everything about secular philosophy, literature, and astronomy, if we are drowning? Everything will be over if we die. If you don't know how to swim, then chances are you will drown if you fall into a river. No matter how much you might have learnt about philosophy, literature, and astronomy, what could you do with this knowledge when you are trying to cross a river? You need a boat to cross a rough river, and if you happen to fall into the river, you need to know how to swim to survive.

Many modern Christians are like the young PhD in this story. They boats are their education, but even if they earn a

PhD in theology, philosophy, or literature, what use is it to them if they do not know the gospel of the water and the Spirit and therefore cannot believe in this gospel? They will just remain as sinners despite believing in Jesus. They will not be able to escape from their sins even though they believe in Jesus. That is precisely why they are trying so hard to be washed from their personal sins through their own efforts, but all in vain.

The many pastors and theologians active in today's Christian communities are incapable of preaching the gospel of the water and the Spirit that has the power to wash away all their sins, and all the sins of their many followers. Because they do not know the gospel of the water and the Spirit that holds the righteousness of God, they cannot solve the problem of sin for their congregations with the dynamite power of this gospel. It doesn't matter how well-educated these pastors might be. Even if they have a doctorate degree in theology, literature, philosophy, or astronomy, if they cannot declare to their congregation that the Lord has taken care of all their sins with the gospel of the water and the Spirit, then they are completely useless to sinners. Those who attend a church led by such people are highly likely to end up in hell, for they still have sins in their hearts even as they believe in Jesus. Although these Christians do believe in Jesus, their faith is completely wrong. Even if they attend church faithfully, volunteer their services, respect their pastors, and make a lot of church donations, it's all totally useless.

It's absolutely important for you to attend a church where the gospel of the water and the Spirit is taught clearly, even if it's led by a pastor who might not be so knowledgeable in secular affairs. Sadly, however, there are so many churches in this age and time that simply cannot teach the remission of sins properly through the gospel of the water and the Spirit. What use is it for there to be 100 million churches in this world, if few of them are actually teaching the gospel of the water and the Spirit? This is akin to having countless doctors, but none of them can actually heal the sick. What's the point of having so many doctors then? It is therefore absolutely indispensable for us to learn about the gospel of the water and the Spirit, preach this gospel to all those who are spiritually ill, and thereby blot out their sins perfectly.

In the old days, when the Korean War broke out, it generated so much dislocation that every major city in Korea was dotted with shanty-towns filled with refugees. Many foreign aid workers came to Korea to assist the downtrodden nation. Some of these foreigners with their flights arriving late in the night were surprised to see many high-rise buildings. They had heard so much about how abjectly poor Korea was and how everyone there was starving, so they wondered why such a poor country had built so many skyscrapers. But, when they woke up the next morning and came out of the hotel, they saw that what they had thought were high-rise buildings were actually shanty-towns up in the hills. The lights they had seen from the plane were actually coming from these shanty-towns, not from any skyscrapers. In the old days, when Korea was poor, shanty-towns had sprung up on the hills, so that's how it looked in the night.

Now there are so many skyscrapers dotting the skyline in Korea that foreigners call it the new Jerusalem. Protestantism has boomed in Korea, so much so that its leaders now claim that Korea has the responsibility to evangelize the world. There are many church buildings all over the world these days, but since the gospel of the water and the Spirit is not being preached there, they are completely and utterly useless. Around the world are found myriad of Christians professing to believe in Jesus as their Savior, but the vast majority of them still have sins in their hearts even though they are very devout and attend every morning prayer service faithfully. Of the many Christians and the many nations on this earth, it's said that Korea has the most zealous of believers. It's also said that no one attends morning prayer services more diligently than Korean Christians.

Korea is the only country where churches pray publicly over the thanksgiving donations and tithes offered by the congregation. In Korea, it's common for a pastor to announce publicly during the worship service which member gave what offering for what reason, and then pray specifically for each of these givers in public. While it's laudable for the believers to thank God, it's very time-consuming to mention everyone making a thanksgiving offering like this. How is the pastor then going to find the time to preach the gospel of the water and the Spirit? The point I am trying to make here is that every church and every pastor ought to preach the gospel of the water and the Spirit to the congregation first and foremost, but sadly, this is not happening. I mentioned a few things about churches in Korea to just emphasize this point.

As mentioned, Korean Christians are extremely diligent when it comes attending morning prayer meetings. They are also very prone to cry easily while worshiping God. It is no exaggeration to say that among all the Christians around the world, Korean Christians are the biggest crybabies. They could easily cry a river during the worship service. Why, then, do these Christians still have their sins remaining intact in their hearts, unable to receive the remission of sins, when they have cried so much during the worship service and offered prayers of repentance so piously? If you are such a Christian, what's the point of attending church? You might have learned under a great pastor, but what benefit does this bring to you if your sins still remain in your heart?

Is such a spiritual phenomenon unique to Korea, or is it something that is happening around the whole world? It is a worldwide phenomenon. The spiritual decay that is plaguing the Christian community in Korea today is also happening around the world, which is the evidence showing that Satan is deceiving many people with his lies. None of us should allow ourselves to succumb to the false beliefs that Satan is offering, nor should we ever be deceived by him. To ensure this, I urge you to find out from the written Word that the righteousness of God is indeed revealed in the gospel of the water and the Spirit, and I hope and pray that with this discovery, you will receive the many blessings God is offering you.

It is ok for us not be knowledgeable of philosophy. Who cares if we are ignorant of philosophy? We are still able to think clearly and argue for our position effectively. What does it matter if we are not well-versed in literature? While we may not be able to express our thoughts as well as novelists and poets, all of us can still appreciate literature when we come across a compelling story or a beautiful poem. Even though you may not be gifted to express your thoughts as beautifully as a Wordsmith, this should not pose an obstacle for you to carry on with your life. You don't need to go to college to appreciate literature or ponder philosophically about life. You can learn about them while tilling the fields. Although work is hard on everyone, it is not only a means of making a living, but also a way to get a sense of fulfillment to your life and appreciate its beauty.

To your life, labor is much more profoundly meaningful than any literature or philosophy you can learn in school. Even if you can't express your thoughts in writing, it does not mean that you are ignorant of literature. What about astronomy then? Do you consider yourself completely clueless when it comes to astronomy? I'm sure that when we were kids, many of us looked up the sky on a summer night and counted the stars until we fell asleep. Most of us probably know at least a couple of constellations, such as the Big Dipper. So we are not entirely ignorant of astronomy either. Besides, no one needs to be an expert in astronomy to carry on with life. After all, the young PhD in the story I told you, after boasting so much about his knowledge and insulting the elderly man for his ignorance, saw absolutely no use for literature and philosophy when the boat was sinking and he was about to drown.

What would have happened to this man if the elderly man didn't save him? He would have drowned. Just as you must know how to swim in order to survive in the water, for us to reach our salvation, we must know the gospel of the righteousness of God that is revealed in the God-spoken Word, the gospel of the water and the Spirit. And we must believe in this gospel. All that we have to do is turn to both Testaments in the Bible, find out exactly how God has set the remission of sins and what His righteousness is, and believe in the Scripture as it is. We can reach our salvation if we know and believe in what the Scripture says about the righteousness of salvation through which God has saved us from the sins of the world, and how God has set the laws of salvation. If we are drowning, all that matters is that we get out of the danger in anyway possible regardless of how we do it, even if we have to resort to the doggy paddle style. Some people might look down on the doggy paddle style of swimming and say that it's not elegant enough, but that's a luxury afforded only to those who are not about to drown.

Let's Turn to Today's Scripture Reading from Leviticus 1:1-9

Let's now examine the statues and law of salvation established by God. The word "Levi" means "unity." Among the twelve sons of Jacob was found a son called Levi, and this name meant unity. The Scripture says that those who have been washed from all their sins by uniting with the righteousness of God - are His people. The Book of Leviticus records the method by which God has blotted out the sins of mankind.

It's written in Leviticus 1:1-4: *"Now the LORD called to Moses, and spoke to him from the tabernacle of meeting, saying, 'Speak to the children of Israel, and say to them: "When any one of you brings an offering to the LORD, you shall bring your offering of the livestock—of the herd and of the flock. If his offering is a burnt sacrifice of the herd, let him offer a male without blemish; he shall offer it of his own free will at the door of the tabernacle of meeting before the LORD. Then he shall put his hand on the head of the burnt offering, and it will be accepted on his behalf to make atonement for him."'"* Having summoned Moses, God began telling him about the requirements of the sacrificial system that the Israelites were obligated to follow. The Book of Leviticus records the Law of God that God told Moses when He called him up to Mount Sinai.

God gave the people of Israel no fewer than 613 statutes and commandments. This number of the commandments has been verified by biblical scholars. But, can any human being really observe all these 613 commandments of God perfectly? If this is not possible, then what is the purpose for which God gave the Law? God gave the Law to mankind so that through it, all people would realize their sins, and made it known to them that they must go to Jesus Christ to be remitted from their sins.

In Exodus chapter 25 God spoke to the people of Israel through Moses to build the Tabernacle for His dwelling. After commanding Moses to build His Tabernacle, God told the people of Israel to come to Him and to receive the remission of sins by faith through the sacrificial system which He was instituting for them. How the people of Israel were to approach God, what kind of sacrifice they were to offer to Him, and how they were to receive the remission of sins by faith are all addressed in the Book of Leviticus.

Leviticus 1:4 says, *"Then he shall put his hand on the head of the burnt offering, and it will be accepted on his behalf to make atonement for him."* It's written clearly here that when a sinner laid his hand on the head of his sacrificial animal, his sins would be passed on this animal, and this is what was meant by atonement. It meant that if a sinner laid his hands on a sacrificial animal as specified by God, then his sins would be passed on to this sacrificial animal. In other words, when the people of Israel offered a sacrifice according to the requirements of the God-established sacrificial system, their sins were passed on to the sacrificial animal. Their sins were removed from them and placed on their sacrificial animal - such as a sheep or a bull.

When the people of Israel broke any of the God-established Laws, they committed a sin, but when they laid their hands on the head of their sacrificial animal, all their sins were passed on to this animal. This was the law of salvation that God had established in the age of the Old Testament. It was the statute God had set in order to save human beings from their sins. It was God's set rule. Therefore, anyone during the age of the Old Testament could receive the remission of sins by believing in the statutes set by God.

Even for the priests, who were the leaders of the people of Israel in the days of the Old Testament, if they failed to live according to the Law of God and sinned against Him, they had to bring an unblemished bull, sheep, or goat, pass their sins this animal by laying their hands on its head, and then sacrifice that animal. Whoever sought to receive the remission of sins had to admit his sins and confess them first. When the person who sinned against God then put his hands on the head of his sacrificial animal and confessed his sins over it, saying, "Lord, I have committed such and such sins. I have worshiped other gods," this person's sins were passed on to the sacrificial animal, and so, he did not have to be put to death. The sacrificial animal, on the other hand, had to be killed in the sinner's place. The person then cut the animal's throat and gave the blood to priest. Then the priest put some of the blood on the horns of the altar of burnt offering, and poured the rest of the blood out on the ground at the base of the altar of burnt offering.

After sprinkling the blood on the four corners of the altar, the priest then cut the animal into pieces, put them on the altar along with its head and fat, and offered them to God by burning it. This was called a burnt offering. The Scripture says that the scent of the burning flesh of the sacrificial animal was a sweet aroma that pleased God. This was the law of salvation that God had established for sinners in order to remit away their sins. To receive the remission of sins, everyone had to offer a sacrificial animal to God for his sins without fail, and this sacrifice had to be offered according to these God-established rules.

When one sinned against another person, how was the washing of this sin obtained? It was obtained through the sacrificial system established by God, who, having set His law of salvation on His own, instituted it so that whoever offered a just sacrifice according to the Law of God could receive the remission of sins. This was the great mercy of God reserved for human beings. God had allowed anyone to receive the remission of sins if they offered a sacrifice by faith according to the requirements of the God-established sacrificial system.

The Remission of Sins for the Priests

How did God promise to blot out the sins of the priests when they sinned? Let's turn to Leviticus 4:1-4 here: *"Now the LORD spoke to Moses, saying, "Speak to the children of Israel, saying: 'If a person sins unintentionally against any of the commandments of the LORD in anything which ought not to be done, and does any of them, if the anointed priest sins, bringing guilt on the people, then let him offer to the LORD for his sin which he has sinned a young bull without blemish as a sin offering. He shall bring the bull to the door of the tabernacle of meeting before the LORD, lay his hand on the bull's head, and kill the bull before the LORD."* God said here that if a priest sinned, he had to bring a young bull without blemish. When the priest brought an unblemished bull and sacrificed it in the Tabernacle, it was absolutely indispensable for him to lay his hands on the bull's head first. God commanded clearly here that the priest should lay his hands on the head of the animal and offer it to God.

The priests were only Aaron's descendants, and if any of them sinned and brought guilt on the people, God commanded that he had to offer a sacrificial animal to Him for his sins and thereby pay of the wages of these sins, and when he did so, he had to offer without fail an unblemished bull according to the

God-established rules. And God also said that the priest had to pass his sins to the sacrificial animal by laying his hands on its head without fail. Only then was the wages of sins paid with the death of this sacrificial animal. So we can see clearly from this that God's law of salvation was built upon righteous and just principles.

For a priest to receive the remission of sins, the first thing he did was to lay his hands on the head of a bull. This was done to pass all his sins to that sacrificial animal. In the Scripture, the laying on of hands has the following spiritual meanings: "to be passed on," "to be transferred," and "to be buried." Even today, if you allow someone possessed by a demon to lay his hands on your head and pray over you, the demons in him or her will be passed on to you. This happens often in Charismatic denominations and at so-called prayer centers which is nothing more than a cult. A long time ago, Brother Bochun Kim once went to such a prayer center, and whenever its director laid his hands on Brother Kim's head, his eyes lit up. This constitutes the evidence showing that the director was demon-possessed. Why would Brother Kim's eyes be lit up like that? Is he a robot? There is something wrong going on if a human being's eyes are lit up. This is the proof that the director of this establishment was demon-possessed, and that the evil sprit had passed on to the brother on whose head the director had laid his hand on to.

For a priest to be saved from his sins, he had to first bring an unblemished sacrificial animal as set by God, and then pass his sins to this sacrificial animal by laying his hand on its head. Secondly, the priest then had to draw the blood of this sacrificial animal, put some of the blood on the horns of the altar of burnt offering, and pour the rest out on the ground.

He prayed as follows, "Lord, I have sinned and brought guilt to the people of Israel. So I am now laying my hands on this sacrificial animal and passing my sins to it. Even though I must die for my sins according to Your Law, You have prepared a sacrificial offering to bear my sins. Thank You for this sacrifice Lord. Instead of me dying, I have now brought an unblemished bull and passed my sins to it by laying my hands on its head, all according to the statutes You have established so that I would receive the remission of sins. And now here is the blood of the animal that died in my place." After this, the priest cut the flesh of the sacrificial animal into pieces, put them on the altar of burnt offering, and offered it to God by burning it according to the requirements of the sacrificial system specified by God. With this, the priest finished giving his sacrificial offering for the remission of his sins.

On the tenth day of the seventh month, when the high priest offered the sacrifice of the Day of Atonement for the people, he sacrificed a bull for the sins of his household first of all according to the requirements of the God-established sacrificial system. For this sacrifice, the high priest put the blood of the sacrificial animal on the horns of the altar of incense inside the Holy Place, and then sprinkled the remaining blood on the Ark of the Testimony, which is also known as the mercy seat. The number Seven here was a number set by God. On this day the high priest could confirm before God that his sins and his household's sins had disappeared, saying to God, "Lord, even though I had to die for my sins, this sacrificial animal bore my sins, shed its blood, and died in my place. Look at this blood Lord."

In likeness, the offerings that we give to God must be given according to the requirements of the sacrificial system as specified by God. There is no other way. Our remission of sins is fulfilled according to how God has set it for us sinners. The priests could confirm that there was no more sin in their hearts when they could say to God, "Lord, I have made my offering according to Your rules. This animal died in my place. Look at its blood." That's how the priests could have the conviction of their hearts that they had received the remission of sins.

My fellow believers, your remission of sins does not depend on just how you feel on any given day, but rather, your salvation is completed when it reaches your knowledge, your conscience, the righteousness of God, His justice, and His merciful love. The remission of sins is not something that's just emotional. Nor is it something that is felt just in your consciences. What is even more important than your own emotions and consciences is the fulfillment of the just love of God, from which the remission of sins is obtained. Receiving the remission of sins is not an emotional affair. Rather, the true remission of sins is received into your heart.

No remission of sins is viable if your conscience still remains guilt-ridden. What would happen to your heart if it remained like this? If you have any sin in your heart, then you will be demanded to pay this sin's wages. In other words, you will still have to come up with some sort of sacrifice for your sin. In contrast, if the wages of your sins has been paid off by someone else' sacrifice, then your conscience would be clear and your heart will be cleansed from your sins. That is why God commanded that if a priest sinned, he had to bring an unblemished bull, lay his hands on its head, cut its throat and draw its blood, and sprinkle this blood before God's Holy Place seven times. This implies that God can say that we are sinless only if we have a sacrificial offering for our sins, as well as the evidence showing to God that this sacrificial offering had actually died in our place.

The Bible says that the priest also had to put the blood of the sacrificial animal on the horns of the altar of incense. Every priest offers interceding prayers for his people. It's written, *"And the priest shall put some of the blood on the horns of the altar of sweet incense before the LORD, which is in the tabernacle of meeting; and he shall pour the remaining blood of the bull at the base of the altar of the burnt offering, which is at the door of the tabernacle of meeting" (Leviticus 4:7).* That the priest put the blood of the sacrifice on the horns of the altar of incense implies that the priests prayed for the people of Israel on their behalf. This altar of incense is actually an altar of prayer. God commanded the priests to put the blood of the sacrifice on the horns of this altar of prayer. This implies that when we pray to God, it's absolutely indispensable for us to have the conviction of faith that because we passed our sins to our sacrificial offering, this offering shed its blood and died. Only then can we come before God and pray to Him.

We can come into God's presence and ask for His help only if we have the conviction that our sins were actually passed on to our sacrificial offering and this animal died in our place. Otherwise our hearts cannot approach the holy God. Without this conviction, we cannot pray to God properly. We will be stuck at the opening of our prayer, calling on the Father but not knowing what to say anymore in our prayer. So, because the priest was someone who prayed on behalf of the people as their representative, and if the priest sinned and brought guilt to the people, he had to first bring a sacrificial offering to God as the price for his sin, lay his hands on the head of this sacrificial animal, draw its blood, and offer this blood to God. As I have already mentioned numerous times before, all of this was set by God which are His rules. It is by believing according to God's statutes that we have received the remission of sins.

It's written in Leviticus 4:11-12, *"But the bull's hide and all its flesh, with its head and legs, its entrails and offal—the whole bull he shall carry outside the camp to a clean place, where the ashes are poured out, and burn it on wood with fire; where the ashes are poured out it shall be burned."* God said here that the sacrificial animal should now be skinned, it's flesh be cut into pieces, all the unclean parts such as its entrails should be removed, and these parts should then be taken outside the camp and burnt. The place where the unclean parts were burnt was located north of the Tabernacle. The unclean parts of the sacrificial animal were taken there to be burnt, while its fat was removed and put on the altar of burnt offering and burnt there. With the fat of the sacrificial animal burning with smoke, God said, "Yes, this sacrificial animal has died in your place. The fat here refers to the Holy Spirit. And the fat of the sacrificial offering implies that thanks to the Holy Spirit we have received the remission of sins by offering our sacrifice to God according to the requirements of the sacrificial system as specified by the Word of God and as commanded by Him, and by faith.

Sadly, many ministers in today's Christian communities are trying to teach without even knowing how Jesus Christ has taken care of their sins. Such efforts do not stem from faith in the righteousness of God, but rather, from the delusional beliefs of their own making.

The Remission of Sins for the Whole Congregation

The sacrificial system instituted by God also had a provision for the whole congregation of Israel, so that when the people of Israel sinned collectively, they could be washed from this sin as well. Let's turn to Leviticus 4:13-21, *"Now if the whole congregation of Israel sins unintentionally, and the thing is hidden from the eyes of the assembly, and they have done something against any of the commandments of the LORD in anything which should not be done, and are guilty; when the sin which they have committed becomes known, then the assembly shall offer a young bull for the sin, and bring it before the tabernacle of meeting. And the elders of the congregation shall lay their hands on the head of the bull before the LORD. Then the bull shall be killed before the LORD. The anointed priest shall bring some of the bull's blood to the tabernacle of meeting. Then the priest shall dip his finger in the blood and sprinkle it seven times before the LORD, in front of the veil. And he shall put some of the blood on the horns of the altar which is before the LORD, which is in the tabernacle of meeting; and he shall pour the remaining blood at the base of the altar of burnt offering, which is at the door of the tabernacle of meeting. He shall take all the fat from it and burn it on the altar. And he shall do with the bull as he did with the bull as a sin offering; thus he shall do with it. So the priest shall make atonement for them, and it shall be forgiven them. Then he shall carry the bull outside the camp, and burn it as he burned the first bull. It is a sin offering for the assembly."*

When the whole congregation of Israel sinned, how were they able to receive the remission of sins? The sacrificial system had a provision for collective sins as well—that is, God had instituted a specific way for the all of Israel to receive the remission of sins when they sinned collectively as a group. It's written here that when the whole congregation of Israel sinned against God, the assembly should offer a young bull for this sin, and bring the bull before the Tabernacle of the Meeting. The elders of the congregations should then lay their hands on the head of the bull before the LORD, and the bull should then be killed before Him.

First of all, when a priest sinned, he personally put his hands on the head of his sacrificial offering. In contrast, when the whole congregation sinned, rather than each and every one of the congregation laying their hands on the head of the sacrificial animal, a number of elders stepped in as their representative, passed the congregation's sins by laying their hands on the head of the animal, and sacrificed it to God according to the same requirements of the sacrificial system that the priests had to follow. That is how the whole congregation of Israel received the remission for their collective sins.

Laying their hands on the head of the sacrificial animal, the elders confessed the sins of the congregation over it, saying, "Lord, we have together sinned. We have committed idolatry, we have harmed others, and we have done these things collectively." What happened when the elders lifted their hands off from the head of the sacrificial after this? What did I say the laying on of hands means? It means "to be passed on" or "to be transferred," and accordingly, the sins of the whole congregation were passed on to the animal. Where, then, did the sins of the congregation rest once the elders laid their hands on the head of the sacrificial animal and lifted them off? They were all passed on to the bull and rested on its head. The congregation then had to deliver the bull that had accepted their sins like this, and offer it to God formally as their sacrifice.

The blood of this animal had to be drawn into a vessel without fail. When this blood of the sacrifice was offered to God, the whole congregation received the remission of sins. This sacrifice had to be ministered in the same way as the sacrifice that was offered by the priests when they sinned. Just as they had done for themselves, the priests had to offer the sacrifice to God by sprinkling its blood, and then burning its fat and flesh for the whole congregation for the remission of their sins. The elders of the congregation had to lay their hands on the sacrificial animal first of all; and then the priest had to cut the throat of the animal and draw its blood, sprinkle this blood on the mercy seat seven times, put this blood of the sacrifice on the horns of the altar, and pour the rest out on the ground. When the priest dipped his finger into the blood of the sacrifice, sprinkled it seven times before the mercy seat, and poured the rest of the blood on the ground at the base of the altar of burnt offering in the Tabernacle of Meeting, atonement was made for the whole congregation and their sins were forgiven.

When the priest himself sinned, he himself had to lay his hands on the sacrificial animal, draw its blood himself, sprinkle the blood himself, and burn the flesh of the sacrifice himself— the priest had to do everything by himself. In contrast, when the whole congregation sinned, the elders to the congregation came out and passed their sins by laying their hands on the sacrificial animal for them, and then the priests took over and ministered the rest of the sacrificial procedure. All the subsequent sacrificial rituals were performed by the priests, from the drawing the blood of the animal to sprinkling it on the mercy seat, putting it on the horns of the altar of incenses, removing the kidneys and the fat, and burning them on the altar of burnt offering. When the priests ministered the sacrifice on behalf of the congregation like this, the congregation received the remission of sins by faith.

The Remission of Sins for the Rulers

The sacrificial system had another provision specifically

set aside for the rulers to receive the remission of sins. It's written here in Leviticus 4:22-24, *"When a ruler has sinned, and done something unintentionally against any of the commandments of the LORD his God in anything which should not be done, and is guilty, or if his sin which he has committed comes to his knowledge, he shall bring as his offering a kid of the goats, a male without blemish. And he shall lay his hand on the head of the goat, and kill it at the place where they kill the burnt offering before the LORD. It is a sin offering."* Who were the rulers? The nation of Israel was composed of twelve tribes descending from the twelve sons of Jacob. The representative of each of these twelve tribes was a ruler. The Bible says here that when a ruler sinned against God, he had to offer a male goat. For this particular sacrifice, the animal used was a male goat rather than a bull.

The Bible says that when a ruler sinned, he should lay his hands on the head of the sacrificial male goat, as it's written, *"He shall lay his hand on the head of the goat, and kill it at the place where they kill the burnt offering before the LORD. It is a sin offering" (Leviticus 4:24).* When the ruler brought an unblemished male goat, laid his hands on its head, and killed it, this ruler's sins were washed away by being passed on to the goat. And as the priests took over from then on and ministered the sacrifice, the ruler's sins were blotted out.

The Scripture says in Leviticus 4:25-26, *"The priest shall take some of the blood of the sin offering with his finger, put it on the horns of the altar of burnt offering, and pour its blood at the base of the altar of burnt offering. And he shall burn all its fat on the altar, like the fat of the sacrifice of the peace offering. So the priest shall make atonement for him concerning his sin, and it shall be forgiven him."* As it's written here, although the ruler himself laid his hands on the sacrificial animal and killed it to take its blood, the rest of the sacrificial procedure was ministered by the priests. But in contrast, when the priests sinned they themselves had to lay their own hands on their sacrificial animal. As happened with the elders of the congregation, once the ruler passed his sins to the sacrificial animal by laying his hands on its head and killed that animal, the priests then took over the rest of the rituals. This is how the people of the Old Testament received the remission of sins.

Sacrifices for the Common People

Let's now look at how the common people washed away their sins when they committed them. It's written in Leviticus 4:27-30, *"If anyone of the common people sins unintentionally by doing something against any of the commandments of the LORD in anything which ought not to be done, and is guilty, or if his sin which he has committed comes to his knowledge, then he shall bring as his offering a kid of the goats, a female without blemish, for his sin which he has committed. And he shall lay his hand on the head of the sin offering, and kill the sin offering at the place of the burnt offering. Then the priest shall take some of its blood with his finger, put it on the horns of the altar of burnt offering, and pour all the remaining blood at the base of the altar."*

When the common people sinned, how did they wash away their sins? These were neither rulers, nor priests, nor the representatives of the congregation, nor its elders; instead, they were just regular folk. How and with what kind of sacrifice did the common people of Israel receive the remission of sins when they sinned against God? It's written, *"If anyone of the common people sins unintentionally by doing something against any of the commandments of the* LORD *in anything which ought not to be done, and is guilty, or if his sin which he has committed comes to his knowledge."* As we carry on with our lives, do we not all sin? Of course we do. Although we might have thought that we were doing the right thing at the time, with the passing of time, it may dawn upon us that we were actually sinning in God's sight. And like this, there are many sins that people commit unintentionally.

As I said in the morning service that the human heart is full of sins by nature, no one can help but sin unintentionally even if they try not to, for everyone was born with and is living in this world in a sinful state. Just as a pear tree bears pears and a persimmon tree bears persimmons, because all human beings were born in this world as sinners, they cannot help but commit all kinds of sins. As Adam's descendant, everyone was conceived in sin and born in iniquities from the womb of the mothers, and consequently, all human beings sin in their lives without even realizing this. That's why people commit so many sins and transgressions.

What did God say the common people of Israel should do when they realized that they broke any of the commandments of the God-given Law prescribing and proscribing what they should and should not do? God said, *"If his sin which he has committed comes to his knowledge, then he shall bring as his offering a kid of the goats, a female without blemish, for his sin which he has committed. And he shall lay his hand on the head of the sin offering, and kill the sin offering at the place of the burnt offering."* In fact, the Bible provides a more detailed description of the sacrifice offered by the common people to be washed from their sins.

When one of the common people sinned and he realized that he had failed to live according to the commandments of

God, that his acts had actually caused him to go astray, that what he thought was a good thing but actually constituted a sin, that he had broken the Law of God, and that he was therefore a sinner, he had to first of all bring a female goat without blemish to the priests. In offering this female goat as his sacrificial offering to God, this person had to pass his sins to the animal by laying his hands on its head just as the priests and the elders had to do. Can anyone recall what the laying on of hands means? It is God's law by which the people of Israel could pass their sins to the head of their sacrificial animal. It means "to be passed on."

Leviticus 1:4 says, *"Then he shall put his hand on the head of the burnt offering, and it will be accepted on his behalf to make atonement for him."* If by chance, any of the common people sinned against God offered a sacrificial animal to Him without laying his hand on its head first, then this person could never be remitted from his sins even if such sacrificial animals' blood flowed like a thousand rivers. It was an absolute must for every sinner to bring a sacrificial offering for his sins, and to pass these sins to the animal by laying his hands on its head. Before handing the sacrificial animal over to the priest, it was absolutely necessary for the sinner to pass his sins to that sacrificial animal by laying his hands on its head according to the requirements of the God-established sacrificial system. The priests then had to draw the blood of this sacrificial animal and minister the rest of the rituals, and only then the sinner could receive the remission of sins from God and return to his home in peace.

The laying on of hands was done by the common people themselves, while the sacrificial animal was killed by the priests at the altar of burnt offering. The animal was sacrificed for the sinner by dying for his sins. It was this sacrificial

animal that bore the sinner's sins and died in his place. In the
Book of Leviticus of the Old Testament it appears that the
primary purpose for which the people of Israel raised livestock
was to use them as sacrificial animals for their sins. It's written
that if someone slaughtered a goat or a sheep in another town,
he should be condemned for the bloodshed as a murderer.
Among the clean animals such as sheep and goats, the
unblemished animals were all used by the people of Israel to
receive the remission of their sins. They offered these animals
to God as the propitiation for their sins. They passed their sins
to these sacrificial animals by laying their hands on them, and
the animals were then killed and condemned before God
without fail. God had allowed the people of Israel to use their
livestock such as sheep and goats to solve the problem of their
sins.

Re-examining the Laying on of Hands

The laying on of hands is extremely important, and so
let's examine it again to make sure that we really know how
the people of Israel passed their sins to their sacrificial animal
by laying their hands on its head. Leviticus 1:4 says, *"Then he
shall put his hand on the head of the burnt offering, and it will
be accepted on his behalf to make atonement for him."* God
commanded Moses and the people of Israel to lay their hands
on their sacrificial offerings, saying, "You must lay your hands
on the sacrificial animal without fail. Unless you lay your
hands on the head of the sacrificial animal, it will be
completely ineffective for the remission of your sins.
Remember this always." This was the God-established statute
of the sacrificial system through which the people of Israel

could receive the remission of sins.

To recap, when any of the common people sinned, they had to lay their hands on their sacrificial offerings and deliver it to the priests. The priests then had to put the blood of the animal on the horns of the altar of burnt offering for them. For the priests, the rulers, and the congregation alike, the blood was put on the horns of the altar of incense. This was done because it was the leaders' duty to pray to God. That's why the blood of the sacrifice was put on the altar of incense. Whoever was a priest had the duty to pray for the people. For these priests to pray to God, it was absolutely indispensable for them to have the conviction of the remission of their own sins before God. In this present age, we are the actual priests. So for us to pray to our God, we must also have in our hearts the full conviction that we have received the remission of sins. We can pray only if we know and are convinced with a clear conscience how our sins were addressed before God. None of us should say that all our sins were taken care of solely on Jesus' Cross. For our sins to be blotted out, we must believe without fail that John had indeed laid his hands on Jesus before He was condemned on the Cross. Only then are we qualified to pray to God unhesitatingly with a clear conscience.

God commanded that the high priest should make atonement upon the horns of the altar of incense. The altar of incense is where the high priest prayed to God, and it was upon the horns of this altar that God commanded the high priest to make atonement. This was done on the tenth day of the seventh month, the Day of Atonement, and once it was done, all the yearly sins of the people of Israel were blotted out once and for all, and therefore they could come to the presence of God with a clear conscience. The remission of our sins is not something that we receive on a daily basis. While the sacrificial system enabled the people of Israel to receive the remission of their daily sins, when we turn to Leviticus chapter 16, we see that it also had a provision for the remission of their yearly sins. This sacrifice of the Day of Atonement was the shadow of the everlasting remission of sins to come for all of us. Just as the people of Israel received the remission of their yearly sins through the sacrifice of the Day of Atonement in the age of the Old Testament, Jesus Christ gave 'one everlasting sacrifice' for us in this age of the New Testament. And just as the people of Israel laid their hands on their sacrificial animals in the Old Testament, so did John the Baptist lay his hands on the head of Jesus just before baptizing Him. This is the principle of the sacrificial system established by God.

It's written in Leviticus 4:30-31, *"Then the priest shall take some of its blood with his finger, put it on the horns of the altar of burnt offering, and pour all the remaining blood at the base of the altar. He shall remove all its fat, as fat is removed from the sacrifice of the peace offering; and the priest shall burn it on the altar for a sweet aroma to the LORD. So the priest shall make atonement for him, and it shall be forgiven him."* When one of the common people handed over his sacrificial animal to the priest after laying his hand on its head, the priest then killed it and drew its blood and put it on the horns of the altar of burnt offering. The altar of burnt offering is where the sacrificial animal was offered to God by burning it. Put differently, it is the place of the judgment of sinners.

The Four Horns of the Altar of Burnt Offering

The horns of the burnt offering are symbolic of the Book of Deeds appearing in Revelation. The Kingdom of Heaven has the Book of Deeds, while the human heart has the Book of conscience. So, whenever you commit any sin, it is recorded in two places without fail, that is, one place being the tablet of your heart, and the other place being God's Book of Deeds. Therefore, the remission of sins must be received at both places, before God and before yourself. Only if you have the full conviction that you have made atonement at both these places can you receive the perfect remission of sins. If you otherwise just arbiterally say on your own that you have received the remission of sins, then you have not really received it. That is why the priest put the blood of the sacrifice on the horns of the altar of burnt offering.

Revelation 20:12 says, *"And I saw the dead, small and great, standing before God, and books were opened. And another book was opened, which is the Book of Life. And the dead were judged according to their works, by the things which were written in the books."* When we finally stand before God and His White Throne of Judgment, there will be two books: the Book of Life, and the Book of Deeds. Those who have received the remission of sins, those who have become righteous by faith while living on this earth now, and those whose hearts are completely sinless both before God, including their conscience will see their names written in the Book of Life. In contrast, those whose hearts remain sinful even after believing in Jesus still have not received the remission of sins, and therefore, they will see their names written in the Book of Deeds instead. All the sins committed by them are recorded in the Book of Deeds. No sinner can therefore claim to be righteous when standing before God. While such Christian sinners may claim to be righteous according to their denominational doctrines, when standing before God or praying to Him, they can never say that they are righteous.

In contrast, those who have become righteous by believing in the gospel of the water and the Spirit can as say with boldness when they stand before God the Father, "Father, I have come to Your presence now. You have blotted out all my sins. Hallelujah. Thank You, Lord. Just as You had blotted out the yearly sins of the people of Israel once and for all, so have You have blotted out all the everlasting sins of this world once and for all by being baptized. I believe in this righteousness of Yours. I believe in the remission of my sins exactly as You have decreed it. By being baptized by John the Baptist, You bore all my sins once and for all." When we pray to God, we can also boldly call Him our Father in our prayer.

Even though we have many shortcomings, we are joyful by the fact that Jesus Christ has blotted out all the sins of this world once and for all with His baptism and the shedding of His blood, and being fully convinced and joyful of what God has done for us, we can pray to Him boldly. When the righteous pray, they pray for all things with the assurance of their salvation and the remission of their sins, whether they are praying for themselves, for others, or for any other cause. This is true for everyone who has received the true remission of sins from God by believing in the gospel of the water and the Spirit.

My fellow believers, God commanded the people of Israel to put the blood of the sacrificial animal on the horns of the altar of burnt offering. These horns of the altar of burnt offering symbolize the Book of Judgment. Because everyone's sins are written in the Book of Judgment, God commanded the people of the Old Testament to put the blood of the sacrifice on the horns of altar of burnt offering, so that He may approve those who put the blood of the sacrifice on these horns by faith as being sinless. The Old Testament says that the life of the flesh is found in the blood, as it's written, *"For the life of the flesh is in the blood, and I have given it to you upon the altar to make atonement for your souls; for it is the blood that makes atonement for the soul" (Leviticus 17:11).*

Verse 14 also says, *"For it is the life of all flesh. Its blood sustains its life. Therefore I said to the children of Israel, 'You shall not eat the blood of any flesh, for the life of all flesh is its blood. Whoever eats it shall be cut off.'"* God says clearly here that the life of the flesh is in the blood. That is why whoever was a sinner in God's sight had to bring a sacrificial animal as specified by God and pass his sins to it by laying his hands on its head. The priest could then minister the sacrifice on behalf of the sinner to wash away his sins, drawing the blood of the sacrificial animal and putting it on the horns of the altar of burnt offering in the sinner's place.

Putting the blood of the sacrifice on the horns of the altar of burnt offering was akin to putting it by faith on the Book of Deeds written in Revelation, demonstrating that the wages of sin was paid in full. The sinner could then say to God, "Lord, look at this blood. With the laying of my hands on this sacrificial animal and the shedding of its blood, all the wages of my sins has been paid, just as Your Law declares that the wages of sin is death." It's for this reason that the blood of the sacrifice was put on the horns of the altar of burnt offering for the common people.

Since the sacrificial animal accepted the sinner's iniquities through the laying on of his hands and shed its blood to death in his place, from then on, God could no longer condemn him for his sins. That's precisely why we say that God is the God of justice. Although God is strict, He has made it possible for us to say that He is also the just and righteous God of mercy. That's because God loves everyone. By right, God had to destroy everyone who had any sin at all. God could not help but destroy everyone who was sinful.

However, through His just sacrificial system, God could wash away everyone's sins. Although people may tolerate another person's sins in their humane way, because God is holy, He cannot just skirt over or excuse a sinner. The holy God must therefore destroy anyone who has any sin. Yet, because God loved mankind so much, He established a way for them to pass their sins to a sacrificial animal and let this animal be condemned in their place, thereby delivering those who walked by faith from their sins. In short, God had saved sinners through His just and righteous law.

That is why God commanded in the age of the Old Testament that after the blood of the sacrifice was put on the horns of the altar of burnt offering, the rest of the blood should be poured out at the base of the altar. The ground of the Tabernacle was composed of sand and dirt. In the Bible, dirt sometimes refers to the human heart. The phrase "from dust to dust" is often used to describe life. The priest poured the blood of the sacrifice on the ground of the Tabernacle. Can you imagine just how bloody the ground of the Tabernacle must have been in the days of the Old Testament? The blood of all those sacrificial animals must have flowed like a river and not to mention the smell.

The court of the Tabernacle where the altar of burnt offering was located was not exactly a beautiful place. It was filled with the smell of blood, thick smoke, and burning flesh, all resulting from countless sacrificial animals being killed and burnt to bear the condemnation of sin. To the north of the tabernacle, the priests were burning filthy parts like animal skin and offal, while on the altar of burnt offering, they were burning fat, kidneys, and pieces of flesh. So the place must have been filled with the smell of burning flesh and smoke.

The fact that sacrificial animals were burnt like this means the condemnation of sin. The animals that were set aside for such sacrifices were all burnt by fire invariably.

When one looked at the blood of the sacrifice in the Tabernacle, one could see that a sacrificial animal was killed in someone's place. A sinner had laid his hands on a certain sacrificial animal, and that animal had then shed its blood and died in the sinner's place. The priests ministering in the Tabernacle performed the rest of the sacrificial rituals on behalf of sinners. The sinner, however, had to lay his hands on the head of the sacrificial animal without fail. Whoever sinned had to offer one of four sacrifices, depending on whether he sinned as one of the common people, part of the whole congregation, a ruler, or a priest. Only in the case of the whole congregation sinning did the elders lay their hands on the sacrificial animal as their representatives; for the rest, they who sinned had to personally pass their sins to the sacrificial animal by laying their hands on its head.

What does this all mean? We believe in every Word of God, and God is telling us to agree wholeheartedly with the righteous work Jesus Christ achieved when He came to this earth, and to believe in it with our whole hearts. Although Jesus died on the Cross, His death would have been completely meaningless if He had not been baptized by John the Baptist. In the age of the Old Testament God could save sinners from their iniquities when they laid their hands on unblemished sacrificial animals in the Tabernacle, and these animals shed their blood and were burnt. The laying of the hands of the sinners on the sacrificial animal was not in vain. Therefore, before Jesus Christ was crucified, it was imperative that He receive baptism from John the Baptist, which was equivalent to the laying on of hands in the Old Testament. God did not accept any sacrificial offering if there was no laying on hands. The Scripture says that God accepted the offering in pleasure only if it came with the laying on of hands.

The Old Testament therefore says that priests would make atonement for the sinner, and the sinner would in turn be forgiven. It's absolutely important for us remember here that the condemnation of sin is not done by us, but it's done personally by our high priest on our behalf. The one thing we have to do as sinners is to pass our sins to the sacrificial offering without fail through the laying on of hands. The rest was taken care of by the high priest ministering for sinners. It's very important to remember this.

We sin because we are weak, but we can still believe in Jesus and the statutes found in the Word of God, and we can consent to the sacrificial system of God. These are the things that we can all do despite our many shortcomings. That God paid off the wages of ours sins by sacrificing Himself, that the Lord was personally baptized by John the Baptist, that He was crucified and shed His blood on the Cross, and that He rose from the dead again—these are the things that the Lord Himself did for us. As sinners, all that we can do is just pass our sins to the sacrificial offering by laying our hands on it. We do not have the prerogative to kill this sacrificial offering or to shed its blood.

Just as the Bible says that *"the wages of sin is death,"* every sinner had to be put to death. That's why the Scripture says, *"So the priest shall make atonement for them, and it shall be forgiven them."* Just how important is the role of the priest then? Without the high priest playing his role, sinners could not receive the remission of sins. They were all doomed to destruction without the high priest fulfilling his role.

For this reason, God called Aaron, Moses' brother, and

made him the high priest. When God delivered the people of Israel from Egypt, Aaron played the role of a spokesman for his brother Moses. Moses received the Law from God and spoke to the people of Israel on His behalf, while Aaron ministered as the priest to blot out their sins. Only Aaron and his descendants could become these high priests. It's absolutely important for us to grasp clearly here that only the descendants of Aaron could minister as the high priest. Today, we got through to the sacrifices offered by the common people. ✉

SERMON

2

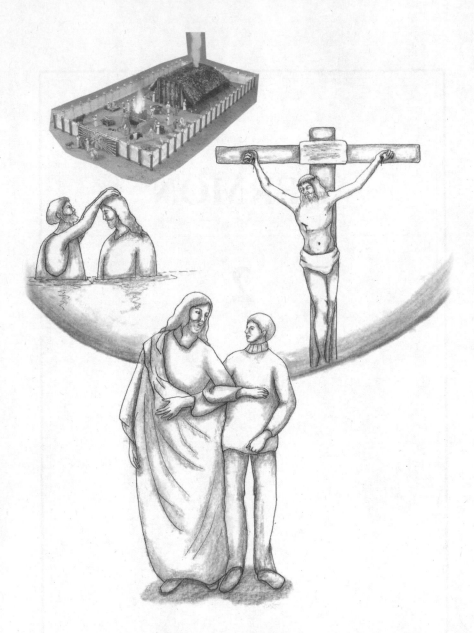

You can download Rev. Paul C. Jong's Christian Books on iPhone, iPad, or Blackberry by going to Amazon's Kindle e-bookstore (www.amazon.com).

Live with Your Heart United with God

< Leviticus 1:1-9 >

"Now the LORD called to Moses, and spoke to him from the tabernacle of meeting, saying, 'Speak to the children of Israel, and say to them: 'When any one of you brings an offering to the LORD, you shall bring your offering of the livestock—of the herd and of the flock. If his offering is a burnt sacrifice of the herd, let him offer a male without blemish; he shall offer it of his own free will at the door of the tabernacle of meeting before the LORD. Then he shall put his hand on the head of the burnt offering, and it will be accepted on his behalf to make atonement for him. He shall kill the bull before the LORD; and the priests, Aaron's sons, shall bring the blood and sprinkle the blood all around on the altar that is by the door of the tabernacle of meeting. And he shall skin the burnt offering and cut it into its pieces. The sons of Aaron the priest shall put fire on the altar, and lay the wood in order on the fire. Then the priests, Aaron's sons, shall lay the parts, the head, and the fat in order on the wood that is on the fire upon the altar; but he shall wash its entrails and its legs with water. And the priest shall burn all on the altar as a burnt sacrifice, an offering made by fire, a sweet aroma to the LORD.'"

We just read Leviticus 1:1-9 for today's Scripture reading. The word "Levi" means "unity." As the name suggests, God made and worked in the Tabernacle because He wanted to be united with the people of Israel by remitting away their sins when they offered Him sacrifices according to the strict requirements of the sacrificial system as recorded in the Book of Leviticus. During that time, just as it's true for us today, not a day went by when the people of Israel did not commit sin. Because the people of Israel sinned constantly without fail, they had to offer sacrifices to God inside the Tabernacle according to the requirements of the sacrificial system, and through this obtain the remission of all their sins, become God's holy people, and receive His help. God instituted this sacrificial system in order to be with the people of Israel, walk with them, watch over them, bless them, protect them from their enemies, solve the problem of all their sins, and be their God. This is also true for you and me today, being so important, receiving such wonderful blessings, and having God on our side.

God's Instruction to Moses

After the Tabernacle was built, God called Moses and said to him, *"Speak to the children of Israel, and say to them: 'When any one of you brings an offering to the LORD, you shall bring your offering of the livestock—of the herd and of the flock. If his offering is a burnt sacrifice of the herd, let him offer a male without blemish; he shall offer it of his own free will at the door of the tabernacle of meeting before the LORD. Then he shall put his hand on the head of the burnt offering, and it will be accepted on his behalf to make atonement for him'"* (Leviticus 1:2-4).

Here, God was teaching the people of Israel how they

could make atonement for their sins, instructing them to prepare a live sacrificial animal and pass their sins on to it by laying their hands on its head. In other words, when the people of Israel laid their hands on their sacrificial animals, all their sins were passed on to this animal to make atonement for them. Once the sins of the Israelites were passed to the sacrificial animal, it was then only slaughtered and its blood shed while bearing all their sins. The priests then put some of *this blood* on the horns of the Altar of Burnt Offering, poured the remaining blood on the ground, and burnt its flesh on the Altar. This was the burnt offering that God demanded from the people of Israel, saying that it was *"a sweet aroma to the LORD" (Leviticus 1:9)*. For God to walk with the people of Israel, they had to give such an offering without fail.

If the people of Israel did not offer this sacrifice that was indispensable for God to walk with them, then God would not have kept His the promise He made to Abraham and his descendants that He would be their God. He could therefore never become their God. That's because while God is the holy God, the people of Israel could not help but sin every day due to their weak human nature. Therefore, to bridge the gap between God and the people of Israel, it was absolutely indispensable for them to pass their sins to their live sacrificial animals by laying their hands on its head, slaughter it, draw its blood, put the blood on the horns of the Altar of Burnt Offering, and burn its flesh, all according to the requirements of the sacrificial system of the Tabernacle. Only then could God fulfill His justice, His love, and His deliverance of the people of Israel. In this way, the people of Israel could become God's own people, and God could become their God, walk with them, protect them, and lead them into the land of Canaan. It is for this reason that God told the people of Israel to offer Him sacrifices in this specific way, and the people of Israel in turn gave their offerings accordingly as instructed.

The Book of Leviticus is named after Levi, who was one of the twelve sons of Jacob, and whose name means "Unity." God entrusted the descendants of Levi with the work of uniting the people of Israel with God, that is, God raised them as the priests to minister the sacrifice on behalf of the Israelites. That's why this particular Book is named the Book of Leviticus, and God spoke about unity through this Book of Leviticus.

Unity with the Righteousness of God Is Very Important for Us the Believers

It's written in Psalm 133:1, *"Behold, how good and how pleasant it is for brethren to dwell together in unity!"* As we can see from this passage also, unity with God is very beautiful and pleasant in His sight. To be one with God, the people of Israel had to give Him the offering of faith, and by giving this offering by faith and in unity, they were able to be saved from their sins and become God's own people. This sacrifice that united the Israelites with God was a tremendous blessing for them.

I'd like to now speak to you about the Tabernacle, and also explain to you step by step the sacrificial system described in the Book of Leviticus. It's absolutely indispensable for us to realize the importance of the sacrificial system. There is a reason why God spoke to Moses about the sacrificial system, and why the people of Israel built the Tabernacle for a year— all of this was done so that the people of Israel could give the sacrifice that was pleasing to God. Moreover, you and I must also unite with God by faith. We must be of one in heart. We must unite by faith, receive blessings by faith, pass our sins over by faith, be judged for our sins by faith, become God's people by faith, and go to Kingdom of Heaven by this faith. No one whose heart is not united with God can go to the Kingdom of Heaven. Heaven can be entered only if we are one with God.

In order to be in unity with God, the people of Israel brought an unblemished animal according to the God-established sacrificial system, passed their sins onto it by laying their hands on its head, slaughtered it and drew its blood. Taking *this* blood, the priests put some of it on the horns of the Altar of Burnt Offering, poured the rest of the blood on the ground, cut the flesh of the animal into pieces, and burnt it on the Altar of Burnt Offering to please God. This was the sacrifice that satisfied God's demand, one that was *"a sweet aroma to the LORD" (Leviticus 1:8)*. Receiving such offerings and sacrifices, God fulfilled everything He promised to Abraham and his descendants. The descendants of Abraham here refer to none other than you and I who believe in Jesus today, implying that we lack nothing to be embraced and loved by God.

The Importance of the Sacrificial Offering

It's absolutely critical for us to realize just how much God desired such a sacrificial offering, and how pleased He was to receive it. This offering was an absolute must for Him, and He was completely satisfied when He received it in this order. We must realize here just how much God was pleased and quenched by every aspect of the sacrifice, from the laying on of hands to the shedding of blood and the smell of the flesh of the sacrificial animal being burnt. God was pleased to receive such an offering as a sweet aroma because through this sacrifice, He was more than able to blot out the sins of the people of Israel. By the same token, God has blotted out all your sins and mine through the sacrifice of Jesus Christ. Words cannot describe how grateful I am for this. It's absolutely important for us to be united with God in oneness of heart. Although we are not 100% perfect in our flesh, at least our hearts must be one with God by faith. In other words, we must believe with all our hearts that even though we were all destined to die for our sins, our Lord loved such wretched sinners like us so much that He bore all our sins through His baptism, died in our place, rose from the dead again, and has thereby made us God's own children.

Like this, God wanted to make us His own people, and we must unite our hearts with Him by faith just as He planned it. In fact, faith itself is unity. Faith is all about trust and unity. So I urge you to have faith, and to live by this faith until the day the Lord returns.

My fellow believers, please pray for our ministry. Preaching the gospel of the water and the Spirit requires a lot of financial resources. Pray to God to give us the resources we need to preach His gopsel. Has any of you here had $10 million in your hand? This may seem like such an unrealistic figure that we can hardly fathom or even imagine it, but in reality, $10 million is not that much money. Once you start spending money, there is no end to how much you can spend. Of course, few people ever see $10 million, $1 million, or even $100,000 in their lifetime. But, regardless of the amount of the money, it is nowhere near enough for our ministry. You might think that there are lots of things you could do with $100,000, but it really is not that much money when you spend it on the righteous work.

At this hour, there is one thing that I would like to ask from everyone of you. I ask you all to be one with God and His righteousness, and to thus reach your salvation. This is my heartfelt desire for all of you. I urge you to also unite your heart with the will of God in everything else you do. When you are one with God, from then on God will walk with you, you will become one of His own people, and you will be blessed by Him. Everything starts from this point of unity. The Book of Genesis explains God's plan, while the Book of Exodus describes how God fulfilled His plan through the Tabernacle. Over half of the Book of Exodus, from chapter 19 to chapter 40, addresses this Tabernacle. And about two-thirds of the Book of Leviticus is all about the sacrificial system.

It's absolutely indispensable for us to realize just how important unity is. Unity with the Church is also extremely important. We need to learn how to be one with God in our hearts by faith, and if we can accomplish this, it will bring tremendous blessings to us. In the course of this journey, we sometimes may be drawn to our own human thoughts, our individual pride may be hurt, and even our hearts may be hurt, but in reality, once we unite with God everything will be taken care of. It's only because we are not one with God that we feel offended and hurt; if we truly are in unity with God, then there would be nothing to be offended or hurt by. This is only a matter of course. In fact, there is nothing wrong that God has ever done to us. If there is anything wrong, it's always our fault. Don't you agree?

You and I must unite our hearts with God without fail. It is right for us to live in unity with God, praying for His gospel to be preached throughout the whole world. Everything we do, from uniting our hearts to devoting our bodies and hearts to pray, work, and raise financial resources, is done for the righteousness of God. That's how we ought to live. If we unite our hearts like this, God will bless us all to prosper. If our hearts are one with God like this, the Lord will ensure that we are prosperous in all things, from our livelihoods and needs to our health. If you really want to be blessed, all that you have to do is live in unity like this.

Unity is absolutely indispensable. Unless our hearts are united, we cannot accomplish anything no matter how hard we try. You and I must unite our hearts. While this may seem simple, it is in fact an extremely important issue.

I Ask You to Be in Unity with the Words "Laying on of Hands"

It's written in Leviticus 1:3-4, *"If his offering is a burnt sacrifice of the herd, let him offer a male without blemish; he shall offer it of his own free will at the door of the tabernacle of meeting before the LORD. Then he shall put his hand on the head of the burnt offering, and it will be accepted on his behalf to make atonement for him."* All that you have to do is to believe in this truth with your heart, "The laying on of hands means passing or transferring sins, and accepting this truth means receiving in joy." Your own emotional feeling is not what's important. What's important is that you believe in the Word of God just as it is. God alone is true. Even if we were to think otherwise a hundred times, could we win over each and every Truth of the Word of God? No, of course not. How could we win over the Word of God when it is the Truth? The God-spoken Word is the forever-unchanging Truth that remains the same yesterday, today and tomorrow and in the future.

If any of you wants to be possessed by a demon, try to get

a demon-possessed person to lay his hands on your head. The demon will come over and possess you for sure. And if you want to be cursed, get someone accursed to lay his hands on your head. You will then be cursed. Stand against God if you wish. You will be cursed. It's a simple principle.

My fellow believers, as those living in such a precarious age, we have no other alternative but to preach the gospel fully before we leave this earth. After living like this, we will go to the Lord when He calls us. If you have any worries troubling your heart, first of all unite yourself with God. If you ask God for His help, He will solve all your problems. It's only because people think of themselves first and rely on their own thoughts that they cannot get their problems solved. For God, for His Kingdom, and for the spreading of the gospel, we must unite our hearts first of all.

For us, God is absolutely indispensable to our lives. I believe with all my heart that God has blessed me. Do you also believe so? Although I've been very busy recently due to some new work that I've been requested to do, I can still work with a joyous heart as I'm convinced that I'm doing this work for the Lord, all to preach His gospel. All of this is the Lord's blessing.

Live with Your Heart United with the Righteousness of God by Faith

God said that He will give us many blessings along with heavy persecution. After removing the dross that's found in our hearts, God sees whether or not our hearts are in unity with Him, and then decides whether to work in our lives or not. Although people judge others based on their outside appearance, God said that He looks at the heart. When God looks into our hearts and sees that we are indeed in unity with Him, from then on He will bless us and bestow His grace upon us. Our faith will then also grow and we will be at peace. That's because our hearts would no longer be torn between our own desires and God's desires.

Once our hearts are in unity with God, all His work will be our own work, everything that concerns Him will be our concern, and therefore we will carry out God's work as our own work. Moreover, there will be nothing we can't accomplish, for God will help us all along the way. Everything will go our way. All our countless worries and troubles will disappear also. God will remove them all for us. That is precisely why we must be one with God by faith.

I cannot emphasize enough just how important this unity is. No matter how much the world changes, we should never let our hearts change along with it. If by chance our hearts seem to go astray for one or other reason, we must return and unite them back with God again. Our hearts must be one with God absolutely and unconditionally. Believing again that we have received the remission of all our sins, because God Himself bore all our sins through His baptism and shed His blood on the Cross for us, we must be one with God. And now that we have received the remission of sins, we ought to follow God by faith in unity, just as He told us, "Seek first His Kingdom and His righteousness." We will then be one with God, as His work will be ours and our work will be His, and ultimately we will be able to solve all our problems. Once all the problems troubling you are solved like this, God will then fulfill your heart's wishes also.

Wouldn't you also love someone who cares about you, and who follows and obeys your will? Wouldn't you want bless such a person? Of course you would. The principle is simple enough, God also loves those who obey Him. God has saved us by giving us the gospel of the water and the Spirit, and He yearns for this gospel to be spread throughout this earth. So, if we pray for this ministry and carry it out in unity, then God will bless us for sure. Whatever we do, if we do everything for the spreading of the gospel of God and live according to His will, then how could God not love and bless us? He can't help but bless and love such people. The principle of unity is that simple. To unite our hearts with God is to be at one with Him. Our hearts must therefore be united with God by faith first of all. Unless our hearts are one with God, we cannot accomplish anything.

It is with some trepidation that I have begun preaching about the Tabernacle, as I am concerned that I might have embarked too hastily on something overambitious. Even if there is much that still remains to be said, it is all useless if the listener cannot understand. In time, some people will eventually come to understand it, but there are so many people in this world who cannot understand. When I think about the latter, I wonder how many of them would be able to understand what I am preaching now. Although it is easy for me to preach to you, it would be twice as difficult for me to give my sermon in a way that these people would really understand.

We must be united to fulfill the will of God. Most of you have done this, but there still are some of you who have not united with God yet. If you are one of them, I ask you to examine yourself and find out in what aspects you are still not united. Like this, when you realize in what ways you are not in unity with God, He will in time give you the heart and the faith to be one with Him. You can then be one with God. Everything will go well for you from then onwards. No matter what, and regardless of your shortcomings, as long as you abide in God, everything will be taken care of. That is what the Word of God is saying.

As long as you and I are united with God in one heart, everything will go well. God's Church throughout the world will prosper if it is united with Him, and you will also prosper if you are one with God. Without this unity, nothing can be accomplished. I cannot emphasize enough just how important this unity is. No matter what our circumstances are and how big or small our faith is, it is only when we are united with the will of God that our faith can grow and we can receive God's blessings.

Unless your heart is upright, everything else is useless. God looks at the center of our hearts. If only we are united with Him, God will bless us so that we would be able to preach the gospel successfully. God will spread the gospel all over the world through us. And He will bless us all. Like His will, God will fulfill all the blessed promises He made to us. Every promise He made to you will be fulfilled by Him. Let us therefore make sure that our hearts are united with God, so that we may all receive His blessings. ✉

SERMON

3

You can download Rev. Paul C. Jong's Christian Books on iPhone, iPad, or Blackberry by going to Amazon's Kindle e-bookstore (www.amazon.com).

Make at All Times a Fragrant Grain Offering To the Lord

< Leviticus 2:1-16 >

"When anyone offers a grain offering to the Lord, his offering shall be of fine flour. And he shall pour oil on it, and put frankincense on it. He shall bring it to Aaron's sons, the priests, one of whom shall take from it his handful of fine flour and oil with all the frankincense. And the priest shall burn it as a memorial on the altar, an offering made by fire, a sweet aroma to the Lord. The rest of the grain offering shall be Aaron's and his sons'. It is most holy of the offerings to the Lord made by fire. And if you bring as an offering a grain offering baked in the oven, it shall be unleavened cakes of fine flour mixed with oil, or unleavened wafers anointed with oil. But if your offering is a grain offering baked in a pan, it shall be of fine flour, unleavened, mixed with oil. You shall break it in pieces and pour oil on it; it is a grain offering. If your offering is a grain offering baked in a covered pan, it shall be made of fine flour with oil. You shall bring the grain offering that is made of these things to the Lord. And when it is presented to the priest, he shall bring it to the altar. Then the priest shall take from the grain offering a memorial portion, and burn it on the altar. It is an offering made by fire, a sweet aroma to the Lord. And what is left of the grain offering

shall be Aaron's and his sons'. It is most holy of the offerings to the Lord made by fire. No grain offering which you bring to the Lord shall be made with leaven, for you shall burn no leaven nor any honey in any offering to the Lord made by fire. As for the offering of the firstfruits, you shall offer them to the Lord, but they shall not be burned on the altar for a sweet aroma. And every offering of your grain offering you shall season with salt; you shall not allow the salt of the covenant of your God to be lacking from your grain offering. With all your offerings you shall offer salt. If you offer a grain offering of your firstfruits to the Lord, you shall offer for the grain offering of your firstfruits green heads of grain roasted on the fire, grain beaten from full heads. And you shall put oil on it, and lay frankincense on it. It is a grain offering. Then the priest shall burn the memorial portion: part of its beaten grain and part of its oil, with all the frankincense, as an offering made by fire to the Lord."

What Is a Grain Offering?

Warm greetings to everyone. Today, I would like to share the Word of God with you regarding the grain offering. The grain offering here refers to a bloodless offering made out of finely ground grain, which was offered with other sacrificial offerings. Spiritually speaking, the grain offering can be said to refer to the offering of devotion that we dedicate to God. After burnt offerings, peace offerings, or sin offerings were made to God, these grain offerings were made by grinding the first harvest of the grain and mixing it with frankincense, salt and oil. That's why they were called grain offerings. The people of

Israel had offered this flour to God along with other sacrificial offerings.

The grain offering holds a very important spiritual meaning. It is spiritually more meaningful for the righteous to offer such offerings to God. It implies our bodies and hearts are offered to God by faith, now that we have been saved and become righteous through the righteousness of God. However, God instructed never to add leaven or honey to this grain offering. Let's all turn to Leviticus 2:11 here: *"No grain offering which you bring to the LORD shall be made with leaven, for you shall burn no leaven nor any honey in any offering to the LORD made by fire."* This means that because we have been saved from the sins of the world and become God's children by believing in the gospel of the water and the Spirit, it is only a matter of course for us to dedicate ourselves to serving the righteousness of the Lord, thanking God for His love. That is why we believe that it is right for us to offer our bodies and hearts for the sake of all those in this world who still do not know the gospel of the water and the Spirit, and are thus unable to become God's children and perishing. In other words, we are offering our physical bodies to serve the gospel of the Lord, so that this gospel may spread to everyone.

The grain offering described in today's Scripture reading refers such an offering, which is made when we serve our Lord's precious gospel. It is for this reason that God commanded not to add any leaven or honey to the grain offering. What then would be the spiritual meaning of leaven and honey? When leaven is added to dough, it makes the dough rise, and adding honey sweetens the bread to make it even tastier. We know this from our everyday life, as we eat bread all the time and use honey quite often for sweetening our food. However, God is telling us, who are living by faith, to eschew or shun such things, spiritually speaking.

For us who live in the New Testiment age, those of us who have received the remission of sins into their hearts by believing in the gospel of the water and the Spirit, God is also telling us not to add leaven or honey when it comes to serving His righteousness. Spiritually speaking, by not adding leaven or honey means, we must not live for or by the teachings or pleasures of the flesh. In other words, God is telling us that when we carry out the work of the Lord, we should not do this for the glory of our own flesh. Put differently, we must do God's work for His righteousness alone, never to inflate ourselves. That is why God said to make the grain offering to Him with just fine flour, mixed with oil, salt, and frankincense.

I hope you can now understand what this means spiritually. We are serving the gospel of the water and the Spirit because we ourselves truly believe in this gospel. And we offer the grain offering in order to spread this gospel to everyone else. This is because we are those who serve the righteousness of God. Because God loves us and has saved us from all our sins, we are serving this gospel out of a truly thankful heart. The Lord also said not to pray to show off to others. So, we are serving God in obedience to His will solely to carry out His desire only. If someone is instead trying to establish his own ego or fulfill the lust of his own flesh, then this person is not making a spiritually sound grain offering to God. When God said not to add any leaven or honey to the grain offering, He was telling us not to devote ourselves to living a fleshly life. Serving God, in other words, is not something that we can do as though it were a hobby.

We know that we are serving God's work spiritually like this because God has saved us first and foremost from all our sins through the gospel of the water and the Spirit. What is absolutely indispensable to all of us who believe in the righteousness of God, however, is none other than the spiritual offering of faith. For this, we must endure all other sacrifices to all the offerings that we make to God, including the grain offering. In other words, to make such offerings that are pleasing to the Lord, we must devote our whole body, heart, and minds to everything we do in order to spread the Lord's gospel of the water and the Spirit. God said that when we offer Him a burnt offering, it is His food. This means that God is happy with us when we the believers in the gospel of the water and the Spirit preach this gospel to people who, because of their sins, garnered God's enmity, they teach this gospel to them, and reconcile them back with God.

It is in the spreading of His gospel of the water and the Spirit that is God's food, not our own self-sacrifice. The same is true for our grain offering. It is because God has saved us from all our sins that we are serving Him. Jesus bore all our sins by being baptized by John the Baptist, He was crucified to death while bearing them upon His shoulders, and He rose from the dead again. If anyone who has received the remission of sins is not preaching this gospel by faith, then the person is someone who is not making any grain offering. Such people are spiritually evil people. Indeed, anyone who does not make the grain offering spiritually is someone who is not one with the Lord. Therefore, it is absolutely critical for all of us to be one with the righteousness of the Lord and serve this righteousness. To do so, we must serve the Lord's righteousness solely out of a thankful heart, rather than trying to establish our own self-righteousness. This is the kind of devotion coming out of a heart that is truly united with the Lord. All of us who believe in the gospel of the water and the Spirit must now lead a life that is one with the Lord spiritually.

It is only a matter of course that those who have received the remission of sins ought to live out their faith in unity with God, making the grain offering. To live such a life of unity with God, we must sacrifice ourselves as peace offerings, burnt offerings, or sin offerings for the sake of others. All of us who have been made righteous have such a duty to God. After all, how could we let everyone else perish in perdition, happy that we alone are loved by God, we alone have been saved from our sins, and we alone will go to Heaven? Anyone who has such thoughts cannot truthfully be said to be someone who is spreading the righteousness of God. Whoever has received the remission of sins must of course serve the righteousness of God in unity with Him.

In fact, if someone has truly received the remission of sins by believing in the gospel of the water and the Spirit, then he cannot help himself but serve the gospel even without anyone asking for it. Because we are so thankful to God for our salvation, we cannot help but serve this gospel of the water and the Spirit. There are countless number of people who have no idea from where they were born and to where they are going. So many people born on this earth do not know the purpose for which they should be living, and as a result, wander around without any direction until they fall into a worldly religion and are trapped there for the rest of their lives, only to be destroyed in the end. Unable to find the true purpose of life, such people face nothing but disappointment and ultimately see their lives end in vain.

Every man and woman must know the gospel of the water and the Spirit, the Word of Truth. What then is this gospel of the water and the Spirit? The truth says, that when we were deceived by Satan out of our weakness and consequently fell into destruction, God Himself who created us, sent the Savior to this earth and saved us. Indeed, God sent His Son to this earth to deliver us from the sins of this world and destruction, making us His children, and let us live forever. Accordingly, Jesus Christ the Son of God came to this earth, and through the gospel of the water and the Spirit, He has saved us perfectly from the sins of the world and judgment. God let us be born on this earth so that He would save us like this, and if we do not realize this will of God, our lives will be all in vain no matter how long we might live and how many riches we might enjoy.

I cannot emphasize enough just how indispensable it is for all of us to know the righteousness of the Lord and believe in it. Look back and think about what has happened to us since we found the Lord's righteousness. God allowed us to be born on this earth so that He Himself could blot out all our sins, and to make it known to us that He has enabled us to enter and live forever in His Kingdom, that He loves us, and that He has made us His own very special children. And to this very day, God has led us in many places and in many ways.

No religion in this world can answer the question, "Why was I born on this earth?" What does Buddhism say? Arguing for reincarnation, it claims that if you are virtuous in this present life, you will be born as a higher being in the next life hereafter, while if you do evil things in this life, you will be born as a lowly being in your next life. The Word of God says in Ecclesiastes 1:2 *"Vanity of vanities, all is vanity."* So what is our Lord saying to us here then? He says, *"For of Him and through Him and to Him are all things" (Romans 11:36).* God is saying that the whole universe and all things in it have come to exist because of Jesus Christ who has saved us from the sins of the world. Why were human beings born on this earth? The Lord said that He made us human beings so that we would live with Him. However, man fell into Satan's temptation and sinned against God. God Almighty Himself then came to this earth incarnated in the flesh of man, was baptized by John the Baptist, died on the Cross, rose from the dead again, and thereby fulfilled the gospel of the water and the Spirit; and in doing so, God has saved once and for all those of us who believe in this gospel from all the sins of the world.

God has, through these works, made us, who were all sinners, His own sinless children. Indeed, this had been God's plan all along for us, who were created in the likeness of His image. In other words, God let all of us be born on this earth and saved us through the gospel of the water and the Spirit so that we would live forever as God's own children and enjoy the same glory as God. If you know this plan of God and this Truth of salvation, you have truly been blessed. Regardless of how many years you have lived thus far, whether 10, 30, or 70 years, you must all realize that making this gospel Truth of the water and the Spirit known to you is the very purpose for which God created you. I am so thankful to you all for listening to and receiving the remission of sins by believing in the gospel of the water and the Spirit, and I hope and pray that you will lead into Jesus Christ not only your very own family members who have not received the remission of sins yet, but everyone else throughout the whole world.

It is by spreading the gospel that the believers in the gospel of the water and the Spirit can make an offering of righteousness to God. Although we may have lived for our own flesh until now, from this moment on, for the sake of mankind who were created in the likeness of the image of God, we must minister the peace offering between them and God, and do so continuously.

What Is the Reason for Us to Live Like This?

It is because we have received the remission of our sins thanks to the righteousness of Jesus Christ. It is because Jesus Christ came to this earth, accepted all our sins once and for all by being baptized by John the Baptist, the representative of mankind, shed His blood on the Cross, rose from the dead again, and has thereby saved us once and for all. By believing in this Truth that has come by the gospel of the water and the Spirit with our hearts, we have received the remission of sins. And by receiving the remission of sins into our hearts by faith like this, we have become God's own children. What should we be doing from now on? We must minister such offerings of righteousness to others.

In other words, we must preach the gospel of the water and the Spirit to other souls so that they would also believe in it. Are you however thinking, "How can I do God's work effectively when I am already so busy with my own life?" It might be agreed that while it would be rather difficult for you to carry out God's work due to your circumstances, God's Church exists on this earth, and in this Church you will find God's servants. There are many ways in which you can take part in God's work, you can make regular financial contributions, you can pray for it, or you can offer your time. God's work is not difficult. If you believe in the righteousness of God and obey His will, then you are someone who can carry out God's work in anyway possible.

If you are truly happy when hearing God's Word of righteousness, I urge you to think about the souls of others, including your own soul. Think again about just how much you had struggled before you met Jesus Christ, who came by the water and the Spirit. Before I found the righteousness of the

Lord, I had absolutely no hope, nor did I have any joy. There was nothing in this world that was worth doing, I had no ability either; and my heart never satisfied even when I tried the work of the world. And I also did not know why I was born in this world nor why I had to live. I thought to myself, "Everyone's life is purposeless. Once born, everyone gets old, falls ill, and dies. What's the point of living then? My grandfather passed away and is now in that grave. Will I not also end up in that grave in time? Is this what my life is all about then? If it is, then my life means nothing. Why do people say, that man is the greatest of all creation? I feel I'm so worthless. In time, everyone will end up in a grave. Young and old, men and women alike, everyone will die at one point. What is the meaning of life then? Isn't life totally meaningless?" I was full of such confusing thoughts.

So, trying to find out the meaning of life, I tried Buddhism at one time, and then I tried Christianity also. However, ten long years went by since I first began believing in Jesus, and, before I came to realize the precious gospel Truth of the water and the Spirit through the Word of God. It was entirely through the Word of God that I came to know the gospel of the water and the Spirit. Once I believed in the gospel of the water and the Spirit, all my sins disappeared from my heart, and from that moment onwards there was no need for me to offer anymore prayers of repentance. At first this all seemed rather dull to me. I had no worries about making a living either, as just a little effort was needed to make my ends meet. There wasn't much else to do. Because everyone is born blind, they do not know what it is that they should be doing in their lives. This was true for me as well. However, once I found the gospel of the water and the Spirit, the gospel of the remission of sins, and received the remission of sins, I reached a clear understanding of what I should be doing in my life.

From then on, I thought to myself, "While it's not easy to make a living, all my basic needs can be met if I just put in a little effort into it. So it's not such a big deal. I want to spread the gospel of the water and the Spirit from now on. Now that my heart's sins have disappeared, I want to preach this gospel of the water and the Spirit to everyone who does not know it." So, from that moment, whenever I met anyone, my mouth opened on its own and I came to preach the gospel of the water and the Spirit at every available chance. When I told people about the gospel of the water and the Spirit, most of them were skeptical at first, but soon I saw many of them rejoicing for having come to know this gospel.

I could not stay still without preaching the gospel of the water and the Spirit. So, as I preached the gospel of the water and the Spirit, I had to also nurture the new believers, and as I began nurturing them, I had to find new things to support the gospel ministry. I had resolved within myself to serve God and other souls. Those who believed in the gospel of the water and the Spirit before you are working for the righteousness of God alone day and night, all to save you from your sins. Is there any pastor here who is living just for himself? Even when travelling, don't all our pastors who believe in the gospel of the water and the Spirit ride with the congregation in a church vehicle? Is there any pastor here who bought his own luxurious car yet and said proudly, "This is my car, so no one else can use it"? No, there isn't!

Although I myself am a pastor, when I see our workers faithfully spreading the righteousness of God, men and women alike, I have nothing but respect for them. How could they be doing what they are doing if they were living just for themselves? See them for yourselves. Are they not carrying out

God's work relentlessly, day and night? Are they not serving God and His gospel of righteousness faithfully like this? At the least, when it comes to those who know and believe in the gospel of the water and the Spirit, there is no one who is working for one's own flesh. I have so much respect for them.

Making this grain offering to God is the natural duty for all who know and believe in the gospel of the water and the Spirit. Right now, it is you and I who are making the grain offering for God and for the people. In other words, we are ministering the offering of righteousness before God for the sake of all those who, still not knowing the gospel of the water and the Spirit, have not received the remission of sins. Just as the actual priests carried out this work during the age of the Old Testament, we now in the age of the New Testament are doing likewise, (all those we believe in the gospel of the water and the Sprit), are ministering these offerings for those who still do not know God's love and the gospel of righteousness.

What then should our tasks be towards ourselves and before God and man? We must sacrifice ourselves. The grain offering was made out of fine flour mixed with oil, and this was sprinkled on the altar of burnt offering along with salt and frankincense. As the flour mixed with salt, frankincense, and oil was burnt on the altar of burnt offering, it emitted a sweet aroma and also produced smoke. This implies that wherever the gospel of the water and the Spirit is preached, such grain offerings are made. In other words, it is our actual workers who are serving the gospel of the water and the Spirit and supporting the gospel ministry that must carry out this work. For instance, when it snows while we are holding a Discipleship Training Camp, there are some people who scatter sand on the road. They do this voluntarily to serve others, not for themselves. The same goes for us. All of us must make the grain offering to God for other people's souls.

Our Lord said, *"Unless a grain of wheat falls into the ground and dies, it remains alone; but if it dies, it produces much grain" (John 12:24).* If we live just for ourselves even after believing in the gospel of the water and the Spirit and receiving the remission of sins, then there would be no reason for us to help others or be helped by them. If a grain of wheat falls onto the ground, it will produce many more grains, if it on the other hand is not buried in the ground, it will remain alone. What will then happen to us? We would remain singled out wicked souls, even after receiving the remission of sins.

If you believe in the gospel Word of the water and the Spirit, and if you believe that the Lord took away all your sins by being baptized in the Jordan River, then the Holy Spirit is bound to dwell in your heart. God is the God of justice, the God of mercy, and the God of truth. He is a good God who is benevolent to mankind, blesses them, and saves them from their sins. Therefore, because this benevolent God dwells in the hearts of all of us who believe in the gospel of the water and the Spirit, we are also capable of doing good to others. As a result, those whose hearts are indwelt by the Holy Spirit cannot help but do God's work of righteousness. For this reason, if you have really received the remission of sins by believing in the gospel of the water and the Spirit, then you cannot live just for your own flesh.

If you are otherwise living for you own flesh, then you are facing a huge problem, as it indicates that you still have not been born again properly yet. We may say that such people do not truly know the righteousness of God and His love. It is not we who loved God first, but it is God who loved us first. Given the fact that such people like us have received the remission of sins once and for all by faith, how could we not do everything we can to support this precious gospel ministry? How could we not minister the grain offering to God spiritually? How could we not sacrifice ourselves so that everyone else may also be saved from sin?

Imagine for a minute that I told you, "Don't do anything to serve the gospel of the water and the Spirit. From now on, do absolutely nothing to lead others to receive the remission of sins." Would you be able to obey my instruction? No, you wouldn't. What would you do if you were prevented from spreading the gospel of the water and the Spirit? Wouldn't you say, "Give me liberty or give me death'? "If you are trying to stop me from spreading the gospel, you might as well take away my life! So many people are in so much pain and struggling with their sins. They do not even know why they were born. You might as well kill me if you want me to stop preaching to such wretched people the beautiful gospel of the water and the Spirit." So don't try to stop me!" Isn't this what you would say? Of course you would say these things.

If we were prohibited from serving the gospel of the water and the Spirit and supporting its ministry, I would be praying like this: "Lord, I've lived long enough, so please take me away soon. If I can't do such a wonderful and good work now, and if I can't carry out Your righteous work, I will just end up wasting the rest of my life eating and sleeping. What's the point of living like this? So please take me away right away." That's how I would pray. Unless we preach the gospel of the water and the Spirit, what hope do we have in this world? I am sure you feel the same. We have no desire to remain on this earth any longer if we can't do God's work.

On the other hand, although countless people have heard and believe in the gospel of the water and the Spirit, there are those who truly want to remain on this earth to support the gospel ministry. What does the Bible say? It's written that even though Jesus healed ten lepers, there was only one leper who returned and thanked the Lord for healing him. A myriad number of people have heard the gospel. In Korea also, many people have heard the gospel. However, caught up in an empty shell of religion, they are still drawn to these mega-churches, and they think that it's ok for their hearts to remain sinful even as they believe in Jesus. Because they believe in the Lord only as a matter of religion, they forsake Him when they feel bad and they look for Him again when they feel better.

In contrast, we are working to spread the gospel of the water and the Spirit to well over 6 billion people living throughout the whole world. We are serving the Lord and other souls. We are therefore the truly blessed ones in God's sight, and we are doing something that is truly benevolent. In Korea, there actually are very few people who believe in the gospel of the water and the Spirit. But, do you know that we have received over 3,000 testimonies of salvation from around the world? Indeed, countless people all over the world are receiving the remission of sins from hearing the gospel preached by us. We ought to be very thankful to God that we are offering ourselves to Him like this. In my sermon today, I explained to you that we must minister peace offerings, and at this evening hour, I would like to emphasize that we must also minister grain offerings by sacrificing ourselves. Those who have received the remission of sins into their hearts must now minister offerings to God often for the sake of other souls. They must do this always. They must serve the Lord's gospel by sacrificing themselves for others.

While we don't speak about it much, just how many sacrifices have we made to serve the gospel of the water and the Spirit? An astounding number of people are sacrificing themselves to support the gospel ministry. But, this is only a matter of course. And how do these people behave while sacrificing themselves? Is there anyone who brags about themselves? While it is ok for us to find it hard to serve the gospel, it is not ok to exaggerate this hardship and demand something back in return. This angers me much. Because grain offerings, peace offerings, and sin offerings are ministered through self-sacrifice for the sake of others, it is only natural for us to find it hard and toilsome. Isn't this so? Don't you think that this is expected? It is only a matter of course that we would find it hard.

However, even if my whole body is ruined, I would be so thankful if only others can receive the remission of sins from hearing this gospel and enter the Kingdom of Heaven. "I would thank the Lord and say to Him gladly, "Lord, even though my effort has been so little and my sacrifice has been so insignificant, You have made it possible to harvest so many fruits. Hallelujah! Thank You, Lord! Despite the fact that I have done so little, You have saved so many people and given them Your glory by making Your love known to them. I am so amazed and thankful that I can't help but give all glory to You." Even if I have to labor until the moment I take my last breath, if more people come to receive the remission of sins from this labor, then I am more than satisfied. I am sure you feel the same way.

As you have received the remission of sins and your faith grows, from now on you ought to live for others rather than just yourself. Of course, those who have received the remission of sins only recently should focus on following their predecessors of faith and growing and learning from this. That is the appropriate thing to do. Just how happy and overjoyed are we to serve the Lord's gospel? I am so happy that words cannot describe it. I trust that you are also happy. Although it's true that serving the Lord is hard on us, at least our hearts are happy. Because of this small labor of ours, everyone throughout the whole world can now be saved. This shows us that God is indeed doing such a great work and blessing us with such a great reward.

I give all thanks to God. Today, at this very hour, I have the following words of admonishment for everyone listening. Let us all serve the gospel faithfully, and let us all support the gospel ministry diligently. It is very wrong for any of us here to slack off and try to avoid God's work when everyone else is working so hard to serve the Lord, saying, "That's it! I can't do it anymore. You can intervene with me up to this point, but no more!" Did the Lord ever say anything like this to us? No, of course not! If the Lord were to say to us, "I will take away the sins that you have committed up to now, but you are responsible for the sins that you commit from now on. You should be thankful that I am even taking away the sins that you've already committed," then we would all end up in hell. However, the Lord is so full of love that He did not this to us.

When He came to this earth, He blotted out all our past, present, and future sins once and for all. Through His 33 years of life on this earth, He has saved us perfectly by being baptized, shedding His blood on the Cross, and rising from the dead again. That is what the Lord has done for us. Therefore, it is only a matter of course that we should sacrifice ourselves to spread the gospel of the water and the Spirit. This is the work that God has entrusted to you and me. It is the task that God has entrusted to us until the day the Lord returns.

I hope and pray that God will bless our lives in both body and spirit. I ask God to protect each and every one of us here and abroad, and to bless them all. If we let ourselves be the

Lord's hands, feet, and lips, and spread His Word just as much as He loves the souls, then the Lord will protect us with even more blessings, so that He may use us as even more precious instruments. In other words, if you and I carry out the work of the gospel, the Lord will give us all His blessings in body, spirit, faith, even in our circumstances. It's because the Lord has blessed us so abundantly that we have made it so far. I ask and pray to our God to bless you all, and I give all my thanks to Him! ⊠

SERMON

4

You can download Rev. Paul C. Jong's Christian Books on iPhone, iPad, or Blackberry by going to Amazon's Kindle e-bookstore (www.amazon.com).

The Righteous Should Fulfill All Their Priestly Duties

< Leviticus 3:1-17 >

"When his offering is a sacrifice of a peace offering, if he offers it of the herd, whether male or female, he shall offer it without blemish before the LORD. And he shall lay his hand on the head of his offering, and kill it at the door of the tabernacle of meeting; and Aaron's sons, the priests, shall sprinkle the blood all around on the altar. Then he shall offer from the sacrifice of the peace offering an offering made by fire to the LORD. The fat that covers the entrails and all the fat that is on the entrails, the two kidneys and the fat that is on them by the flanks, and the fatty lobe attached to the liver above the kidneys, he shall remove; and Aaron's sons shall burn it on the altar upon the burnt sacrifice, which is on the wood that is on the fire, as an offering made by fire, a sweet aroma to the LORD. If his offering as a sacrifice of a peace offering to the LORD is of the flock, whether male or female, he shall offer it without blemish. If he offers a lamb as his offering, then he shall offer it before the LORD. And he shall lay his hand on the head of his offering, and kill it before the tabernacle of meeting; and Aaron's sons shall sprinkle its blood all around on the altar. Then he shall offer from the sacrifice of the peace offering, as an offering made by fire to the

LORD, its fat and the whole fat tail which he shall remove close to the backbone. And the fat that covers the entrails and all the fat that is on the entrails, the two kidneys and the fat that is on them by the flanks, and the fatty lobe attached to the liver above the kidneys, he shall remove; and the priest shall burn them on the altar as food, an offering made by fire to the LORD. And if his offering is a goat, then he shall offer it before the LORD. He shall lay his hand on its head and kill it before the tabernacle of meeting; and the sons of Aaron shall sprinkle its blood all around on the altar. Then he shall offer from it his offering, as an offering made by fire to the LORD. The fat that covers the entrails and all the fat that is on the entrails, the two kidneys and the fat that is on them by the flanks, and the fatty lobe attached to the liver above the kidneys, he shall remove; and the priest shall burn them on the altar as food, an offering made by fire for a sweet aroma; all the fat is the LORD's. This shall be a perpetual statute throughout your generations in all your dwellings: you shall eat neither fat nor blood."

Our Present Duties

You and I are leading our lives of faith in God's Church, and accordingly are serving the gospel of the water and the Spirit united together with one heart so that sinners may be reconciled with God. We all believe in the gospel of the water and the Spirit, and we are all serving it diligently even at this very moment. But this gospel work will not end so easily anytime soon, for it is something that we must carry on until the end of this world. We are therefore determined to continue to carry out this work into the future. Even though we sometimes get weary from our work, and we feel worn out in both body and soul, we must still bear the burden of this work by placing our faith in the righteousness of God. That's because the salvation of so many souls now depends on us. Because there are so many sinners in this world, it is incumbent upon us to preach to them the gospel of the water and the Spirit that reveals the righteousness of God.

Most Christians living in this world today are perishing away in silence because of their sins. Having turned into God's enemies, they have nothing waiting for them except their own destruction, and therefore they must return to the gospel of the water and the Spirit if they want to prevent this outcome. In contrast, we are now preaching the gospel of the water and the Spirit to the people of this world. When we complete God's work that each of us are doing now, there will be still more work waiting for us. For instance, our Christian book series has continued to expand endlessly, from the Book of Romans to Revelation, 1 John, Genesis, the Gospel of John, and the Gospel of Matthew. This literature ministry must continue on into the future, producing yet more gospel books to enrich our fellow saints all over the world.

That's because just as you are listening to the Word of God continuously, so do our brothers and sisters and our coworkers abroad need to listen to the Word of God in their lives of faith, and this is made possible through our gospel books. That is why we are so devoted to our literature ministry all the time. Through our print and electronic ministry, we hope to proclaim the gospel of the water and the Spirit and nurture God's people all over the world. Even though we have preached the gospel of the water and the Spirit to the people of the world, if we fail to nurture them continuously through our literature ministry, we will also fail to spread the gospel completely. We will then bring disappointment to God. We have given birth to many spiritual children of faith by spreading the gospel of the water and the Spirit, but unless we share our spiritual bread with them, these souls will end up perishing. We therefore cannot afford to take a break from God's work, that is, spreading the gospel through our literature ministry.

Once we complete the spreading of the gospel of the water and the Spirit to people all over the world, it will be an absolute necessity for us to nurture them with our gospel books. Of course, no one here in God's Church is doing anything superfluous; everyone is indeed doing something necessary and useful. Our literature ministry is that much more important, an absolutely critical task for God's Church. That's because when a spiritually immature baby is born, we need the milk to feed this baby right away. Don't you agree with this? If a spiritually immature baby never eats anything, this baby is bound to get seriously ill. When people fall spiritually ill, they need spiritual nourishment to restore them, but if there is no spiritual food, then these souls will end up perishing. What is the bread of our souls then? This spiritual bread is found in the gospel Word of the water and the Spirit written in the Old and New Testaments.

And this gospel of the water and the Spirit written in the Bible is explained in our sermon books, and we need to spread and share these sermon books with everyone in this world. Only then can the dying souls live and find new strength to grow. This is precisely what we are doing right now. We are working to reconcile every sinner with God. We are doing something tremendously joyous, for this work is absolutely indispensable and priceless.

The Sin Offering Desired by God

Take a look at the peace offering described in today's Scripture passage. It explains how sacrificial offerings were made to reconcile sinners with God. Every peace offering mentioned in the Bible was an offering made to reconcile sinners with God. All those gathered here today have received the remission of sins by believing in the gospel of the water and the Spirit, and therefore we will focus on what we must do as God's servants to spread this gospel.

Leviticus 3:1-2 we just read describes how the people of Israel and its priests passed their sins on a sacrificial animal by laying their hands on it, slaughtered it, put its blood on the horns of the altar of burnt offering, and burnt the body of the animal by fire. The passage shows us how the Israelites passed their sins on their sacrificial animal by laying their hands on it, and what the priests did for their people once this sacrificial animal was handed over to them. What the priests did is recorded in verse 3 and onwards: *"Then he shall offer from the sacrifice of the peace offering an offering made by fire to the LORD. The fat that covers the entrails and all the fat that is on the entrails, the two kidneys and the fat that is on them by the flanks, and the fatty lobe attached to the liver above the kidneys, he shall remove; and Aaron's sons shall burn it on the altar upon the burnt sacrifice, which is on the wood that is on the fire, as an offering made by fire, a sweet aroma to the LORD"* *(Leviticus 3:3-5)*. These are the things that the priests did continually in the Tabernacle. They offered peace offerings day and night.

During the age of the Old Testament, the priests ministered in the Tabernacle to blot out the Israelites' sins, but inside the Tabernacle there wasn't even a chair for them to sit down. So the priests had to always stand while working. It's written in Leviticus 3:6-11: *"If his offering as a sacrifice of a peace offering to the LORD is of the flock, whether male or female, he shall offer it without blemish. If he offers a lamb as his offering, then he shall offer it before the LORD. And he shall lay his hand on the head of his offering, and kill it before the tabernacle of meeting; and Aaron's sons shall sprinkle its blood all around ·on the altar. Then he shall offer from the sacrifice of the peace offering, as an offering made by fire to the LORD, its fat and the whole fat tail which he shall remove close to the backbone. And the fat that covers the entrails and all the fat that is on the entrails, the two kidneys and the fat that is on them by the flanks, and the fatty lobe attached to the liver above the kidneys, he shall remove; and the priest shall burn them on the altar as food, an offering made by fire to the LORD."* It's written here that the Israelite's sacrifice was an offering made to God. That the sacrifice was an "offering" made to God means that God accepted this sacrificial offering and remitted away the Israelites' sins in return.

The priests of the Old Testament fulfilled God's desire by ministering these peace offerings, while in the age of the New Testament, when Jesus came to this world, He bore all the sins of this world once and for all through the baptism He received from John the Baptist, shed His blood on the Cross, and thereby saved sinners from their sins and iniquities—an offering accepted by God the Father. It's such an offering that God is demanding from sinners. The sacrifice that God the Father wants is the sacrifice of faith that blots outs sins; He demands nothing else. Therefore, in the age of the New Testament, God is pleased when we offer Him the sacrifice of faith, that is, faith in the gospel of the water and the Spirit—rather than any sacrifice of the old Testament.

If we have indeed received the remission of sins by believing in the gospel Word of the water and the Spirit, then we must continue to spread this true faith so that others may also receive the remission of sins. This is indeed the right thing to do. As those who have now received the remission of sins by believing in the gospel of the water and the Spirit, we must offer the sacrifice of faith ceaselessly for those who still have not heard this gospel. Those who offer such sacrifices have come to know the righteousness of God and believe in it, and therefore they must minister to offer the sacrifice of faith that saves the souls of sinners from sin. We must preach the gospel of the water and the Spirit to the countless people living in this world, and for us to achieve this, we must teach them about their salvation from sin, the righteousness of God, and His judgment.

For this to happen, who are the people that should make a peace offering for these sinners? Who should minister to make such offerings as burnt offerings, grain offerings, and sin offerings for them? It is none other than us who are living in the age of the New Testament and believe in the gospel of the water and the Spirit; it is us that must fulfill this priestly duty by placing our faith in the righteousness of God. This is the responsibility of those making peace offerings.

It Is All Thanks to the Righteousness of God That We Can Continue to Carry out Such Blessed Works in Our Lives

God's Church, where we are abiding, is supporting the work of spreading the gospel of the water and the Spirit in various ways, and we are serving this work from our individual positions. The righteous are indeed laboring hard for God's work. However, while it is admirable that we are carrying out God's work diligently, it is also exhausting to our flesh and we sometimes feel very weary and tired. As a result, there are some people among us who are taking an easy approach to God's work and neglecting the work of spreading the gospel of the water and the Spirit. In other words, although God's workers are indeed carrying out His work, some of them are working with a careless and an unspiritual heart.

What should we then do when such fleshly thoughts come to our minds? Since this would mean that our minds are tainted by the flesh, we must overcome it by placing our faith in the righteousness of God. It's true that among the laborers serving God's righteousness, there actually are some people who are not spiritual enough. It's also true that some of them are trying to protect their own privileges to live for their own fleshly desires. So these people think to themselves, "I am doing enough for God's work, and so no one should expect anything more from me, I will do only so much and no more." These people care more about their own flesh than the work of God or His righteousness.

If we have really received the remission of sins into our hearts by believing in the gospel of the water and the Spirit, then all of us should be happy to carry out God's work. The problem, however, is that some of us do not have this disposition. There are various departments within the Church serving the gospel of the water and the Spirit, but some people want to do just what they like, trying to pick and choose their preferred departments and positions. Such people challenge the Church leaders endlessly, thinking to themselves, "I have my rights and privileges, and so why are these rights not recognized then?" What do they do eventually, when they can't suppress their fleshly thoughts? They refuse to be led by the Church, saying, "I've been carrying out the Lord's work as a faithful believer in the gospel of the water and the Spirit, but no one has given me any recognition." Many of them come to think, "I will live my own life from now on," and as a result, they end up leaving God's Church, wanting to live for their own desires rather than serving the gospel of the water and the Spirit for the sake of God's Church.

Still others may think, "I'll attend the worship service at God's Church and listen to His Word, but the rest of my time will be spent on my own fleshly affairs. I'll no longer devote myself exclusively to God's work alone, but I'll also live for myself." It's actually possible for everyone, young and old, including even ministers, to have such fleshly thoughts. However, although it's true that all of us have such carnal thoughts, we don't live according to the flesh because it can't make God pleased and we will be destroyed.

The righteous who believe in the gospel of the water and the Spirit have the duty to preach this gospel to all the sinful souls that still do not know or believe in it. It is then only a matter of course that all of us should indeed serve God's work by faith. Yet despite this, there still are some people even in God's Church that refuse to do His work and instead follow their own flesh. They think to themselves, "I'm sure that I've received the remission of sins by believing in the gospel of the water and the Spirit. So don't pester me with all these requests. What has God's Church done for me lately? I've served the Church more than enough, what more can anyone demand from me?" All these are fleshly thoughts do exist within the righteous. Before God, carnal thoughts only leads to death, both spiritual and physical.

As those who have been made righteous, we must know

the will of the Lord and His righteous work which He entrusted to all of us clearly, and we must faithfully carry them out. The Book of Leviticus explains the sacrificial system through which the Israelites made sacrificial offerings to God. What do these offerings mean? Do they mean that you and I have to continue to carry out what the priests did literally? Or do they mean that now that we have become spiritual priests by believing in the gospel of the water and the Spirit, we must fulfill our spiritual duties as priests until the end? Not just those of us who have been entrusted with God's work, but all of us who believe in the gospel of the water and the Spirit are spiritual priests. Therefore, each and every one who believes in the gospel Word of the water and the Spirit must carry out spiritual work. This duty extends to everyone in Gods' Church, from the kids in the Sunday school to teenagers, young adults, men and women, lay believers and ministers alike. All of us must preach the gospel of the water and the Spirit, and all of us must serve this work of proclaiming the gospel.

As the righteous, we must make peace offerings time after time for the sake of all those who still do not know the righteousness of God. Is anyone then especially exempted or excluded from this work? No, that is not the case. Everyone must partake in this work. It is something that must be participated in by all. Each and every one of us must serve and preach the gospel of the water and the Spirit, no one is exempt from this. Remember this clearly, if you have indeed been remitted from your sins, thanks to the righteousness of God, then you have this duty, you are not excluded.

When we received the remission of sins by believing in the gospel of the water and the Spirit, how was this all made possible? We were able to born again because of the peace offering made by the priests who believed in the gospel of the water and the Spirit before us and were serving to proclaim this gospel. As such, we must also devote ourselves to the spreading of the gospel of the water and the Spirit and share our faith with others. It is none other than you who must work spiritually to serve and proclaim of the gospel of the water and the Spirit.

No righteous person is ever exempt from serving this gospel. If a three-year old child has really received the remission of sins by believing in the gospel of the water and the Spirit, then even this child must serve the spreading of the gospel of the water and the Spirit in whatever capacity that's appropriate for his or her age. In whatever way, whether by being a good-mannered child or in some other way, the child must serve the gospel. So even among our kids at the Sunday school, when I see some kids not serving the gospel, I say to them, "Although you are young, you still should serve the gospel. Shouldn't you do so if you have received the remission of sins by believing in the gospel of the water and the Spirit, and if you really believe in this gospel?" Don't you agree with this? What about our adult believers? Don't they also have the same duty to serve the gospel? If you and I have indeed received the remission of sins, then whether we like it or not, both of us have the rightful duty to serve and spread the gospel of the water and the Spirit by faith, which is the gospel of the Lord. This is right and fitting. It's the destiny of the righteous to carry out this work. It is something that's only a matter of course for all of us.

In God's Church, it's not acceptable for only some people to serve the gospel of the water and the Spirit while others are neglecting it. Even if you are a teenager, you shouldn't think to yourself, "Now that I've reached adolescence, I don't want to serve the gospel anymore. I am a free person, and so don't try to suppress my freedom." Every adolescent student must still continue to work to spread the gospel of the water and the Spirit. Likewise, the elderly must still serve the gospel of the water and the Spirit. Whether young or old, strong or weak, everyone must serve equally to spread the gospel of the water and the Spirit. You can't say, "Well, since you are strong and healthy, you should serve the gospel diligently, but I don't have to serve the gospel since I am not healthy." There are such exemptions. Each and every one who has become a priest before God must minister to offer spiritual sacrifices for sinners.

How Did the High Priest of the Old Testament Minister?

On behalf of sinners, the high priest of the Old Testament had to lay their hands on live sacrificial animals such as lambs and goats, slaughter these sacrificial animals, and burn them with fire. To show His power to Moses, God had brought fire down from the sky to ignite the altar of burnt offering, but He did this only once. All offerings, including burnt offerings, peace offerings, and sin offerings, were made to God by the priests, putting firewood under the altar of burnt offering and igniting it to burn the sacrificial animals. A huge amount of firewood was thus needed for this. The priests had to bring the dry firewood and ensure that it would burn well. Even when the smoke stung their eyes, they couldn't complain about it. They also had to make sure to cut the flesh of the sacrificial animals into pieces. This wasn't all. Once high priest laid his hands on the sacrificial animals head, he had to kill it and remove all its unclean parts.

You can imagine just how revolting it was to see what was inside this animal. When an animal dies, it defecates, and the priests had to clean up all the feces. All of this required a tremendous amount of water and firewood, both of which had to be prepared by the priests. The priests had to minister the sacrifice of the remission of sins for countless Israelites before God. To accomplish this, they had to keep the fire burning constantly under the altar of burnt offering.

All these things were done by the priests of the Old Testament. Today, if one has received the remission of sins, I believe that this person must serve to spread the gospel of the water and the Spirit, whether he is a Sunday school kid or the elderly. Isn't this true? What do you think will happen if someone with a sound body and mind says, "Though I've received the remission of sins, I won't serve the gospel"? Do you actually feel that God's Church has not served you well enough? But if you have indeed received the remission of sins by believing in the gospel of the water and the Spirit, then isn't it obvious that you were saved because those who had become priests before you had served you?

I am sure that you are well aware of the fact you and I are serving the righteousness of God. Do you think that our ministers and our supporting workers are laboring hard because they have a tough heart? Even ministers struggle in their flesh from time to time. Some evangelists are overheard praying like this when they go out to preach the gospel: "Lord, please allow me to come across good people whose hearts are prepared to receive the mercy of God, so that I may preach the gospel of the water and the Spirit to them. "Every evangelist wishes this sincerely, praying to God to bring good people to them. If you put yourself in the evangelist' shoes, you will also find yourself praying like this. No matter what, all of us must serve the Lord and preach His gospel of righteousness. This duty belongs to all of us equally, none of us are exempt. However, when I say things like this, some of people still can't understand and just blink their eyes. So whenever I say anything, I have to explain it in detail.

How Do Today's False Pastors Pray to God?

Today's false prophets pray to God like so, "Our holy, merciful, and omnipotent God, Your people have committed many sins in the past week, whether knowingly or unknowingly. Please forgive them." Some of them also say, "Everyone is a priest before God. Because the Lord Jesus Christ has saved us by shedding His blood on the Cross for us, we have been delivered by our faith, and therefore we are all priests. Now that we have been saved, we should live happily. God had come to this earth to love us. We were born on this earth to be loved by Him."

However, if we have indeed received God's love of salvation, then we ought to love everyone else's soul in turn as well. Yet despite this, some people just insist on their own rights when they attend church, saying to their pastor, "If I stop giving donations to this church, you will probably have some serious trouble. You may be the chair of the board of directors at this church, but I am also a member of the board. So what will you do? Are you willing to make some compromises with me? If not, I will have your salary reduced." How would a pastor who hears something like this preach then? This pastor will have no choice but to bless his congregation and say, "May you prosper in all things and be in health, just as your soul prospers. I want you all to receive material blessings. I wish you all to become rich." Why is it unavoidable for this pastor to minister like this? Why must he say things like this? That's because only then can he get paid and make a living. In other words, false pastors get paid only if they curry favor with the members of the church board or its Eldership.

What will such pastors do to their congregation in the end? They will turn their congregation into arrogant people, wanting to be served in the church rather than serving, thinking to themselves, "I have been saved by believing in Jesus' blood on the Cross. All that I have to do in this church is just give a tithe and make various thanksgivings and special offerings." Many Christians taught under such false pastors consider that this way of thinking is only natural. God's truth, however, teaches very differently.

The Word of God Says That the Believers in the Gospel of the Water and the Spirit Should Never Live Like the False Christians

The Bible teaches that those who have received the remission of sins from God must be, from that moment on, faithful to God and His gospel to death. As those who believe in the gospel of the water and the Spirit, all of us must be fully devoted to God's work on this earth until the day we go to the Lord's Kingdom to enjoy everlasting life. This means that in order to deliver the souls that have not been saved from the sins of the world yet, we must make these offerings, such as the peace offerings, grain offerings, burnt offerings, and sin offerings spiritually on their behalf, all with the gospel of the water and the Spirit. And we must also lead these souls to the Church and continue to offer peace offering for them through the gospel of the water and the Spirit. In other words, we must carry out God's work continuously to serve these souls. This is what every priest must do without fail.

It would be deplorable if any of us were to fail to realize this and think, "I've done my share of work since receiving the remission of sins. What more can anyone ask from me? I've done everything I should as a minister. So how can anyone expect anything more from me?" Such people will render it meaningless that they have received the remission of sins by believing in the gospel of the water and the Spirit. Of course, it's not completely implausible for us to say, "There are well over 6 billion people living in this world. When will we ever preach the gospel of the water and the Spirit to all these countless number of people? I've done my best, and this is all that I could achieve. What more can I possibly do?" However, my fellow believers, we must serve the righteousness of God ceaselessly, placing our faith in the gospel of the water and the Spirit and being empowered by God.

Think about it for a moment. Just because a priest has offered a sacrifice once for his people, does this then mean that he is done with all his work? No, that is not the case. You must continue to abide in God's Church and carry out His work. And when you go home, you must return after taking care of your family affairs and resume God's work. In the Old Testament, priests were required to fulfill their priestly duties until the age of 50. But what about us? If priesthood were to end at 50, many of us should have retired long ago. Pastor Kim should have retired, and I myself should have retired as well. But this is neither tenable nor acceptable. The priests of the New Testament must fulfill their priesthood from the moment they first believed in the gospel of the water and the Spirit to the very day they pass away.

You and I Have the Same Priestly Duties

I am no exception when it comes to my priestly duties. I must also continue to carry on with my spiritual priesthood. I also know very well just how hard you are working, but this gospel work must continue. Countless sinners are stretching their hands out to us for help, asking us to save them, and we have the duty to preach the true gospel of the water and the Spirit to them. After all, are we not doing God's work? Haven't you seen newly hatched chicks opening their beaks to be fed, even when their parents are not around? Aren't the sinful souls all over the world opening their mouths to be fed just like these chicks? Aren't they begging us to preach the gospel of the water and the Spirit to them? Given this, it is simply impossible for us to avoid this work. We must continue to spread the Word of life through our sermon books.

What will happen when the chicks grow up? Won't their flap their wings and venture out, and with enough courage, soar into the sky? What will happen when more time passes by? Having matured into fully-grown birds, they will hatch their own chicks and they will have to continue to bring food to their offspring. Haven't today's believers in the gospel of the water and the Spirit also become spiritual parents, doing the work of God until their time comes? Isn't this true having given birth to our spiritual children? We therefore cannot neglect them. How can any parent say, "My life is mine to live," and neglect to feed the children to seek one's own pleasure?

You are carrying out God's work faithfully now, and you will continue to do so even without my admonishment, but even so, I want all of us to fully realize just how important this work is, and to do it even better. If you carry out God's work without realizing its importance, you will think to yourself,

"I've done enough work." That is why I am calling all of us to set our minds firmly on God's work, renounce all other pursuits, and continue to do God's work faithfully.

Do you think there is anyone among the workers serving the righteousness of God who is free of any health problems? Even if we are physically ill, we must still continue to serve the Lord even while treating our illnesses. Only then can we preach the gospel of the water and the Spirit to everyone in the world. You and I were born on this earth with this mission of spreading the gospel of the water and the Spirit. This mission has not just been imposed on us, but it is something that we have willingly taken on out of gratitude, because we are so very happy to have received the remission of sins by believing in the gospel of the water and the Spirit. It is out of this heart of gratitude that we have come to nurture our spiritual children and make many more preparations to continue to carry out this work. And once we began to live in this way, we have also come to realize how we should live as Christians.

Ultimately, we have realized how we ought to live. The Lord said, *"It is enough for a disciple that he be like his teacher" (Matthew 10:25).* Having come to this earth, the Lord has given us His own life, thus making it possible for us to receive true life. We are then Jesus' disciples, and if we really want to live according to the will of Jesus our Lord, then we ought to live with Christ and die with Christ. How should we then live and die? We should live to spread the gospel of the water and the Spirit, and we should also die for the proclamation of this gospel.

My fellow believers, everyone who has become a priest and received the remission of sins by believing in the gospel of the water and the Spirit must serve the work of spreading this gospel. Regardless of who you are, man and woman, young and old, all of us must spread this gospel throughout the whole world. It doesn't matter whether or not you hold an office in God's Church. As long as we are in God's Church, all of us must work from each of our positions. Only then will this gospel of the water and the Spirit be preached completely to the ends of the world. Only then can every soul all across the world be saved. As such, I believe that we must live in obedience to the will of the Lord from the very moment we realize and believe in the gospel of the water and the Spirit.

We should no longer think or expect that life would get easier once we are elevated to a higher position in the church. In reality, when you are offered a higher position in God's Church, you will actually be even more busier. The higher your church office is, the more work of God you must do. Perhaps some of our junior ministers are thinking, "Since my church office is still low, I think what I am doing is enough for now. I'll serve more when I'm promoted to a higher office. When I become a senior minister, I'll enjoy more privileges." But this is not the case. You'll find this out once you actually become a senior minister. There will be even more work for you to do, as you will have to be sensitive to the needs of the saints, lead them, and build a sound foundation for them to serve the gospel well. Perhaps you will have a slightly more authoritative voice, but you will still have to carry out the same work of God as you had done before.

So, my fellow believers, do not think what you are doing for the gospel right now is enough. Instead, prepare yourself to work a hundred times more than what you've been doing thus far. Your mind will then be at ease. If you think that you are already doing more than enough for the gospel, then you will react adversely and have even a tougher time when more work of God is entrusted to you. But this doesn't mean that you should do nothing but work.

I believe that all our saints must serve the gospel of the water and the Spirit in unity, at least if they have indeed received the remission of sins. Am I right here? I ask you all to believe so also, and carry out the work of the Lord without fail by this faith. All those who have become spiritual priests must serve the Lord's gospel, and I believe that this readiness is something that all of us should have as a matter of course. Let me then close by giving all thanks to the Lord for His righteousness. ✉

SERMON

5

Restoring Our Relationship with God

< Leviticus 4:1-12 >

"Now the Lord spoke to Moses, saying, 'Speak to the children of Israel, saying: "If a person sins unintentionally against any of the commandments of the Lord in anything which ought not to be done, and does any of them, if the anointed priest sins, bringing guilt on the people, then let him offer to the Lord for his sin which he has sinned a young bull without blemish as a sin offering. He shall bring the bull to the door of the tabernacle of meeting before the Lord, lay his hand on the bull's head, and kill the bull before the Lord. Then the anointed priest shall take some of the bull's blood and bring it to the tabernacle of meeting. The priest shall dip his finger in the blood and sprinkle some of the blood seven times before the Lord, in front of the veil of the sanctuary. And the priest shall put some of the blood on the horns of the altar of sweet incense before the Lord, which is in the tabernacle of meeting; and he shall pour the remaining blood of the bull at the base of the altar of the burnt offering, which is at the door of the tabernacle of meeting. He shall take from it all the fat of the bull as the sin offering. The fat that covers the entrails and all the fat which is on the entrails, the two kidneys and the fat that is on them by the flanks, and the fatty lobe attached to the liver above the kidneys, he shall remove, as it was taken from the bull of the sacrifice of the peace offering; and the priest shall burn them on the altar of the burnt

**offering. But the bull's hide and all its flesh, with its head
and legs, its entrails and offal—the whole bull he shall
carry outside the camp to a clean place, where the ashes are
poured out, and burn it on wood with fire; where the ashes
are poured out it shall be burned."""**

If We Sin against God, What Should We Do to Address It?

The Book of Leviticus is the Word of God writing about
the union between God and man. How and what kind of
sacrifice should we offer in order to be united with the
righteous God? For us to be one with God, we have to offer the
sacrifice that God desired. The same was true for the people of
the Old Testament, from the priests to the leaders of the
congregation, to the common people, and to the elders. The
Scripture reading we read today describes what had to be done
when a priest brought guilt on the people.

It is written in Leviticus 4:2-4: *"If a person sins
unintentionally against any of the commandments of the LORD
in anything which ought not to be done, and does any of them,
if the anointed priest sins, bringing guilt on the people, then let
him offer to the LORD for his sin which he has sinned a young
bull without blemish as a sin offering. He shall bring the bull to
the door of the tabernacle of meeting before the LORD, lay his
hand on the bull's head, and kill the bull before the LORD."*

As we can see here, the priests of the Old Testament could
also bring guilt to the people. This means that just like the
people of God, the priests could also go astray by sinning. God
said that everyone sins against Him, including the elders of the
congregation and the common people alike. However, our Lord

wanted to blot out our sins forever. How can we restore our relationship with God when we actually sin? For the people of Israel, to address the sin blocking them from God, they had offer a sacrifice to God without fail and get that sin resolved by faith. In the Old Testament, when the people of Israel sought to address their sins, they laid their hands on the head of the sacrificial animal and killed it, and then the priest took this blood of the sacrifice with his finger, put it on the horns of the altar of burnt offring, and pour all the remaining blood out at the base of the altar.

By believing in the gospel of the water and the Spirit, we can be washed from all our sins. However, when we commit a sin our hearts become darkened. When even a little bit of dirty water is poured into clean water, it can cloud the whole body of water. In a similar vein, our transgressions can darken our hearts even if for a short while. This can happen even though we the believers in the gospel of the water and the Spirit now have absolutely no more sin. But, if we continue to commit sins, then our hearts will be darkened by these sins. As a result, our relationship with God can no longer be what it used to be. Whenever we commit a transgression against God, our hearts become darkened.

In times like these, we must think of and trust in the righteousness of Jesus Christ, who has become our own propitiation for sin. It is by our faith in the gospel of the water and the Spirit that we should restore our relationship with God. We must return to the Lord's gospel of the water and the Spirit, and reaffirm that all our sins were indeed passed onto the Lord once and for all through the baptism He received from John the Baptist. In other words, we must reaffirm that our Lord carried all our sins of the world once and for all by being baptized. This is because it is through the baptism He received from John the Baptist that the Lord took upon all our sins once and for all. And while shouldering the sins of the world, He was crucified and shed His blood for us.

We believe in this work done by the Lord, and we have received the remission of sins by this faith. It is quite possible for us to sin while living on this earth, but whenever we do so, we should remember that the Lord bore all the sins of this world once and for all by being baptized by John the Baptist, remind ourselves again of His condemnation as well, and thank Him with our faith. Unless we trust in and look towards the righteousness of God, our relationship with God will encounter problems. Of course, as long as we look towards the righteousness of God, there shouldn't be any big problem. So, whenever we commit a sin, we should once again look at the gospel of the water and the Spirit, and reaffirm that even that sin has disappeared. Only then can our relationship with God be restored.

Where can we realize this truth? We can realize it in the gospel of the water and the Spirit as recorded in the Scripture, of both the Old and New Testaments. This realization is reached when we make the offering of the remission of sins to God by faith. Such an offering is not the offering that is made to receive the remission of sins by believing in the gospel of the water and the Spirit, but rather, it is an offering that that must be made by reaffirming this gospel once more. Therefore, we must return to and search through the Word of God again, which records the righteousness of our Lord Jesus, who bore all our sins through His baptism. We must reaffirm that the Lord took upon our sins through the baptism He received from John the Baptist, that He was crucified while shouldering the sins of the world, and that as a result, our sins have been judged and blotted out. Our relationship with the Lord can be restored only if we reaffirm that the Lord was baptized by John the Baptist for us, died on the Cross, and rose from the dead again.

The High Priest of the Old Testament offered the Sacrifice of the Day of Atonement Only Once a Year

In the Old Testament, on the tenth day of the seventh month, the high priest firstly offered a sacrifice of atonement for himself and his own family by laying his hands on the head of a sacrificial animal and passing his sins and the sins of his family to it. After this, he then passed the sins of all the people of Israel to another sacrificial animal by laying his hands on its head. However, when the people of Israel sinned against God before the Day of Atonement arrived, they had to offer a sacrifice to God for such sins, for their hearts were darkened by their sins. Likewise, whenever our hearts are darkened by the transgressions we commit after being saved, we must offer the sacrifice of the Day of Atonement by reaffirming our faith in the gospel of the water and the Spirit. Spiritually speaking, we can do this because all our sins were already passed onto Jesus Christ once and for all through His baptism. In other words, we make such an offering by ruminating on the fact that Jesus Christ took away all the sins of each and every one of us once and for all by being baptized by John the Baptist.

This offering is all about reaffirming once more that our hearts are sinless, and thereby restoring our relationship with God. It is by our faith in the righteousness of God that we pass all our sins to Him. We must lay our hands spiritually, by believing in the righteousness of God. We must reaffirm in our heart that all our sins were passed onto Jesus Christ once and for all. With our hearts and our faith, we must uphold the grace of the remission of sins fulfilled by the Word of God.

Because we have received the everlasting remission of sins by believing in the gospel of the water and the Spirit with our hearts, we have absolutely no sin, and therefore we have no hesitation to approach God. That's because the Holy Spirit in us acknowledges that we are indeed sinless. What must we then believe for this to come about? We must return to the written Word of God and believe in the gospel of the water and the Spirit. And by once again reaffirming our faith through the Word of God, we get the approval of the Holy Spirit dwelling in our hearts for our faith in the gospel of the water and the Spirit. The Holy Spirit says to us, "Yes, I have blotted out your sins. You are right. Do not worry, for I have washed away all your sins and cleansed you with the Word of God."

The Holy Spirit says that all our sins are washed away with the baptism Jesus received, and that this is the Truth. We must wash away our hearts' sins by believing in the baptism Jesus received from John the Baptist like this. When we look at the Word of God in John 1:29, *"Behold! The lamb of God who takes away the sin of the world,"* we can verify that our Lord indeed took away all the sins of this world. We know the following from this passage: we the believers have no sin, for our Lord took away all our sins by being baptized and was condemned for them on the Cross. Knowing that our Lord was baptized and condemned for our sins, and therefore we have no sin in our hearts, is the correct knowledge.

Therefore, by reaffirming the gospel of the water and the Spirit recorded in the Word of God, we can be freed from all darkness even if we commit transgressions by chance. That is how we restore our relationship with God. Even those who have received the everlasting remission of sins by believing in the gospel of the water and the Spirit may suffer a momentary setback in their relationship with God. However, once this relationship is restored, they can continue to live for the righteousness of God. To have such a faith that leads us to restore our relation with God, we have to make the offering of faith with the gospel of the water and the Spirit. Only then can our hearts be freed from darkness when we sin. And only then can we restore our relationship back with God. Therefore, we must always live by our faith in the gospel of the water and the Spirit.

Even though we have received eternal redemption once and for all by believing in the gospel of the water and the Spirit, we must still maintain a healthy relationship with God. Why? It's because we stumble over our transgression often, for we are weak. It's all because we are weak. In fact, when the righteous commits a transgression, even their hearts, which had been sharing fellowship with God amid bright light, are darkened temporarily. For us to restore our relationship with God in our hearts, we must believe in the gospel of the water and the Spirit and make an offering of faith spiritually. We must know what is it that we have done wrong in God's sight, and we must also recognize that the Lord bore even such sins and washed them away with the gospel of the water and the Spirit. To believe in the gospel of the water and the Spirit is to pass our sins on to the Lord by believing in His baptism. We must also reaffirm with the Word of God that Jesus Christ shouldered all our sins once and for all and was condemned for them on the Cross. That is how we ought to revitalize and restore our hearts.

When a priest sinned unintentionally against any of the commandments of the Lord in anything which ought not to be done, the way to restore his relationship back with God was offering a sacrifice according to the requirements set by Him. This implies that by giving the offering of the remission of sins to God, we are restored to once again sharing fellowship with God. It's written in Leviticus 4:8-9: *"He shall take from it all the fat of the bull as the sin offering. The fat that covers the entrails and all the fat which is on the entrails, the two kidneys and the fat that is on them by the flanks, and the fatty lobe attached to the liver above the kidneys, he shall remove."* What does the Bible emphasize when it comes to the sin offering that brings the remission of sins to us? It is none other than the Holy Spirit. It's written here that the priest should take the two kidneys, the fat that is on them by the flanks, and the fatty lobe attached to the liver above the kidneys, and offer them to God by burning them on the altar of burnt offering. Spiritually speaking, the fat here refers to the Holy Spirit. This implies that we must burn the sins that are in our hearts with the sin offering.

Although we have made the everlasting sin offering by believing in the gospel of the water and the Spirit, this does not mean that we can continue to sin. Rather, whenever we become weary, we must reaffirm how God has blotted out our sins. God approves our faith only when we believe that God Himself bore our sins through His baptism and blotted them out. Because we are all human, it's possible for us to sin, but we cannot solve away such sins with our own thoughts no matter how hard we try. We must therefore reaffirm our salvation once again by trusting in the gospel Word of the water and the Spirit that has cleansed us. By reaffirming once more that the Lord has blotted out our sins, we can restore ourselves to this grace of salvation and drive out the darkness that had come because of our transgressions. Unless we reaffirm our salvation with the Word of God, our lives will be seized by darkness.

What Should We Do When We Sin?

Darkness descends on us when we sin. In times like these, we end up turning into darkness, even though God is the light. How can we then restore our relationship back with God again? We can restore it by making an offering of faith. We must cleanse ourselves and restore our fellowship with God, so that we can put away our temporary uncleanness to once again serve the Lord, renew our lives of faith, and receive God's blessings anew.

It is because we are weak that we make our offering of faith. It's because we will perish spiritually unless our relationship with God is restored. If we are cut off from God, then we will be ruined spiritually. Our lives would then become meaningless. Although we have received the remission of sins, there is no one amongst us that can commit no more sin while living on this earth? Who among us will not face darkness at one point or another? No one!

Jesus has blotted out our sins once and for all with the gospel of the water and the Spirit. We must look towards the righteousness of Jesus Christ often. The Book of Hebrews admonishes us to *"look unto Jesus, the author and finisher of our faith" (Hebrews 12:2). "Jesus Christ is the same yesterday, today and forever" (Hebrew 13:8).* If we do not fix our eyes on Him, we will fall into and be bound by darkness, our flesh, and our weaknesses, only to perish in the end. We must look towards the righteousness of the Lord always. We must look towards the righteousness of the Lord who has made us perfect. We must look towards it by trusting in the Word of God. This means we must look towards the righteousness of God that is written in His Word, not according to our own thoughts.

The Word of God has tremendous power. The Bible says in John 1:29, *"Behold! The Lamb of God who takes away the sin of the world!"* Let's all memorize this passage. Most of us know this passage without even turning to the Bible. In fact, most of us know it so well that we can probably cite it effortlessly even while asleep. However, just knowing it like this is different from reaffirming it once more. At the moment we read the Word of God, we can reaffirm in our hearts that Jesus took away our sins once and for all by being baptized by John the Baptist. While it is important for us to know the Word of God, it is also indispensable for us to once again reaffirm our salvation with the gospel of the water and the Spirit. That's because our darkened hearts are then cleansed by the Word of God.

Let's turn to Ephesians 5:25-27 here: *"Husbands, love your wives, just as Christ also loved the church and gave Himself for her, that He might sanctify and cleanse her with the washing of water by the word, that He might present her to Himself a glorious church, not having spot or wrinkle or any such thing, but that she should be holy and without blemish."* The "washing of water" mentioned here refers to the baptism of Jesus. This baptism of Jesus came by the Word of God. That God has washed us with water means that He has washed away our sins with His Word. What washes our filthy hearts is none other than the baptism Jesus which He received from John the Baptist, and the blood He shed on the Cross. The Scripture speaks of this issue quite often, so whenever our hearts become soiled, we must wash them again with the Word of God by reaffirming it.

This is how we must restore our relationship with God, so

that we may fulfill our priesthood. Standing at the entrance of the Tabernacle with a heart that is always sinless, we ought to reaffirm that the Lord is the One who has blotted out all our sins, He is the One who created us, He is the One who helps us, He is the One who blesses us, and He is God Himself who is our Judge. It is on account of this righteousness of God that we are able to truly ask Him for His help. This is how we are renewed everyday. By cleansing our darkened hearts with the Word of the righteousness of God, we can walk with the Lord everyday brightly, spotlessly, and in holiness.

As we carry on with our lives in this world, especially in social settings, there are many times when our hearts become darkened. There are times when our hearts or acts go astray. Whenever this happens, we must wash ourselves by trusting in the righteous Word of God. If your heart becomes darkened for some reason, then it's because you have sinned, even if you are not sure exactly what sin you committed. In times like these, you must reaffirm that the Lord took away this sin also. Because we are sinless, we can share fellowship with the Lord. And we can have the boldness to pray to God.

In 1 John, God said that He will give us whatever we ask with a good conscience. What makes us unable to have a good conscience before God? It's such things as fleshly thoughts and transgressions. Washing away these things with the Word, we must always pray to God boldly. Because Jesus has saved us from the sins of the world and become our Lord, and because He is God Himself, He will answer us whenever we pray to Him to help us. We ought to pray to God boldly with a clean heart to help us. We ought to wash our hearts with the Word of the Lord, pray to Him, and become the people of faith. So let us live in this world by trusting in the Lord.

The more time goes by since we first received the

remission of sins by believing in the gospel of the water and the Spirit, the more weaknesses are exposed. But, by what faith do the righteous live? In the Old Testament, if the priests sinned, if the congregation sinned, if the elders sinned, and if the common people sinned, they all had to offer a sacrifice to God to be washed from their sins. Just like that, in the New Testament, we can share fellowship with Him on account of this faith because we believe in the righteousness of the Lord, and because we believe in the Lord who has blotted out the sins of this world washing us clean. The Book of Leviticus speaks about unity with God. To be one with the Holy God, the very first step is to receive the remission of sins. This remission of sins is obtained by sacrificing a sin offering. Our relationship with God is restored according to the rules set by God. So, we must offer sin offerings to God often by believing in His Word. The Scripture says that when Job's son sinned, Job made a sin offering and a burnt offering for his son. This offering was an offering of sacrifice. God Himself described Job as a righteous man.

When we return to our everyday lives, we must make the offering of faith to God by trusting in His righteousness. We are spiritual priests. We are holy priests in God's sight. What should we then do when we sin? When those who have received the everlasting remission of sins commit a sin again, what can they do about this sin? They can restore themselves by once again making their sin offering spiritually. Such offerings are needed every day and every moment. Why? It's because the world is filthy and full of wickedness.

A long time ago I once read a weekly magazine called *Sunday Seoul*, and there were all kinds of nasty things written in that magazine. And flipping through the pages, I also saw many sexually suggestive pictures. We come across such things all the time. We can all access them easily if we make up our minds. Sometimes, such things are seen by our eyes inadvertently, even if we don't want to see them at all and have absolutely no intention to see them. Like this, our flesh commits transgressions often. In such times, we cannot come to the presence of God for a short while. For us to once again come to the presence of God, we must make the offering of faith that reveals the righteousness of God.

Therefore, whenever we make the offering of faith, we must do so with a clear understanding of what it is that we have done wrong before God. We must live in this world by trusting in the Lord, being always holy and sinless in God's sight. We are able to live now because we have heard the offering of faith, the Word of the offering of redemption. But, although we are now hearing the Word of redemption often in our lives, what should we do if we can no longer hear it? Even in a day, we ought to make the sin offering of faith in our daily lives. Only then will our hearts be restored. God's Church makes sin offerings all the time.

Even for those whose hearts have been corrupted by the world, their hearts will also be cleansed if they come into the Church, sit quietly in the pew, and listen to the Word of God. The Lord has cleansed away our sins once and for all and made us spotless with the gospel of the water and the Spirit. He has saved us from the sins of the world. He has turned us into holy people who can share fellowship with God. What about you then? Have you been washed from your sins by believing in the gospel of the water and the Spirit? I give all my thanks to God! ✉

You can download Rev. Paul C. Jong's Christian Books on iPhone, iPad, or Blackberry by going to Amazon's Kindle e-bookstore (www.amazon.com).

SERMON

6

You can download Rev. Paul C. Jong's Christian Books on
iPhone, iPad, or Blackberry by going to Amazon's Kindle
e-bookstore (www.amazon.com).

The Death Jesus Suffered on the Cross

< Leviticus 4:13-21 >

"Now if the whole congregation of Israel sins unintentionally, and the thing is hidden from the eyes of the assembly, and they have done something against any of the commandments of the Lord in anything which should not be done, and are guilty; when the sin which they have committed becomes known, then the assembly shall offer a young bull for the sin, and bring it before the tabernacle of meeting. And the elders of the congregation shall lay their hands on the head of the bull before the Lord. Then the bull shall be killed before the Lord. The anointed priest shall bring some of the bull's blood to the tabernacle of meeting. Then the priest shall dip his finger in the blood and sprinkle it seven times before the Lord, in front of the veil. And he shall put some of the blood on the horns of the altar which is before the Lord, which is in the tabernacle of meeting; and he shall pour the remaining blood at the base of the altar of burnt offering, which is at the door of the tabernacle of meeting. He shall take all the fat from it and burn it on the altar. And he shall do with the bull as he did with the bull as a sin offering; thus he shall do with it. So the priest shall make atonement for them, and it shall be forgiven them. Then he shall carry the bull outside the camp, and burn it as he burned the first bull. It is a sin offering for the assembly."

Warm greetings to all of you. Today, I would like to share the Word with you on how the people of the Old Testament received the remission of sins from God by offering a certain kind of sacrifice. When we read the Book of Leviticus, we can experience it being very difficult to understand. The Book of Leviticus records in great detail how people in the age of the Old Testament received the remission of sins. If the people of the Old Testament received the remission of sins according to the Word on the sacrificial system, then I believe that all of us living in this age are likewise can receive the remission of sins by believing in the Word of the gospel of the water and the Spirit.

In today's Scripture reading drawn from Leviticus 4:13-21, it's written how the people of Israel received the remission of their sins when they sinned against God as a whole. When the people of Israel sinned against God collectively, and when they realized this sin later on, they had to sacrifice a bull as their sin offering. To be remitted from their sins, the people of Israel selected a man amongst themselves to be appointed as the leader of the congregation. And this leader passed the sins of the people of Israel by laying his hands on the head of the sacrificial animal. In other words, a representative of the people of Israel passed their sins on their behalf to an unblemished bull chosen as their sacrificial offering.

What We Must Know about the Sacrificial System

It's very important for us to be knowledgeable of the Word of God. To once again summarize the sacrificial system of the Old Testament in rudimentary terms, acting as the representative of the whole congregation of Israel, the High priest passed their sins to a live goat by laying his hands on its head; he then drew the blood of the goat by cutting its throat; taking some of this blood into the Most Holy Place, he then sprinkled it seven times on the mercy seat; and then the High priest put some of the blood on the Altar of Incense. In addition, the High priest also poured the rest of the blood out under the Altar of Burnt Offering. After this, the flesh of the bull was cut into pieces, and they were burnt on the Altar of Burnt Offering and offered to God. This is how the people of Israel received the remission of sins when they sinned. Today, I would like to expound on this sacrificial system through which the people of Israel were remitted from their sins by passing their sins onto the sacrificial offering through the laying on of hands.

It is from the Scripture that we can find out how the remission of sins is received. For a sinner to receive the remission of sins, he must first of all pass his sins to a sacrificial offering by laying his hands on its head without fail. The offering that enables one to pass and transfer all his sins to his sacrificial animal is called the "sin offering." Let me first explain here what this sin offering means.

A "sin offering" is an offering that is made to make atonement for one's sins. When one seeks to receive the remission of sins from God, he himself must pay a price for it, and this price is paid by offering a sacrificial animal in lieu of himself. In other words, the "sin offering" here means that something else is sacrificed to make atonement for one's sins, by killing such animals as a lamb, a goat, or a bull." That's why it's known as the "sin offering." To illustrate, instead of a sinner dying for his own sins, these sins are passed on to a bull, and the bull instead pays for them by being killed in the sinner's place to pay the wages of his sins. It's very important for you to fully grasp this point, as only then can you believe in the Word as I go on to explain it to you.

Various Offerings Were Meant to Fulfill the Law

Apart from such sin offerings, there also are various other offerings such as burnt offerings and peace offerings. There is a common attribute to all these different offerings, and it is that they all require one's sins to be passed to a sacrificial animal. That's because instead of a sinner dying, a commensurate offering has to be made to God without fail. Put differently, instead of putting the sinner to death, an animal is killed. This was God's justice and His fair salvation. You all know that there are 613 commandments in the Law of God, right? You also know that you are incapable of keeping all these commandments? But you still try to keep them, don't you? It is indeed absolutely mandatory for us to keep these God-given laws.

If we cannot keep this Law, then we must be put to death as the price for failing to do so. Therefore, the conclusion to draw here is simple and straight-forward: if we fail to keep the Law of God, we have no choice but to face death. However, although God has to kill us sinners who cannot keep His Law, but because He loved us so much, He could not bring Himself to put us to death; and for this reason, God fulfilled the salvation of atonement, of the water and the Spirit, by accepting a live sacrificial offering in our place. God is just and absolute. He is perfect. His Word is therefore the absolute Truth that is fulfilled without fail.

Through Moses, God made a promise to the people of Israel with blood. And the people of Israel pledged that they would keep the God-given Law. God told Moses to call the children of Israel out before him. And proclaiming His Law to the people of Israel, God made the congregation of Israel to kill a bull and sprinkle this blood together, saying to them, "I have given you My Law, and you have promised to keep this Law. If you fail to keep the Law, then you will be put to death, just as this bull's blood was shed and it was killed." At the same time, however, God knew beforehand that the people of Israel were incapable of keeping the Law, and even so God still loved them. Therefore, instead of putting the people of Israel to death, God made them prepare sacrificial offerings in their place. This is God's just law of salvation. The key point for you to grasp here is that absolutely no sin whatsoever can ever be remitted away without paying its full price.

Sin is absolutely intolerable to God. The wages of sin is death without fail. This means that sin is blotted out only if its wages are paid off through death; it is not something that can be forgiven without a price. Because we commonly think of God as the God of love, it's very easy for us to delude ourselves into thinking that when we sin against God, out of His goodness He would just forgive us without demanding anything in return. But in reality, God never forgives any sinner freely, and instead He demands a price for it without fail, for He is perfect, holy, and just. Put different, because God does not lie, because God is holy, and because God is sinless and cannot tolerate any sin, He must put all sinners to death.

However, behind such wrath God shown towards sin, there is His just love, His love of salvation. As we can see from Scripture, this love of salvation has been manifested to us through the sacrifice made by Jesus Christ, that is, that which has been revealed to us by God the Father by passing all the sins of every human being to Jesus Christ through His baptism, which is a form of the laying on of hands; putting Him to death; and washing away our sins through this death of atonement. Let me explain this by drawing an example from everyday life.

Let's say that you were pressed for money and bought some food from a store on a tab. Can you settle your tab just by saying to the store owner that you've paid it all off already, without actually paying the money you owe him? No, of course not! You cannot settle your debt just with your words, nor is this acceptable to your creditor. All debts must be paid off in reality to be settled. If you have no ability to pay them off, then someone else must make that payment on your behalf. This is only fair and just. God has such a just mind. And man also has such a sense of justice. Because we human beings were made in the likeness of the image of God and after His heart, we are also drawn to justice.

As shown in today's Scripture reading, the people of the Old Testament received from God such a system to get their sins remitted away. When the High priest passed all the sins of the people of Israel to the sacrificial animal as their representative, killed it, drew its blood, and burnt its flesh as an offering to God, God accepted this offering and remitted the sins of the people of Israel.

The Death Jesus Suffered on the Cross

If this is the way the remission of sins was received in the age of the Old Testament, then you and I living in this age of the New Testament should also receive the remission of sins by the same principle. But, do we have any bull or lamb that we can readily offer? To my knowledge, none of us is really raising cattle. Nonetheless, even if we don't have any lamb, bull, or goat, we must still give something to God as our sacrificial offering in our place. Who then came to this earth as our propitiation for sin? It is none other than Jesus. Like the bull here in today's Scripture passage, Jesus had to accept all the sins of this world including yours and mine, and He had to be put to death as our offering to God, just as the bull had to shed its blood and be put to death. That is why Jesus came to this earth.

Having thus come to this earth, and when Jesus turned 30, He was baptized by John the Baptist in the Jordan River. When we turn to Matthew 3:15 and read further, we see Jesus being baptized. By being baptized by the representative of mankind named John the Baptist (Matthew 11:11), Jesus accepted all the sins of mankind. He accepted each and every sin of every human being from the beginning of the world to its end, leaving none behind. And in doing so, Jesus could become the sacrificial offering for all sinners, for you and me alike, just like the bull in today's Scripture reading.

Even though you and I had to die for our sins, Jesus bore all our sins through His baptism. When reading Matthew 3:15 in the original Greek text it says, "Αποκριθεις δε ο ιησους ειπεν προς αυτον αφες αρτι ουτως γαρ πρεπον εστιν ημιν πληρωσαι πασαν δικαιοσυνην τοτε αφιησιν αυτον." We have to pay attention to the underlined words, "ουτως" and "πασαν δικαιοσυνην." The Greek word "ουτως" (hutos) means 'just in this way,' 'most fitting,' or 'there is no other way besides this.' And the words "πασαν δικαιοσυνην" (pasan dik-ah-yos-oo'-nayn) means in the fairest state that has no defect at all. Therefore, this verse means that Jesus took all the sins of mankind irreversibly onto Himself in the most proper way by His baptism which He received from John the Baptist. Let me repeat once again here that Jesus was baptized for you and me to bear all your sins and mine.

Some of you have heard this blessed Word, 'that Jesus took upon all the sins of the world from its beginning to its end,' while some of you are hearing it for the first time. But, regardless of whether it's the first time you are hearing this or you've already heard it several times, it is the Truth clearly written in the Scripture.

Matthew 3:15 writes clearly that Jesus fulfilled all righteousness when He was baptized, that is, He has blotted out everyone's sins by being baptized. He was then crucified to death. As we see in today's Scripture reading, for the bull to die in lieu of the people of Israel during the age of the Old Testament, it also had to accept their sins first of all. But, did this bull know any sin? Did it know the Law of God? No, of course not. Only human beings know sin; it is not something that any animal knows. The bull therefore actually had no reason to die.

As I mentioned just a short while ago, because human beings were born on this earth in the likeness of the image of God and take after His holy character, they are capable of realizing their sins when they break the Law of God. That is why so many people try so hard to get their sins remitted away by praying to God. To compensate for the sins they committed, some people do good deeds such as volunteering at a seniors' residence, helping the poor, or giving a lot of donations to their churches, all in the name of God. They do these things because they think God would then somehow gloss over their sins. While their intention is worthy, their method is wrong.

Our sins do not disappear just because we do good deeds for other people or pray long and hard. Rather, the wages of our sins must be paid without fail. To pay the wages of our sins according to the law of God, we the sinners must be put to death. If this requirement were met right now, there would be no one left alive on this earth. But the people of this world are still alive. Spiritually speaking, all people are already dead because of their sins. That is precisely why Jesus was baptized in the Jordan River, to deliver you and me from this condemnation of our sins. It is for our sake that Jesus was crucified to death. He shed His blood on the Cross just as the sacrificial bull of the Old Testament had its throat cut and shed its blood.

Whenever you and I commit any sin, we feel wretched in our hearts. When we sin against God, we feel so down that we don't feel like living in this world anymore. It's because the wages of sin is death that we feel so depressed. This is because the Law that God spoke of thousands of years ago still applies to our hearts fully even now. That is why we must be saved by believing in the baptism of Jesus and His blood.

For those who believe in Jesus, it is a wonderful blessing that Jesus died on the Cross. One may wonder what is so blessed about Jesus suffering such a wretched death on the Cross, but even so, some of you still wear a cross around your neck. What is there to like so much about the Cross that you are wearing it on your neck? Crucifixion was one of the most cruel capital punishments reserved only for the most appalling criminals. So what is so lovely about the Cross of Jesus that you are wearing it around your neck? You wear it because Jesus died on the Cross in your place even though you had to die for your sins every time you sinned, and because you are so grateful for this; and that is why it's such a wonderful blessing that Jesus died for you.

It's not because people commit many sins that they must be put to death. Rather, the just law of God demands that anyone who commits any sin at all, even the tiniest of all sins, must be put to death for the wages of this sin. Just a short while ago today we sang a hymn called "At Calvary." I love this hymn. I love it because Jesus died for you and me in our place. Do we not all sin? Does everyone in this world sin, Christians and non-Christians alike? By their fundamental nature, human being cannot help but sin constantly. It is in their nature to sin every time they are awake. Today, I am speaking to you about the death Jesus suffered on the Cross in our place.

You and I, and all the people in this world, commit countless sins, but we are just glad that Jesus died on the Cross. Some people might think, "Jesus died on the Cross all on His own without even asking us about it, so how is this relevant to us? What is there to be so thankful about?" However, I know and believe that when Jesus died on the Cross, He died in my place. Although I believe in Jesus, because I am weak, I cannot help but sin while living in this world, and even if these sins of mine are small, whenever I commit them my conscience is still tormented. That is why I'm so grateful that Jesus has saved me by dying in my place rather than putting me to death. When we have this faith that Jesus died for our sins, it's then that we can truly pray to God with thanksgiving.

You all believe in Jesus, right? And you all pray to God, right? But, do you always find it easy to pray? Sometimes it's not so easy to pray. Is there then sin in your heart? Everyone's heart has a sinful desire. Are there any sins engraved in your heart that you just cannot forget, that just won't disappear? Some of you may deny this. However, although human beings are more than capable of easing their own conscience and hiding their worries from others, if they have any sin in God's sight, they cannot hide this sin.

It's written in Jeremiah 17:1, *"The sin of Judah is written with a pen of iron; with the point of a diamond it is engraved*

on the tablet of their heart, and on the horns of your altars."
God is saying here that He writes everyone's sins on the tablet
of one's heart and in God's Book of Judgment. That is why so
many people still have their sins remaining intact even after
believing in Jesus. It's not just a mere saying. Even after
believing in Jesus, countless number of Christians actually do
remain sinners. It's true that everyone sins constantly, but the
fact that so many Christians' sins remain in their hearts all the
time means that there is something wrong with their faith, and
it's all because they do now know the gospel of the water and
the Spirit.

If one really believes in Jesus, then this person should be
filled with peace, just as a hymn goes, "I've got peace like a
river, I've got peace like a river, I've got peace like a river in
my soul." Yet, instead of having peace like a river, countless
Christians are weighed down by heavy sins. God therefore
exposes people's sins so that they may not hide in their hearts
away. By exposing your sins, God is pointing out clearly to
you that there are sins in your heart, and that these sins are
written in two tablets. God is asking you to come forth and
admit your sinfulness to Him. And God is asking you to
believe that He Himself was baptized and crucified to death for
you.

Oftentimes we think simply that any wrongdoing we
commit against another human being is what constitutes a sin.
But this is a misunderstanding, indicating one's failure to grasp
what sin is really is all about. We can realize our sins before
God only when we realize that we have failed to live according
to the Word of God as written in the Bible.

It's written in today's Scripture reading, *"When the sin
which they have committed becomes known" (Leviticus 4:14).*
This passage implies that you must first of all realize what sins

you have committed against God, and that only after you have done this are you qualified to receive the remission of sins by believing in Jesus. When nonbelievers do something bad, such as getting into a fistfight, they just think that they made a small mistake rather than thinking that they actually committed a sin. They think of their wrongdoings as simple "mistakes" rather than as "sins." However, when people learn about the Word of God and come to believe in Jesus, they come to realize their sins. For some people, this realization takes a long time after they first began to believe in Jesus. In fact, many people truly recognize themselves as sinners only after believing in Jesus.

Like this, for many people it takes a long time since first believing in Jesus to admit to God sincerely that they are sinners, and to finally reach their salvation by believing in the gospel truthfully. That is why it took the Apostle Paul such a long time before being born again, and this is true for God's servants today also, many of whom were not born again until after ten, twenty years had gone by since they first believed in Jesus. In some cases, they were not born again until well after they finished they seminary training and were ordained as pastors. So, even if you have believed in Jesus for a long time, there is nothing to be ashamed of if it's only now that you realize your sins, and started to believe in the baptism of Jesus and His blood on the Cross, and thereby receive the remission of sins. On the contrary, this is something that you should be proud of.

In fact, I could be born again only after ten years had gone by since first believing in Jesus, around the time I was nearing the completion of my seminary training. But, I consider it extremely fortunate that I was born again even if belatedly. Had I not been born again, I would have turned into a crook doing nothing but defrauding you to make a living. How could

I have preached the Word, when I would have remained a sinner if I were not truly born again? So, let me take this opportunity to make the following admonishment: no matter how long you might have believed in Jesus, examine yourself right now to see just how much you really know about Jesus, and how correctly you understand and believe in the Word.

Receive the Remission of Sins through Your Faith

I admonish you all the time to receive the remission of sins. That's because the remission of sins is the greatest gift God has given us human beings. Before coming to God's Church, you did not know that Jesus had taken all your sins by being baptized in the Jordan River. Is there anyone here who already knew this? Worldly churches just teach that Jesus was baptized to demonstrate his humanity, to show us that He lived on this earth like every other human being. This, however, is ignoring the Word of God. Let's turn to God's Word here for a moment.

Let's all turn to Matthew 3:13-17 and read it together: *"Then Jesus came from Galilee to John at the Jordan to be baptized by him. And John tried to prevent Him, saying, 'I need to be baptized by You, and are You coming to me?' But Jesus answered and said to him, 'Permit it to be so now, for thus it is fitting for us to fulfill all righteousness.' Then he allowed Him. When He had been baptized, Jesus came up immediately from the water; and behold, the heavens were opened to Him, and He saw the Spirit of God descending like a dove and alighting upon Him. And suddenly a voice came from heaven, saying, 'This is My beloved Son, in whom I am well pleased.'"*

The word "then" in verse 13 the time when Jesus turned

30. After spending some time near the Sea of Galilee, Jesus stepped into the Jordan River and stood before John the Baptist, seeking to be baptized by him. This must have shocked him, as he said to Jesus in response, *"I need to be baptized by You, and are You coming to me?"* However, Jesus said to him, *"Permit it to be so now, for thus it is fitting for us to fulfill all righteousness."* As Jesus rebuked John the Baptist severely like this, he obeyed Him and baptized Him.

Do you know the meaning of the baptism Jesus received? Some of you are probably thinking that Jesus' immersion in the water symbolizes His death, while His emergence symbolizes His resurrection. Does anyone else know more about the baptism of Jesus? - Beyond this, most Christians think that baptism symbolizes the making of a new person. When I was baptized, I prayed to God to take away all my sins before getting immersed in the water. However, I did not know at that time what it really meant to pass my sins on when being baptized.

The Importance of the Word of God

What is more important: man's word, or the written Word of God? I have a question to raise here, but doing so, let's turn to Matthew 3:15 first: *"But Jesus answered and said to him, 'Permit it to be so now, for thus it is fitting for us to fulfill all righteousness.' Then he allowed Him."* Amen!

Didn't Jesus say clearly here, *"Permit it to be so now, for thus it is fitting for us to fulfill all righteousness"*? Now then, it's very important for us to pay close attention what Jesus mentioned here. Where it's written, "thus it is fitting for us to fulfill all righteousness," Jesus was saying that it was fitting for

Him to be baptized by John the Baptist, for John the Baptist to baptize Him, and for them to thereby fulfill all righteousness. Let me explain what the word "thus" means here. This word is "πασαν δικαιοσυνην" (pasan dik-ah-yos-oo'-nayn) in Greek. It refers to the way of fulfilling all righteousness, and this way is the baptism of Jesus. Jesus had come to this earth to blot out the sins of every sinner in this world. Having come for this purpose, He sought to be baptized by John the Baptist. Receiving baptism from John the Baptist was the only way to save all the people of this world from their sins. That's because by being baptized by John the Baptist, Jesus would accept all the sins of the world by them being passed to Him.

Let's return to Leviticus 4:13-21 in the Old Testament. When the sins of the people of Israel were passed to the bull, were hands laid on its head or not? It is written that hands were laid on its head without fail. This "laying on of hands" means, first of all, "to be passed on"; secondly, "to be transferred and planted': and thirdly, "to be buried." When the high priest representing the people of Israel confessed their sins and laid his hands on the head of the bull on the day of atonement, and through his hands all the sins of the people of Israel were passed on to that bull. That is why the bull was put to death, because the sins were passed to it. And that's why the laying on of hands implies burial.

In the New Testament, baptism involves getting immersed in under the water. Very importantly, the meaning of baptism is the same as that of the laying on of hands that I have just mentioned here, which is: "to be washed," "to be buried," and "to be passed on." In other words, the laying on of hands in the Old Testament and the baptism mentioned in the New Testament has the same meaning. The role of the bull that was sacrificed in the Old Testament is the same of the role of Jesus, the lamb of God in the New Testament.

The Book of Leviticus explains the sacrificial system. "Levi" was actually one of the twelve sons of Jacob. The name "Levi" means unity. It refers to a union, like the former Soviet Union that was created out of the union of various nations and ethnicities. So, the Scripture, especially the Book of Leviticus, is explaining to us how human beings can become one with the holy God through the sacrificial system.

While God is holy, human beings are unholy because of their sins. It is therefore absolutely indispensable for there to be a sin offering between mankind and God. To blot out the sins of mankind, an offering was necessary, and this offering had to be an unblemished animal such as a goat or a bull. By making the High priest lay his hands on this sacrificial animal and kill it instead of the people of Israel, God made it possible for them to become one with Him. It is through this sacrificial system of the Tabernacle that God blotted away the sins of the people of Israel making them clean. Not only did God blot out their daily sins, but on the tenth day of the seventh day, God also blotted out their yearly sins through the offerings on the Day of Atonement.

When we turn to Leviticus 16:21-22, we see how the high priest passed all the yearly sins of the people of Israel to one of two goats by laying his hands on the head of the goat. The first goat was killed in the Tabernacle, with its blood sprinkled on the mercy seat and its flesh offered to God by burning. The other goat, after accepting all the sins of all the people of Israel through the laying on of hands, was led out far into the wilderness to die for these sins. In the age of the Old Testament, God made the people of Israel the only sinless nation in the whole world through this sacrificial system.

Let's turn to Leviticus 16:21-22 here: *"Aaron shall lay*

both his hands on the head of the live goat, confess over it all the iniquities of the children of Israel, and all their transgressions, concerning all their sins, putting them on the head of the goat, and shall send it away into the wilderness by the hand of a suitable man. The goat shall bear on itself all their iniquities to an uninhabited land; and he shall release the goat in the wilderness." Amen!

It's written here that Aaron should lay both his hands on the head of the live goat, confessing over it all the iniquities of the children of Israel and all the transgressions committed by them, and putting them on the head of the goat. Aaron was Moses' big brother. He was also the high priest, and he confessed all the sins of the people of Israel by laying his hands on the head of the goat while they were watching him. I've already explained to you that the "laying on of hands" means "to be passed on," haven't I? It's because the high priest laid his hands on the head of the goat like this that the sins of the people of Israel were passed to it. In this, the people of Israel in the age of the Old Testament received the remission of their sins through the sacrifice of the Day of Atonement offered on the tenth day of the seventh month every year. They were remitted from all their yearly sins in this way.

After the high priest laid his hands on the goat, confessing all the sins of the people of Israel and passing them to the sacrificial animal, this goat was then led out into the barren desert. All the people of Israel saw the goat being led into the wilderness. As they saw the goat disappearing into the horizon, they sighed in relief and joy. Thinking that the goat had left with their burdensome sins, they celebrated this and praised God. It's very important not to think of the burden of sin in the same way that we think of other burdens. The weight of sin is determined by God, and all sins, big or small, are equally sins.

That's because there is the Law established by God to blot out the sins of mankind. The "laying on of hands" means "to be washed," "to be passed on," and "to be buried." What the Scripture says is the most important.

Let's then return to Matthew 3:15 again. The Scripture says that as Jesus was baptized, all our sins were passed to Him so that they could disappear. It's also written in the Epistle to Romans, *"For in it the righteousness of God is revealed from faith to faith" (Romans 1:17)*. The righteousness of God here means that God has done the most right thing. How? He has done it by passing all the sins of mankind to His Son Jesus through baptism, and making His Son bear all these sins and be condemned for them. None other than this is the "righteousness of God," that is, the right thing done by God. Therefore, by believing in the baptism that Jesus received, we can wash away all the sins of our hearts.

Jesus has fulfilled the righteousness of God by being baptized. He has blotted out all our sins. That is precisely why Jesus said to John the Baptist when He was being baptized that the righteousness of God would thus be fulfilled: *"Thus it is fitting for us to fulfill all righteousness."* Do you now understand what this passage means? Do you believe that when Jesus was baptized by John the Baptist like this, all the sins of mankind, including all your sins, were passed on to Jesus? That is what I believe. I believe that all my sins were passed to Jesus at that moment. All your sins were also passed to Jesus at that time. They were all passed on already over 1,900 years ago in the past tense. By bearing all our sins through His baptism 1,900 years ago, Jesus washed them away and saved us, and we are now hearing this Truth at this hour after 1,900 years. Whether you believe in this Word of Truth that you are now hearing is entirely up to you. If you believe in it with your heart, then you will be saved for sure.

The righteousness of God is that He loved human beings and has therefore made them sinless. In Romans 10:3 God rebuked the Jews by saying, *"For they being ignorant of God's righteousness, and seeking to establish their own righteousness, have not submitted to the righteousness of God."* We must believe in God's righteousness, which is this joyful gospel that God took away all our sins by being baptized and ultimately died on the Cross in your place and mine. We must believe in this good news. Jesus could die on the Cross and be buried because He had accepted all our sins by being baptized in the Jordan River. The Jordan River is the river of death. This river flows into the Dead Sea. Because Jesus accepted all our sins in this Jordan River and washed them all away, all those who believe in this salvation can go to Heaven. However, whoever does not believe in what happened in the Jordan River, that is, the Truth that all the sins of mankind were passed on to Jesus through His baptism—will go to hell.

Let's turn to Hebrews 9:27 here: *"And as it is appointed for men to die once, but after this the judgment."* Like this, the Scripture says that everyone must face the judgment, and to avoid this judgment, one must be born again of water and the Spirit. By being baptized, Jesus bore all the sins of every human being, including yours and mine; He then shed His blood and died on the Cross; and He rose from the dead again in three days. He is the Holy Spirit and God Himself. Those who believe that Jesus is their Savior and their God will go to Heaven. It's such people who are born again of water and the Spirit.

Do you now understand that Jesus was baptized for every sinner? Do you now realize that all your sins were passed on to Jesus? By believing in this gospel of the baptism and the Cross of Jesus with your heart, you can pass all yours sins to Him at this very hour. This is not my own words. Far from it, I am just preaching the God-spoken Word exactly as it is written in the Scripture. So I urge you all to believe.

"Behold! The Lamb of God Who Takes away the Sin of the World" (John 1:29)

Do you then have any sins in you or not? You don't have any. All the sins you've committed so far have been passed on to Jesus, right? They have indeed all been passed on. Then about the sins you commit today, or the sins that you will commit in the future until the very last day of your life? Have these sins also been passed on to Jesus? Yes, they have! If we believe in this truth, then have we not been made holy also? Indeed, we have been made holy. However, it is not by not sinning that we have been sanctified, but rather, it is because we believe in this Truth that we have become sinless and therefore holy. In other words, we have no more sin because Jesus took away all our sins.

Let's then turn to John 1:29 here: *"The next day John saw Jesus coming toward him, and said, 'Behold! The Lamb of God who takes away the sin of the world!'"* Referring to Jesus, John the Baptist bore witness of Jesus here, testifying clearly to everyone that He was the Lamb of God who took away the sins of the world. John the Baptist then bore witness again in verse 36: *"And looking at Jesus as He walked, he said, 'Behold the Lamb of God!'"* Having come to this earth to blot out your sins and mine, Jesus accepted all our sins by being baptized by John the Baptist in the Jordan River, and thereafter He preached the gospel of Heaven for three years.

The Lord said that He is the way, the truth, and the life, and that no one can come to the Father except through Him. As shown in John chapter 6, the Lord also said that He is the bread of life from Heaven, and that whoever ate this bread would be saved and receive everlasting life. Saying that He is greater than Moses who brought the manna to the people of Israel, Jesus also said that He has saved sinners by accepting all their sins through His baptism and giving up His body on the Cross. Urging us to believe in what He has done for us, the Lord expounded that we are to receive the remission of sins and become righteous and sinless by this faith.

Jesus took away the sins of the world. Do you then have any sin left? No, you are sinless! That is why the Scripture says that whoever believes in Jesus is saved, as it's written, *"There is no other name under heaven given among men by which we must be saved" (Acts 4:12).* Because Jesus alone accepted all our sins through His baptism and died on the Cross in our place, only those who believe in Jesus are saved. How many sins then did Jesus take away when He took away the sins of this world? He took away each and every sin that has ever been committed and will ever be committed from the beginning of this world to its end. This world will end one day, and Jesus took away all the sins that have been and will ever be committed until that day. It's because Jesus took away every sin forever that John the Baptist bore witness of Jesus as *"the lamb of God who takes away the sin of the world."* It is indeed impossible to count all the sins that Jesus took away.

Our Lord took away all the sins that every human being commits throughout the entire lifetime, regardless of how long or short one lives. And by accepting this joyous God-given news into our hearts, we have become the children of the Kingdom of Heaven. Let's us all read Hebrews 9:11-15 together here: *"But Christ came as High Priest of the good things to come, with the greater and more perfect tabernacle not made with hands, that is, not of this creation. Not with the blood of goats and calves, but with His own blood He entered the Most Holy Place once for all, having obtained eternal redemption. For if the blood of bulls and goats and the ashes of a heifer, sprinkling the unclean, sanctifies for the purifying of the flesh, how much more shall the blood of Christ, who through the eternal Spirit offered Himself without spot to God, cleanse your conscience from dead works to serve the living God? And for this reason He is the Mediator of the new covenant, by means of death, for the redemption of the transgressions under the first covenant, that those who are called may receive the promise of the eternal inheritance."*

Do you believe in this Word of God? The Scripture says here that Christ has made an everlasting atonement for us. This means that Jesus has saved us forever and perfectly by taking upon all our sins through His baptism and shedding His blood to death on the Cross. Let's then turn to Hebrews 10:9-18 now and read it with one voice: *"Then He said, 'Behold, I have come to do Your will, O God.' He takes away the first that He may establish the second. By that will we have been sanctified through the offering of the body of Jesus Christ once for all. And every priest stands ministering daily and offering repeatedly the same sacrifices, which can never take away sins. But this Man, after He had offered one sacrifice for sins forever, sat down at the right hand of God, from that time waiting till His enemies are made His footstool. For by one offering He has perfected forever those who are being sanctified. But the Holy Spirit also witnesses to us; for after He had said before, 'This is the covenant that I will make with them after those days, says the LORD: I will put My laws into their hearts, and in their minds I will write them,' then He adds, 'Their sins and their lawless deeds I will remember no more.' Now where there is remission of these, there is no longer an offering for sin."*

Do you now believe without a doubt that Jesus has blotted out all our sins by being baptized, dying on the Cross, and rising from the dead again? Is there then any need for us to receive the remission of our sins from God again? No, of course not! While it is only a matter of course that we should all continue to serve God, there is no longer any need for us to beg Him again to forgive our sins. Now, all of us who have received the remission of sins ought to serve God alone. We ought to live for this gospel. Having heard and believed in this gospel, you are no longer a sinner, but you have become righteous.

From now on, we must pool our strengths to spread this joyful news of the Kingdom of Heaven to all those who still do not know the gospel. So I urge you to spread that this Word that I am preaching to you to all those around you who still have not heard this blessed Word. You will then become God's precious worker. You will become His witness. Just how grateful are we all that Jesus died for us on the Cross in our place, and that He bore all our sins by being baptized in the Jordan River? Jesus is now sitting at the right hand of the throne of God, and He is forever alive. If you accept into your heart that this Jesus has blotted out all your sins, that is, accepting the gospel of the water and the Spirit—then Jesus will dwell with you in your heart. That is precisely how you receive the Holy Spirit (Acts 2:38-39).

Do you then have any sin? No, of course not. Who did I say dwells in the hearts of those who are made sinless? The Holy Spirit dwells in their hearts. The Holy Spirit dwells in the hearts of all those who accept the joyful news of Heaven, the news of salvation, saying to them, "You are My children. You are Mine. You are My people." None other than this is the way to receive the remission of sins and the Holy Spirit at the same time.

Whoever claims to have received the remission of sins without accepting this gospel Word is invariably a liar. By our nature, we cannot help but sin while living on this earth. Precisely because that's who we are, and because we should have all died for our sinfulness, I am all the more thankful that Jesus died in our place. That is why I believe only in Jesus. Jesus has saved us through the water and the Spirit, His baptism and His blood on the Cross; and believing in this Jesus alone and holding on to Him alone, I give all glory to God. I hope and trust that you are doing the same. Once again, I give all my thanks and glory to God for saving you and me from all our sins, for saving everyone in this world. Hallelujah! ✉

SERMON

7

Forgiveness of sins

You can download Rev. Paul C. Jong's Christian Books on iPhone, iPad, or Blackberry by going to Amazon's Kindle e-bookstore (www.amazon.com).

The Everlasting Remission of Sins

< Leviticus 4:27-31 >

"If anyone of the common people sins unintentionally by doing something against any of the commandments of the Lord in anything which ought not to bc done, and is guilty, or if his sin which he has committed comes to his knowledge, then he shall bring as his offering a kid of the goats, a female without blemish, for his sin which he has committed. And he shall lay his hand on the head of the sin offering, and kill the sin offering at the place of the burnt offering. Then the priest shall take some of its blood with his finger, put it on the horns of the altar of burnt offering, and pour all the remaining blood at the base of the altar. He shall remove all its fat, as fat is removed from the sacrifice of the peace offering; and the priest shall burn it on the altar for a sweet aroma to the Lord. So the priest shall make atonement for him, and it shall be forgiven him."

The Spiritual Offering of Faith That We Must Give To God

Today I would like to examine the sacrificial offering that the people of Israel gave to God in order to receive the remission of sins during the age of the Old Testament. In the days of the Old Testament, the people of Israel offered a sacrifice to God to blot out their sins, and in this way the remission of their sins was obtained. By examining the requirements, forms, and contents of the sacrifices offered by the people of the Old Testament, we can think about the proper way to believe in Jesus. In those days, whenever the people of Israel broke the Law of God, they receive the remission of their sins by bringing a sacrificial animal and offering it to God. This world and the whole universe were all made by God. Although God is not visible by our naked eyes, there is no question that He is alive and with us. God has also given human beings His Law. It is through this Law of God that we have come to realize not only the sins of our acts but also the sins of our hearts.

In today's Scripture reading, we can see how the people of Israel were able to receive the remission of sins when they failed to keep the Law of God. When the people of Israel sinned against the God of love, that is, when their hearts, acts, or thoughts went astray—how did they obtain the remission of such sins and wash them away? They received forgiveness by offering a sacrifice according to the requirements set by God. God gave them the Law so that whenever they sinned against Him, they could obtain the remission of their sins by offering a sacrifice to God. To this end, God made the people of Israel build a house called the "Tabernacle," and He made them offer their sacrifices inside this Tabernacle. In other words, God had given them the sacrificial system whereby the people of Israel were to bring an unblemished animal such as a lamb or a goat, and sacrifice it to God as their offering. Let's then take a closer look at today's Scripture reading and find out exactly how the people of Israel offered their sacrifices to God in order to receive the remission of sins.

It's written in Leviticus 4:27-29: *"If anyone of the*

common people sins unintentionally by doing something against any of the commandments of the Lord in anything which ought not to be done, and is guilty, or if his sin which he has committed comes to his knowledge, then he shall bring as his offering a kid of the goats, a female without blemish, for his sin which he has committed. And he shall lay his hand on the head of the sin offering, and kill the sin offering at the place of the burnt offering."

This is the very first thing that an Israelite had to do when he sinned against God. He had to bring an unblemished female goat and pass his sins to it by laying his hands on its head. The reason why an unblemished female goat had to be brought is simply because this is what God had commanded for them. That the sinner brought a female goat means that this goat was sacrificed in the sinner's place. Because God loved the people of Israel so much, in order to save them from their sins, God accepted the female goat in their place and so forgave them. It's not because God somehow liked meat that He commanded the Israelites to bring the female goat. To repeat, God commanded them to bring an unblemished female goat in order to save them from their sins by them passing their sins to the goat and letting this goat die in their place, in this order.

Why was it necesssary for the Israelites to lay their hands on the head of the female goat? They laid both their hands on the head of the goat because this was the way in which they could pass their sins to that animal as set by God. When their hands were laid on the goat by faith, all their sins were transferred to the goat. The laying on of hands means "to be passed on," "to be transferred," and "to be buried." It has the same meaning as the baptism of Jesus. In short, the people of Israel laid their hands on the head of their sacrificial animals in order to pass their sins to them. Laying their hands on the sacrificial animal meant passing and planting all their sins on to that animal. It was the ritual by which the sins of the people of Israel were passed to these sacrificial animals, and as a result of this these animal were put to death instead of the people of Israel dying for their sins. So, in effect, instead of the people of Israel dying for their sins, this unblemished female goat accepted their sins and was killed before God, even though it was sinless. That's why it was called a sacrificial animal. The goat had accepted the sins of the Israelites and died in their place for their sins. This was the God-established way for saving the people of Israel from their sins, and furthermore, for the entire human race as well. Because God loved all of us human beings, He instituted this sacrificial system in order to save us from our sins.

To blot out the sins of the people of Israel, God set the requirement that they should lay their hands on their sacrificial animals without fail and thereby pass their sins to them. Accordingly, to blot out their sins, the people of Israel by faith had to lay their sins on the sacrificial animal by laying their hands on its head without fail. That's because unless they laid their hands on the sacrificial animal and passed their sins to it, it was impossible for them to receive forgiveness or become sinless. Only if the people of the Old Testament did this could they be born again as sinless people. This was God's law it could not be changed.

Now then, when an Israelite realized that he had sinned against God, and passed his sins to the sacrificial animal by laying his hands on its head, what happened to this animal? Once the goat accepted these sins, it lost its life. The goat had to die because it had accepted someone else's sins. This was all in accordance to the way of salvation that God had set for the people of Israel. Even in the secular world, once a law is in place, everything must follow this law as long as the law remains intact. The legislators create laws, and the people must follow these laws. In the same vein, God Himself, the Creator who made everything, set the law of salvation for the people of Israel, and when they passed their sins to their sacrificial animals by laying their hands on its head and killed it in their place according to this law, God saved them from their sins. Like this, to be remitted from their sins, the people of Israel first passed their sins to the live goat, and then cut its throat and drew its blood. The goat was put to death precisely because it had accepted the Israelites' sins.

The Inescapable Consequences of Sin

Every sin has consequences, and no sinner can ever escape from them. Let me illustrate this with a story. Long ago, there was once a king in a certain kingdom. Adultery was so rampant among the people of this kingdom that the king, in an effort to stamp out adultery, set a very strict law in place. The king decreed that anyone caught for adultery would be punished by having one of his eyes plucked out. He then proclaimed this new statute to all the people throughout the kingdom.

However, it so happened that the very first person facing punishment under this new law was none other than the king's own son. The prince was the first to be caught for adultery since the decree was proclaimed. The king was facing a very difficult situation. Since he was the one who established the decree against adultery, he had to enforce it, but this meant punishing his own son. To uphold this law, the king would have to pluck out one of his son's eyes, but he couldn't bring himself to do this as he loved his son very much. No matter how strict the law of his own making was, it could not overcome the king's love for his son. So the king was tormented by the fact that he would have to remove his own son' eye. At the same time, because the king's decree was still in place, he had to enforce the law. The king had to punish his son according to the law.

Yet, the king could not bring himself to remove his own son's eye. In the end, the king ordered the executioner to remove one of his own eyes instead of his son's eye. He did this because his son's crime had to be punished according to the law no matter what. So, the king gave up one of his eyes for his son, and the executioner thus plucked out the king's eye instead of the prince's before the people. In this way, by removing his own eye in lieu of his son's eye, the king could protect the prince and at the same time uphold his law. As a result of this, adultery fell precipitously across the kingdom.

As illustrated by this story, someone must pay the price of any and every sin committed against God without fail. God established His law for mankind, and therefore the wages of their sins must be paid in His sight. That's because God decreed that anyone with any sin would be put to death without fail, just as He said, "The wages of sin is death." However, because God loved even sinners, He did not have the heart to put them to death. That is why God enabled the people of Israel to be saved by passing their sins to a live goat and then kill it in their place. God had saved them from their sins through such a sacrifice.

It was all carried out in this way that the people of Israel in the Old Testament received the remission of sins. Whenever they sinned, they brought an unblemished animal such as a goat, a lamb, or a bull to the House of God, that is, to the

Tabernacle. They then passed their sins to this animal by laying their hands on its head, drew its blood by cutting its throat, and then gave this blood to the priests ministering in the Tabernacle. This was the way by which the remission of sins was received.

The people of Israel sinned day in and day out. They had to therefore offer a sacrifice every day. When they sinned in the morning, they brought an animal and sacrificed it to God. When they committed another sin at noon, they brought another animal to be sacrificed. When they sinned again in the evening, they brought yet another animal, passed their sins by laying their hands on its head, and once again received the remission of sins from God. But, they found themselves sinning again even before going to bed. In principle, the people of Israel would have to offer not just one but several goats or lambs every day just to be washed from their daily sins.

Although the people of Israel knew the law of God, they couldn't help but sin constantly, and therefore it was impossible for them to remain sinless. So, God established another law for them. Since it was not viable for the people of Israel to receive the remission of sins individually by bringing a sacrificial animal and passing their sins every time they sinned, so God provided them with an alternative. This new law was for the people of Israel to raise someone amongst them as their representative and offer a sacrifice to God through this representative once a year, rather than offering a sacrifice day in and day out. According to this law, these representatives of the people of Israel could pass all the people's yearly sins to a sacrificial goat once a year, and as a result of this one offering, Israel's sins could be remitted from all the sins they committed for that year.

The Everlasting Sin Offering

Let's turn to Leviticus 16:6-10 here, *"Aaron shall offer the bull as a sin offering, which is for himself, and make atonement for himself and for his house. He shall take the two goats and present them before the LORD at the door of the tabernacle of meeting. Then Aaron shall cast lots for the two goats: one lot for the LORD and the other lot for the scapegoat. And Aaron shall bring the goat on which the LORD's lot fell, and offer it as a sin offering. But the goat on which the lot fell to be the scapegoat shall be presented alive before the LORD, to make atonement upon it, and to let it go as the scapegoat into the wilderness."* Amen!

Aaron was chosen and raised up by God as the high priest to represent the people of Israel. The high priest's ministry was all about offering sacrifices to God on behalf of the people of Israel. So, Aaron the high priest first passed his own sins, his wife's sins, and his children's sins to a bull by laying his hands on its head, killed this bull, drew its blood, and offered the bull to God. In this way, Aaron firstly made atonement for himself and his household. Only after after this was completed did he have two live goats brought to him. These had to unblemished goats. Having brought these two goats, Aaron then cast lots for them.

Why were two goats brought to Aaron? Aaron had to lay his hands on both of these goats to pass all the yearly sins of the people of Israel to them, one of the goats was to be offered to God in His Sanctuary, while the other goat was for the people of Israel to see this in actually and believe that their sins were indeed passed on. Simply put, one goat was sacrificed to God for the atonement of the people of Israel, while the other goat was offered to make this atonement known to the people of Israel.

So, in this way, Aaron brought one of the two goats to the Tabernacle. He then laid both his hands on the head of this goat and prayed, "Lord, the people of Israel have sinned against You like this. They, Your own people, have committed all kinds of sins. They have failed to worship You faithfully; they have blasphemed against You; they have committed murder; they have committed adultery; they have stolen; they have been lustful; and they have been greedy." Like this, Aaron passed all the sins that the people of Israel had committed over a year by laying his hands on the goat according to this God-established law. After removing his hands from the goats head, he cut its throat with a knife.

In the Tabernacle, there was a place where God dwelt, namely, the Most Holy Place. Aaron entered into this place where God's Ark of the Testimony was located, dipped his finger into the vessel holding the blood of the goat, and sprinkled this blood on the mercy seat on the east side seven times, as is written in verse 14: *"He shall take some of the blood of the bull and sprinkle it with his finger on the mercy seat on the east side; and before the mercy seat he shall sprinkle some of the blood with his finger seven times."* As the Scripture explains, in the days of the Old Testament, goats were not the only sacrificial animals that accepted the sins of the people of Israel to wash them away, but other animals such as bulls and lambs were also used as sacrificial offerings. These animals were taken as the sin offerings that accepted and bore all the yearly sins of the people of Israel, and as a result of which they had to be killed.

Aaron sprinkled the blood of these goats seven times as a ritual to testify to God that this goat had in fact died instead of the people of Israel. Instead of the people of Israel dying for their sins, the high priest took the blood of the sacrificial goat, their propitiation, into the Most Holy Place and sprinkled it there to signify that the wages of the sins of the Israelites was paid by the blood of the goat in their place. It meant that the price of their sins was now paid before God.

In fact, the people of Israel had to be put to death in God's sight if they had any sin at all. However, on account of the sacrificial system, the high priest passed the sins of the people of Israel to the sacrificial animal, cut its throat, drew its blood, and sprinkled this blood before God. This signaled that the sacrificial animal paid off the wages of the sins of the Israelites in their place. In effect, the high priest was saying to God, "Lord, look at this blood. The sacrificial goat was killed instead of the people of Israel. Look at this blood and see that all the sins of the people of Israel have been blotted out and remitted away according to Your law." This was the significance of the first sacrifice offered to God on the Day of Atonement. When God saw the blood sprinkled by the high priest in His presence, He forgave and approved the people of Israel as being sinless, saying, "This sacrificial animal was put to death instead of the people of Israel. The wages of their sins have now been paid off according to My law. The people of Israel are now cleansed and become sinless."

Like this, the sins of the people of Israel were blotted out through the laying on of the hands of the high priest and the blood of the sacrificial animal. When God saw this blood, He knew that the high priest had laid his hands on the sacrificial animal. Of course, animals do not even know what sin really is. Since God did not establish any law for them, they are thus without sin. However, because the sacrificial animal accepted the sins of the Israelites, it had to die in their place. Like this, when God saw the blood of the animal brought by Aaron, He forgave the people of Israel from all their yearly sins.

Without the laying of hands and the shedding of blood, there can be no remission of sins. For us to receive the remission of sins from God, we must pass our sins to a sacrificial offering by laying our hands on its head without fail. We must then kill this offering in our place. And we must sprinkle its blood before God.

Now that we have seen how the sacrifice of the Day of Atonement was offered to God in the Sanctuary, let's turn to the sacrifice that was offered while the people of Israel were watching. Verse 21 says, *"Aaron shall lay both his hands on the head of the live goat, confess over it all the iniquities of the children of Israel, and all their transgressions, concerning all their sins, putting them on the head of the goat, and shall send it away into the wilderness by the hand of a suitable man."* The tenth day of the seventh month was a day of rest for all the people of Israel. It was like today, that is, it was like the Lord's Day, Sunday, when we do not work.

The tenth day of the seventh month, which was the Day of Atonement, was the day when the people of Israel received the remission for their yearly sins. As a result of the high priest ministering the sacrifice of the Day of Atonement, the people of Israel were remitted from all their yearly sins, but it took seven days to minister this sacrifice instead of just one. That the people of Israel passed all their yearly sins on the tenth day of the seventh month is not just my own claim, but it is written clearly in the Scripture for all to see. This is found in Leviticus 16:29. Let's read verses 29 and 30 together: *"This shall be a statute forever for you: In the seventh month, on the tenth day of the month, you shall afflict your souls, and do no work at all, whether a native of your own country or a stranger who dwells among you. For on that day the priest shall make atonement for you, to cleanse you, that you may be clean from all your sins before the LORD."*

As it's written clearly here, God determined that on the tenth day of the seventh month, the high priest would make atonement for the people of Israel, that is, the high priest would cleanse them and make them sinless by laying his hands on the head of the sacrificial animal and passing their sins to it, so that they may be clean before God. With a reminder that all of this was set by God Himself, let's turn to the preceding verse: *"Aaron shall lay both his hands on the head of the live goat, confess over it all the iniquities of the children of Israel, and all their transgressions, concerning all their sins, putting them on the head of the goat" (Leviticus 16:21).* It's very important for us to pay close attention to this passage, where God commanded Aaron to confess all the sins of the people of Israel and put them on the head of the goat.

When the high priest laid his hands on the head of the live goat, all the yearly sins of the people of Israel were passed on to this goat. This is not just my own claim or the claim of our church, but it's what the Scripture says. When Aaron laid his hands on the sacrificial goat, all the yearly sins of the Israelites were passed on to the goat, just as the Bible says here, *"putting them on the head of the goat."* The sins of the people of Israel were passed on to the goat because that was what God had determined would happen. Like this, the sins of the people of Israel were passed on to the head of the sacrificial goat trough Aaron's hands when he laid them on the head of the goat on their behalf and confessed their sins, saying, "Lord, the people of Israel have sinned. They have committed murder. They have committed adultery. They have stolen. They have envied. They have committed idolatry before You." That is why the laying on of hands means "to be passed on," "to be transferred," and "to be moved and planted elsewhere."

Like this, once all the sins of the people of Israel were passed on to the sacrificial goat, the goat was led into the barren wilderness and abandoned there. For the people of Israel, the fact that all their sins were passed on to the scapegoat and this goat was led far into the wilderness and abandoned there signified that their sins were removed from them as they were taken away by the scapegoat. This fulfilled the Word of God saying, *"The wages of sin is death."* While all the people of Israel were watching, small and tall alike, the high priest passed their sins to the scapegoat by laying his hands on its head, and then one of the Israelites led this scapegoat out into the wilderness. Those who were too short probably could not see it well, while those who were tall probably could see it further. Do you now believe that sins are passed through the laying on of hands? The people of the Old Testament received the remission of sins in this way.

Knowing all these truths how can we receive the remission of sins in this present age? Everyone living in this age, that is, everyone in the age of the New Testament—can receive the remission of sins by none other than believing in Jesus. When we turn to Matthew 1:21, we see that God the Father sent His Son to this earth to blot out all our sins. He had sent His Son to this earth through the body of the Virgin Mary. That Jesus was conceived by a virgin had already been prophesied by God through His servants. This is clearly written in Isaiah 7:14: *"Therefore the Lord Himself will give you a sign: Behold, the virgin shall conceive and bear a Son, and shall call His name Immanuel."*

God said here that He would give us a sign to indicate the coming salvation of everyone in this world. This sign was that a virgin would conceive the Son of God, and that this Son of

God would become the Savior on this earth. God had said so clearly through His servant, the Prophet Isaiah, about 2,700 years ago, promising us, "I will send My Son, so that I may save everyone in this world. I will send you the Savior, who will be born into this world conceived by a virgin. I will save you all through this Son."

Just as God had promised, Jesus indeed came to this earth about 1,900 years ago. The birth year of Jesus marks 1 AD. The calendar used by everyone nowadays, that is, the Gregorian calendar—is based on this birth year of Jesus. Everything is fulfilled according to God's promised Word.

Just a short while ago, I mentioned that when a sacrificial offering was given, it had to be an unblemished offering. But, is there anyone who is unblemished? No, there is no one! This then means that no human being can save any other human being, and that is precisely why God sent His own Son to this earth, made Him accept our sins and die in our place, and thereby made us sinless. That is how God has saved us. No human being can save another human being. So God promised that Jesus would bear the sins of mankind, die in our place, rise from the dead again, and thereby save us.

Let's turn to Matthew 3:13-17 here: *"Then Jesus came from Galilee to John at the Jordan to be baptized by him. And John tried to prevent Him, saying, 'I need to be baptized by You, and are You coming to me?' But Jesus answered and said to him, 'Permit it to be so now, for thus it is fitting for us to fulfill all righteousness.' Then he allowed Him. When He had been baptized, Jesus came up immediately from the water; and behold, the heavens were opened to Him, and He saw the Spirit of God descending like a dove and alighting upon Him. And suddenly a voice came from heaven, saying, 'This is My beloved Son, in whom I am well pleased.'"*

The passage here describes what happened when Jesus was baptized by John the Baptist. As it's written here, Jesus sought out John the Baptist to receive baptism from him. He sought to be baptized by John the Baptist in order to become our own sacrificial offering and accept all the sins of this world, just as Aaron the high priest in the Old Testament had passed the sins of the people of Israel to the sacrificial goat by laying his hands on its head. What is the importance of the relationship between John the Baptist and Jesus? Also, what is the role of John the Baptist? John the Baptist was the representative of all mankind. And Jesus was the propitiation for the entire human race in this world. In other words, Jesus was to become the sacrificial offering for our sins. That is why He sought to be baptized by John the Baptist and no one else.

What is the meaning of "baptism" then? The word "baptism" means "to be washed," "to be buried," "to be transferred," or "to be passed on." Its meaning is the same as that of the laying on of hands in the Old Testament. In other words, the fact that Jesus was baptized means that our sins were passed on to Him, transferred, buried, and washed away. Just as water is used to wash something, the baptism of Jesus implies that the sins of mankind were indeed washed away. Whose sins were then washed away once John the Baptist baptized Jesus? This baptism washed away all the sins of everyone who truly believes in Jesus. That is how our sins were passed on to Jesus. It is through His baptism that the sins of mankind were passed on to Jesus and planted on His body of sacrifice. And it is because Jesus was baptized by accepting all the sins of mankind, He was put to death. It's for this reason that Jesus sought to be baptized by John the Baptist.

It's written in Mathew 3:14-15: *"And John tried to prevent Him, saying, 'I need to be baptized by You, and are*

You coming to me?' But Jesus answered and said to him, 'Permit it to be so now, for thus it is fitting for us to fulfill all righteousness.'" Jesus said this because He was God Himself, whereas John the Baptist was the representative of mankind. No matter how virtuous the representative of mankind might be, it's only a matter of course that he would be lower than God. However, Jesus the Son of God accepted all our sins by being baptized by John the Baptist with the laying on of his hands. It was to blot out all our sins that Jesus, God Himself who had come as our Savior was baptized.

Matthew 3:15 says, *"But Jesus answered and said to him, 'Permit it to be so now, for thus it is fitting for us to fulfill all righteousness.'"* By this, Jesus was saying that it is right for Him to free everyone from all the sins of the world by being baptized by John the Baptist. What do you think was the most right thing that Jesus did for mankind when He came to this earth? It was blotting out all the sins of mankind by being baptized John the Baptist by the laying of his hands, and then bearing the condemnation of all these sins, for human beings could not come to the presence of God, nor go to Heaven, nor receive God's blessings because of their sins. That is why Jesus was baptized and was condemned. He had come to this earth to blot out your sins. And to this end, He was baptized by John the Baptist. The word baptism has the same meaning as the laying on of hands. By being baptized by John the Baptist like this, Jesus accepted all the sins of everyone once and for all.

It's written in verse 16, *"When He had been baptized, Jesus came up immediately from the water."* Through this baptism received from John the Baptist, Jesus accepted all the sins of the entire human race in this world, each and every sin ever committed by any and all human beings until the day they die, whether committed with their thoughts, hearts, or acts. In the age of the Old Testament, salvation was reached through the scapegoat. Likewise, in this present age, we the sinners are saved through Jesus. That is why Jesus was baptized by John the Baptist.

When Jesus was baptized by John the Baptist in this way, all the sins of mankind, each and every sin of everyone on this planet earth, were passed on to Jesus. While no one knows when this world will end, all the sins until the end of the world were passed on to Jesus when John the Baptist baptized Jesus. Every sin ever committed by all human beings since the day they were born to now were passed on at that time. If you have not known God until now, then this also constitutes a sin, but this sin was passed on to Jesus as well, just as all the other sins that you have ever committed were passed on to Jesus, regardless of whether or not they were committed knowingly or unknowingly, and with your thoughts or acts.

Do we then still have any sin left with us, or do we have no more sin? We have no more sin! It was to bear all the sins of this world that Jesus came to this earth. And according to the will of God, Jesus indeed bore all our sins. This is the Truth. Jesus took upon all my sins when He was baptized. And He bore not only my sins, but also all the sins of everyone at that time.

God is holy. God is just. And God loves us all. Human beings were made in the likeness of the image of God. God said, "I am the Alpha and the Omega." He also said, "I am the Beginning and the End." God is the Creator who made this world in the beginning, and He is sovereign over all things until the end. God is forever alive.

Does everyone here know dayflies? Dayflies are insects, named so because they live for only a day. Since they live just for one day, their entire lifetime spans only 24 hours. In contrast, God is forever living. He can therefore do everlasting things once and for all. He can bear the sins of those who died long ago, just as He can bear all the present and future sins of every human to come as well. God can transcend time and space. He is never restricted by any constraints of time or space. God is omnipotent like this. That is why when God came to this earth, He could bear at once all the sins of those who passed away long ago, as well all the sins of those who are alive now.

God also knows when this earth will end. All of us are under the sovereignty of God. Jesus Christ could bear all the sins of mankind once and for all because He is God Himself. That's why Jesus lived on this earth only until 33. Until He turned 30, He was raised in an ordinary family and led an ordinary life. Why was Jesus then baptized at the specific age of 30? Why did Jesus receive the baptism through which He bore all the sins of the people of the world when He turned 30? There was a reason for this. In the age of the Old Testament, the son of Aaron the high priest could succeed him as the representative of the people of Israel when he turned 30. Likewise, Jesus could accept all the sins of mankind as their Savior only after He turned 30.

In the days of the Old Testament, the remission of sins was received by passing them to a sacrificial animal, but in the age of the New Testament, Jesus accepted our sins on His own body. In other words, in contrast to the past when God had remitted away the Israelites' sins by passing them to sacrificial animals, now in this age of the New Testament, Jesus accepted our sins on His own body rather than using an animal. Because He is forever living and immortal, He accepted all the sins of this world on His body of sacrifice and forever remitted away everyone's sins once and for all. That is why Jesus was baptized at the age of 30.

Jesus could personally bear all the sins of mankind and remit them all away Himself rather than using any sacrificial animal because He is immortal. Because He is forever living, He could take away the sins of mankind forever. Because Jesus is God Himself rather than a human being like us, and because He had only put on the flesh of man for a short while, He could bear all our sins forever. In this way, He was able to take upon all our sins and all the sins of the entire human race.

Jesus bore all the sins of this world. He took upon the sins of mankind once and for all by being baptized. In doing so, He has saved us from all our sins. All our sins, from my sins to Pastor Kim's sins, Deacon Park's sins, and my beloved wife's sins, were passed on. Because Jesus loved us, and because He had to save us out of this love, Jesus bore all our sins personally by being baptized. Because God loved Deacon Park, because He loved us, and because He loved everyone made in the likeness of His image, God Himself came to this earth and bore each and every sin by being baptized. That is how God has saved us. It is through His baptism that Jesus has saved us. All the sins of this world were passed on to Him when He was baptized.

In this way, Jesus has fulfilled all righteousness. He bore all the sins of every human being, not just the sins of everyone living on this earth right now, but also the sins of everyone who ever lived and who will ever live in the future. All the sins of this world were passed on to Jesus completely. If we believe in this, then we can all realize that our sins were passed on to Jesus. God Himself bore all our sins and all the sins of this world. Because we are full of shortcomings, we cannot help but continue to sin in the future. Nonetheless, we have still received the remission of sins by believing with our hearts that

Jesus bore all our sins.

We are inadequate on our own. We are all weak. But despite this, Jesus took upon our sins. Therefore, by believing in this truth with our hearts, we can all reach our salvation. There is nothing else that we have to do. For that matter, there is nothing that we can do by ourselves to reach salvation either. The only thing that we have to do, the only thing that we can do, is to know and believe that God Himself bore all our sins. To do so, we must of necessity first of all cast aside our own thoughts. Even though in our thoughts it may be difficult to understand how Jesus took away all the sins of this world, this does not change the fact that Jesus indeed took away all our sins. So, you need to consider here what is right, whether you should stick to your own thoughts, or cast them aside.

In late the 1970s there were numerous Japanese soldiers from the Pacific War hiding in various island jungles such as Guam. Everyone knows that the Pacific War ended in 1945, right? However, these Japanese soldiers held out and were in hiding for decades, believing that they were still at war. In fact, the war had already ended long ago. Just as it's a fact that the Pacific War ended in 1945, it's also a fact that the sins of the world were passed on also. This world's sins have ended already. They were already (in the past tense) passed on to Jesus 1,900 years ago, just as the Pacific War ended long ago. What about your sins then? Were they not also passed on to Jesus, or are they still around? They ended already 1,900 years ago. It's extremely important for you to know clearly that your sins were passed on to Jesus. I'm not asking you to just believe it blindly, but rather, to grasp it clearly first.

"The next day John saw Jesus coming toward him, and said, 'Behold! The Lamb of God who takes away the sin of the world!'" By then, Jesus had already accepted all the sins of this

world, and He was now carrying them to the Cross. That Jesus took away the sins of the world means that He took away each and every sin of the world, big and small alike, including the twelve sins that everyone has inherited from the womb of one's mother. The "Lamb of God" here refers to the sacrificial lamb of the Old Testament, and at the same time to Jesus as well. Jesus as John the Baptist testified, *"Behold! The Lamb of God who takes away the sin of the world,"* Jesus indeed took away the sins of the world. He shouldered all the sins committed by us in this world. And He was condemned for our sins on the Cross. The sins that we will commit in the future are also part of the sins of the world. Jesus took away all these sins some 1,900 years ago.

John 19:17 says, *"And He, bearing His cross, went out to a place called the Place of a Skull, which is called in Hebrew, Golgotha."* Jesus was crucified because He had borne all the sins of this world. It's because of this that He was killed with both his hands and feet nailed to that cruel Cross. As the nails pierced through His arteries, He bled to death with all the blood that was in His heart pouring out. For human beings, the blood is life itself. Yet, because Jesus had borne all the sins of the world, He was crucified in our place, and He shed His precious blood to lay down His life for us. It was for all our sins that Jesus was crucified. In the age of the Old Testament, once a sacrificial animal such as a goat or lamb accepted the sins of the people of Israel through the laying on of hands, it had to shed its blood and be killed. In the same manner, once Jesus took upon all the sins of the world through His baptism, He had to face death on the Cross Himself.

Now then, let's turn to John 19:28-30 and read the passage together in unity, *"After this, Jesus, knowing that all things were now accomplished, that the Scripture might be fulfilled, said, 'I thirst!' Now a vessel full of sour wine was sitting there; and they filled a sponge with sour wine, put it on hyssop, and put it to His mouth. So when Jesus had received the sour wine, He said, 'It is finished!' And bowing His head, He gave up His spirit."* The Lord said here, "It is finished!" He said this because He had borne all our sins through His baptism, and was now dying on the Cross to bear the condemnation of these sins in our place. In this way, Jesus paid off all the wages of our sins. When Jesus said, "It is finished," He meant that He had completed all His work of salvation from the beginning to the end. In other words, Jesus had finished the work of salvation completely, so that there would be no more work ever again.

Let's now turn to Hebrews chapter 10 and read verses 9-12: *"Then He said, 'Behold, I have come to do Your will, O God.' He takes away the first that He may establish the second. By that will we have been sanctified through the offering of the body of Jesus Christ once for all. And every priest stands ministering daily and offering repeatedly the same sacrifices, which can never take away sins. But this Man, after He had offered one sacrifice for sins forever, sat down at the right hand of God."* The Scripture says clearly here that Christ, after offering one sacrifice for sins forever, sat down at the right hand of God. It says without a trace of doubt that Jesus offered one everlasting sacrifice for all our sins.

Let's read just one more passage before closing. It's written in Hebrews 10:17-18, *"Then He adds, 'Their sins and their lawless deeds I will remember no more.' Now where there is remission of these, there is no longer an offering for sin."* When God said here, *"Their sins and their lawless deeds I will remember no more,"* He was telling us that He will no longer condemn or judge us for the sins we commit out of our weaknesses, for Jesus had already borne all our sins and was condemned for them fully. The Scripture also says here, *"Now where there is remission of these, there is no longer an offering for sin."* This means because Jesus has blotted out all the sins of this world by being baptized and dying on the Cross, there is no longer any need for us human beings to try to be remitted from our sins through our own efforts. This is what Jesus has done for us. He is our Savior. He has fulfilled our salvation completely as our true Savior. Once more, I give all my thanks to our Lord! ⊠

SERMON

8

You can download Rev. Paul C. Jong's Christian Books on iPhone, iPad, or Blackberry by going to Amazon's Kindle e-bookstore (www.amazon.com).

This Is the Remission of Sins the Lord Has Fulfilled for Us

< Leviticus 4:27-35 >

"If anyone of the common people sins unintentionally by doing something against any of the commandments of the Lord in anything which ought not to be done, and is guilty, or if his sin which he has committed comes to his knowledge, then he shall bring as his offering a kid of the goats, a female without blemish, for his sin which he has committed. And he shall lay his hand on the head of the sin offering, and kill the sin offering at the place of the burnt offering. Then the priest shall take some of its blood with his finger, put it on the horns of the altar of burnt offering, and pour all the remaining blood at the base of the altar. He shall remove all its fat, as fat is removed from the sacrifice of the peace offering; and the priest shall burn it on the altar for a sweet aroma to the Lord. So the priest shall make atonement for him, and it shall be forgiven him. If he brings a lamb as his sin offering, he shall bring a female without blemish. Then he shall lay his hand on the head of the sin offering, and kill it as a sin offering at the place where they kill the burnt offering. The priest shall take some of the blood of the sin offering with his finger, put it on the horns of the altar of burnt offering, and pour all the remaining blood at the base of the altar. He shall

**remove all its fat, as the fat of the lamb is removed from the
sacrifice of the peace offering. Then the priest shall burn it
on the altar, according to the offerings made by fire to the
Lord. So the priest shall make atonement for his sin that he
has committed, and it shall be forgiven him."**

Our Lord has blessed us so that we can preach the gospel
of the water and the Spirit. I can't help but thank our Lord
whenever I think about the blessed gospel of the water and the
Spirit that the Lord has given us. So, although I am extremely
busy with so much work and my everyday life is not so easy
for me either, but I am still thankful that the Lord has become
my everything, for He is alive in my heart. The Lord has
enabled us to spread the gospel of the water and the Spirit
alone without any other asistance. The Lord and His
righteousness is everything to me. I am sure you believe like
this also. To you and me alike, the Lord is the Savior who has
blotted all our sin, who is the Judge, and the Creator. We
believe that by laying down His own life, He has given us new
life. Our Lord has given us everything that is good. Whatever
we have, there is nothing that we obtained on our own. All
things were given to us by our Lord. When we think of the
God-given salvation, we can realize that there is nothing that
has not come from God.

Everything we have, from our salvation to the new life we
are now enjoying and the Kingdom of Heaven to come, were
all given to us by God thanks to the righteousness of the Lord.
Even our condemnation of sins was borne by our Lord. We
know that it is our Lord who has brought salvation to us, and
who has given us everything we now have. Even at this very
moment, you and I are living, all thanks to the righteousness of

the Lord. If the Lord had not given us new life through the water and the Spirit, we would not be able to live forever. In other words, unless our Lord saved us, we could not have obtained everlasting life. Do you also think so? No matter how much we think about it, there is nothing that came from us. There is nothing that we can do on our own. Everything has been given to us by our Lord. After all, what could we ever achieve through our own efforts? Would our sins be blotted out if we tried hard enough? Everything has come about by our Lord's permission, and through the water and the Spirit. It is the Lord Himself who accomplishes all things, and never through our own strength.

Have We All Received the Remission of Sins?

Today's Scripture reading describes the sacrifice through which the sins of the common people were blotted out. It explains how the common people were to receive the remission of sins. However, in this passage also, the Lord made it clear that the remission of sins was to be received by offering a sacrificial animal in a sinner's place according to God's command. It's recorded here in Leviticus 4:27-29: *"If anyone of the common people sins unintentionally by doing something against any of the commandments of the LORD in anything which ought not to be done, and is guilty, or if his sin which he has committed comes to his knowledge, then he shall bring as his offering a kid of the goats, a female without blemish, for his sin which he has committed. And he shall lay his hand on the head of the sin offering, and kill the sin offering at the place of the burnt offering."*

Today's Scripture passage explains what kind of offering

should be sacrificed and how it should be offered by the common people when they sinned against God. The people of Israel often broke God's commandments and did what He had told them not to do. For the common people to be washed from their sins on those occasions, they had to first realize the sins they had committed, and then only offer a sacrificial animal. Once they realized that they had sinned against God and broken His commandments by doing something He had told them not to do, then the way to be remitted from this was offering a sacrifice of faith to God according to the sacrificial system established by Him, as it is written, *"If his sin which he has committed comes to his knowledge, then he shall bring as his offering a kid of the goats, a female without blemish, for his sin which he has committed. And he shall lay his hand on the head of the sin offering, and kill the sin offering at the place of the burnt offering" (Leviticus 4:28-29).*

A "sin offering" was made when a sinner passed his sins to a sacrificial animal and blotted them out. In other words, when the Israelites committed sins, these sins remained in their hearts, but they could get them blotted them out by passing them to a sacrificial offering as set by God. The common people themselves did not blot out their sins, but rather, their sins were blotted out through an unblemished female goat, by them laying their hands on its head, drawing its blood, and sacrificing it as an offering. There was nothing extraordinary that the common people had to do to get their sins blotted out. All that they had to do was just realize their sins and offer a sacrifice to God according to the God-spoken sacrificial system of justice. The sacrificial female goat then bore the common people's sins once and for all through the laying on of their hands, was condemned in their place, and as a result their sins were blotted out. Again, it was not the common people themselves that blotted out their sins on their own. Rather, their sins were blotted out as the female goat accepted these sins and was condemned in their place.

This implies that the salvation of mankind is fulfilled by our Lord Himself. It's written here that when the people of Israel realized their sins, they had to offer a sacrificial animal to God, and in such burnt offerings and sin offerings, female goats were used as sacrificial offerings. The sacrificial offering here speaks about our Lord Jesus Christ in the New Testament, that is, it explains how the Lord would bear all our sins once and for all by being baptized by John the Baptist, shed His blood as our own sacrificial offering, and thereby save us. Put differently, it is because our Lord bore all our sins once and for all by being baptized by John the Baptist that He could shed His blood on the Cross. We all had sins, but just like the unblemished female goat mentioned here in the age of the Old Testament, our Lord came to us, took upon our sins once and for all by being baptized, shed His blood, and has through this saved us. The Lord Himself accepted our sins once and for all through the baptism He received from John the Baptist, and the Lord Himself bore the punishment for our sins on the Cross once and for all in our place.

Therefore, it is by faith that we are saved from all our sins, and this means salvation is reached only by believing in the righteousness of the Lord. There is no sin that can ever be washed away through our own human efforts, such as offering prayers of repentance or seeking sanctification. In other words, God has made it clear that our salvation is not reached through our own prayers of repentance. Because everyone is born as a descendant of Adam, everyone is born as a sinner automatically. Everyone, however, is created by God. Therefore, there is only way for human beings to obtain the washing away of their sins from God. They must confess themselves to God, saying, "Lord, I have sinned against You. I am a sinner by my nature. I have failed to live according to Your Word all this time." One must then believe in the gospel of the water and the Spirit. This is how the remission of sins can be received. There is nothing more. All that we have to do is believe in the gospel of the water and the Spirit with which our Lord has blotted out our sins. Put differently, to blot out all our sins personally, the Lord Himself bore all the sins of everyone once and for all by being baptized by John the Baptist, shed His own blood on the Cross, and has thereby saved all those who believe in this.

The Lord has delivered us from all the sins of this world through the gospel of the water and the Spirit, and this is the Truth. What enables us to be saved from the sins of this world is knowing and believing in the gospel of the water and the Spirit. All that we can do is keep committing sins time after time, keep realizing our sins time after time, and keep confessing them time after time, but the Lord has saved us through the gospel of the water and the Spirit, so what else could we do but believe? Born as sinners under the Law of God, we can't help but sin all the time. Yet, our Lord loved such people like us even more and saved us through the gospel of the water and the Spirit. Having come to this earth to blot out our sins once and for all, the Lord bore them by being baptized by John the Baptist. And by shedding His blood on the Cross to death, our Lord bore the condemnation of our sins in our place.

The Scripture says that the common people had to offer an unblemished female goat for the remission of sins, but spiritually speaking, every human being is blemished. In this entire universe the only unblemished One is Jesus Christ. There is no one else unblemished but Jesus Christ, who created the heavens and the earth and came to save us from our sins once and for all. Our Lord never committed any sin while on this earth. He never sinned, not even once. The Bible says that even though people tried to push our Lord over the cliff to death, He walked through them unflinchingly and went on His way.

Jesus Christ has neither any weakness nor any blemishes. Our unblemished Lord came to this earth, and to blotted out all the sins of the entire human race, He bore all the sins of this world once and for all by being baptized by John the Baptist, who fulfilled the last high priesthood of the Old Testament; He was then crucified to death while shouldering the sins of the world, and He rose from the dead again. To blot out everyone's sins, the Lord Himself had become the sin offering by being baptized. In other words, the Lord accepted all the sins of this world by being baptized by John the Baptist. We have done nothing but commit sins since being born on this earth, but our Lord had already established a way to blot out all the sins of this world, so that He may save us from them. Let's turn to Leviticus 4:28-29, *"If his sin which he has committed comes to his knowledge, then he shall bring as his offering a kid of the goats, a female without blemish, for his sin which he has committed. And he shall lay his hand on the head of the sin offering, and kill the sin offering at the place of the burnt offering."*

When the people of the Old Testament committed sins, and when these sins came to their knowledge, they brought a sacrificial animal to the altar of burnt offering and passed their sins to it by laying their hands on its head. This laying on of hands was the method that God had set to remit away all the sins of the world. To save us from our sins, in other words, God fulfilled His will through this method of the laying on of hands. Having established the way of saving us from our sins, our Lord has saved us according to this way. Since God Himself had established that our salvation would come in this way, it was fulfilled accordingly. God Himself had come and set the way of saving us and remitting away the sins of mankind.

God said that the common people should bring an unblemished female goat and lay their hands on its head. Like this, when the people of Israel laid their hands on the head of their sacrificial animal, their sins were passed onto this sacrificial offering.

Now Let Us Look at How Sacrifices Were Offered on the Day of Atonement

Let's turn to Leviticus 16:2, *"Aaron shall lay both his hands on the head of the live goat, confess over it all the iniquities of the children of Israel, and all their transgressions, concerning all their sins, putting them on the head of the goat, and shall send it away into the wilderness by the hand of a suitable man."* As it's written here, Aaron the high priest laid both his hands on the head of the goat, confessed all the iniquities and sins of the children of Israel over it, and sent the goat away out into the wilderness by the hands of a suitable man. This means that the high priest passed all the iniquities and sins of the children of Israel to the scape goat by laying his hands on its head. The "laying on of hands" means "to pass on," "to transfer," or "to bury."

The Day of Atonement in the Old Testament implies that the Lord Himself had set and promised us a method and a way to blot out all our sins, and when the time came, He came to this earth and personally accepted all the sins of mankind by being baptized by John the Baptist, the representative of all mankind. In other words, the Lord Himself had set the way of blotting out our sins, and He had also said that He would make us righteous by thus blotting out our sins completely. Let me repeat here again, there is nothing that human beings can do on their own to blot out their sins.

It's written, *"And he shall lay his hand on the head of the sin offering, and kill the sin offering at the place of the burnt offering. Then the priest shall take some of its blood with his finger, put it on the horns of the altar of burnt offering, and pour all the remaining blood at the base of the altar"* *(Leviticus 4:29-30)*. God said here that the sacrificial animal should be killed at the place of the burnt offering. When one entered into the Tabernacle through its gate, the first thing that you encountered was the place of the burnt offering. This was the place where sacrificial animals were offered to God by burning them. It was the place where sins were passed onto the sacrificial animal, and it was also the place of judgment. When an ordinary sacrifice was made, the sinner passed his sins to the sacrificial animal by laying his hands on its head, drew its blood by cutting its throat, gave this blood to the priest, and the priest put some of this blood on the horns of the altar of burnt offering and poured the rest out on the ground.

Then the sacrificial animal was cut into pieces and burnt on the altar of burnt offering. The burnt offering signified the following for the sinner: "Instead of me dying for being a sinner, this sacrificial animal accepted my sins and died before God in my place." What would happen to us if we were judged? What would happen to sinners when they are judged for their sins? If people were to be judged for their sins and perish in the end, what is the point of being born on this earth in the first place, and why do we need the universe and all things in it? Without our existence, this universe and all things in it are completely useless. It's because of our existence that everything in this universe needs to exist, and why God needs them also.

Likewise, who then took upon our sins for you and me in the age of the New Testament, and who bore the condemnation of sins in our place? It is the Lord who took upon our sins and bore the condemnation in our place. Just as the unblemished female goat accepted the sinner's sins and died at the place of the burnt offering, so did our Lord bear the sins of the world once and for all by being baptized by John the Baptist; and just as God said that the wages of sin was death, so the Lord was crucified to death in our place, for He had shouldered our sins through His baptism. What is it that we did out of all these things? It is the Lord who did everything to blot out our sins, there is nothing that we ever did. That is why it is the grace of God and His gift that we have received the remission of sins by believing in the gospel of the water and the Spirit.

Is Only by Believing in the Gospel of the Water and the Spirit That We Have Been Saved from Our Sins

We have done nothing but commit sins under the Law of God ever since we were born. The remission of our sins is all God's doing. It is the Lord who let us be born on this earth, and it is also the Lord who let us be weak on this earth. Why did He bear all our sins and blot them out by being baptized? He did so to make us His children and let us live forever in glory in the Kingdom of Heaven, in His glorious Kingdom. There is nothing that we have done to achieve this. It is entirely the

Lord's doing. Instead of you and me being condemned for our sins, our Lord took upon all our sins and bore all their condemnation on the Cross. The unblemished female goat here refers to none other than our Lord. What then have we done? Nothing at all.

Until the age of 44 I had tried very had to accomplish something on this earth, but there was nothing that I could achieve in my own strength. Yet, the Lord fulfilled salvation through the water and the Spirit to save me from all my sins. He let me be born on this earth as a weak human being, and knowing that I would sin, the unblemished Lord came to this earth to blot out all my sins. The Lord Himself bore all my sins by being baptized by John the Baptist, and He was condemned for them on the Cross in my place. There is nothing that I did for my salvation.

Similarly, there is nothing that man has done to receive the remission of sins. What we must grasp here that you and I have received the remission of sins by believing in the gospel of the water and the Spirit and will go to Heaven, but this has nothing to do with our own efforts. Our salvation has been fulfilled by our Lord alone, who let us be born on this earth, bore all the sins of this world by being baptized by John the Baptist, and was condemned for our sins on the Cross. The only thing we can do is confess with our mouths that the Lord is the Lord of our life, the One who loves us, and the One who has given us everlasting life. And we can do no more than thank Him. In times past, however, people did all kinds of things trying to be remitted from their sins.

During the Middle Ages, the Catholic Church used to sell indulgences claiming that this would remit away people's sins. The claim was that the moment people purchased an indulgence, a soul that had already been cast into hell would go to Heaven. Even today, countless people foolishly try to receive the remission of sins through their own efforts, such as offering prayers of repentance, until that is, they come to know the gospel of the water and the Spirit. But, does anyone really receive the remission of sins by offering prayers of repentance or fasting? Can anyone be saved from his sins by trying so hard on his own like this? No, of course not. All the offerings and donations that Christians make to their churches go into building bigger and opulent churches. There are countless such opulent churches around the world.

These things happened in the past as they are happening now. If it were possible to be washed from our sins and enter the kingdom of heaven by offering money like this, why would it be necessary to believe in the gospel of the water and the Spirit? But, as I just mentioned, there is nothing that we can do for our salvation. The only thing that we can do is believe in the gospel of the water and the Spirit. Were we born on this earth because of our own efforts? Were we born because we wanted to be born? No, in reality, we were born all under the plan of the Lord. When we received the remission of sins into our hearts by believing in the righteousness of the Lord, all the will of God towards us is fulfilled.

Let's turn to Leviticus 4:31, *"So the priest shall make atonement for him, and it shall be forgiven him."* For the priest to address the sins of the people, he must work according to God's command. Our spiritual Priest is none other than our Lord. That's why we call our Lord the "High Priest of Heaven." The High Priest of Heaven has saved His people from all their sins by offering His own body to God the Father.

It's written, *"He shall remove all its fat, as the fat of the lamb is removed from the sacrifice of the peace offering. Then the priest shall burn it on the altar, according to the offerings made by fire to the* LORD. *So the priest shall make atonement for his sin that he has committed, and it shall be forgiven him"* (Leviticus 4:35). The common people received the remission of sins only if the priest put the blood of the sacrificial animal on the horns of the altar of burnt offering, took its fat, and burnt it on the altar on behalf of the people. Our Lord is the unblemished High Priest of the Kingdom of Heaven. The earthly high priest was a shadow of Jesus Christ, while the Lord is God Himself. As the Priest, the Lord bore all our sins by being baptized and died on the Cross.

Can anyone not commit any sins just by planning and determining himself not to sin anymore? No, of course not. While making the determination not to sin is itself a noble thing, when God made us mere human beings, He did not make us as such being that can avoid committing any sins just by determination. Rather, God made human beings as imperfect beings. Why? It's because we could be saved by believing in the gospel of the water and the Spirit that constitutes the righteousness of Jesus Christ. God made us as such imperfect beings so that He would make sinners righteous, turn them into His holy people, and let them live with Him forever in the Kingdom of Heaven.

Ephesians 1:4 says, *"Just as He chose us in Him before the foundation of the world, that we should be holy and without blame before Him in love."* This means that God let us be born as weak beings because He had planned that Jesus Christ would come to this earth personally, blot out all our sins, and make us His perfect people. That is why God allowed us to be born as imperfect beings from the beginning. Is there then anything that we can protest to God? No, of course not. Anyone who says, "Why did God make me so wretchedly weak?" is really challenging God the Creator. Such people might as well say to their own parents, "Why did you give birth to me? Since you gave birth to me anyways, you should treat me well and leave me a large inheritance." Perhaps one can say such things to his parents of the flesh, but can any of us say it to God who created us? Can we really say to God, "Why did You create me so weak? You should have made me strong, so that I would not commit any sin if I just resolved myself not to sin".

It is precisely because God made us as imperfect beings that we could become His precious children by believing in the gospel of the water and the Spirit. Angels can never become God's children. Everything is decided by the Creator. Can this cup that you see here say, "I don't like being a cup. I want to be a plate"? No, vessels are made according to the maker's desires. If the maker decides to make a cup out of clay and use it for drinking water, the cup cannot protest. The same principle applies when it comes to the purpose for which God made us.

By bearing our sins and being condemned for them, God Himself has blotted out our sins once and for all. By taking upon all our sins and bearing all their condemnation once and for all, God Himself has saved us from all our sins. Given the fact that God has determined that the remission of sins would be received if we believe in the gospel of the water and the Spirit, how can we reject it? Why would we grumble when God has enabled us to enter and live in His Kingdom if only we would have faith in His righteousness? On the contrary, we ought to be thanking God and believe in the gospel of the water and the Spirit with gratitude.

A while ago, I had a chance to visit the University of Gangwon and see an art exhibition. Sister Haesook Heo had invited me to the exhibition, as it was held by her friend. There, I saw a painting with this title, "Are All These Things

Predetermined?" The painting portrayed Heaven on one side and hell on the other side. So I scribbled a few words next to the painting. You know, some people think that who goes to Heaven or hell has already been predetermined, so they say that this is irrational. But, I wanted to make the point that God did not make human beings so that He would send them to hell.

As we saw in today's Scripture reading, when the common people needed to receive the remission of sins, all they had to do was just realize their sins, and upon this knowledge, pass their sins to an unblemished female goat by laying their hands on its head, kill it, and give its blood to the priest. The female goat then accepted all their sins and shed its blood in their place, its fat was burnt on the altar of burnt offering in their place, and its flesh was discarded outside of the camp. All these things were done by the unblemished goat on behalf of the common people. There was noting that the common people did. All that they did was simply to believe in God's Word just as it was and to obey it.

I mentioned just a few minutes ago about writing a few words next that painting. I can't recall the exact words that I wrote, but I wrote something to the following effect: "God does not love just some people while hating others. Nor did God make some people just to cast them into hell and others to send to Heaven. But whoever believes in the righteousness of God is made into a righteous person, while hell was made for those who challenge the righteousness of God." My point is that God did not make hell for people exclusively.

For whom then did God make hell for? When we turn to the Book of Revelation, we see that it is for the Devil who will be cast into the Abyss. As you know, the Devil is an angel that fell from grace. This angel fell because he challenged the righteousness of God by trying to become greater than God.

Angels were right below God, so they were made to give God much honor. Despite this, one angel challenged God and tried to climb up above Him. So God made hell at that time, saying to Satan, "Will you be exalted to the end of the heavens? You shall be brought down to Hades."

Like the angels that are spiritual beings, so God made us humans as very honorable beings. And God has given us personalities and a free will. Words cannot describe how thankful it is that we were made by God as such precious beings and are used by Him for His precious work. So how could anyone challenge the righteousness of God? How could a mere creature challenge God the Creator? What is so great about human beings, even if they are capable of greatness? Computer technology has advanced so much lately that we are now capable of making artificial intelligence. In sci-fi films, we even see computers controlling human beings, but no matter how much progress computer technology makes and how much computer capacity increases, a computer is just a computer and it can never be a creator. In other words, it cannot be better than human beings. No matter how capable a computer is, it is a child of the human brain, something that is made by man, not a self-existing being. Who then made man? It is God. It is the Lord who made or created us and who fulfills everything.

Can we reach salvation from our sins just by bowing down and offering our own prayers of repentance? Some Christians are deluded into thinking that they can receive the remission of sins if they go to church after sinning in the world, kneel down, and cry out to God in tears, "Lord, I have wronged. Please forgive me." If this were the case, then why did the unblemished female goat in today's Scripture reading have to die? If God were to forgive our sins like this, then there would have been no need for the unblemished female goat to die in place of the sinner. Whenever the common people sinned, they could have just said to God, "Lord, I am sorry that I have wronged You. Please forgive me."

If forgiveness could be obtained by begging like this, then why did the unblemished female goat have to shed its blood to death, and why did it have to be burnt on the altar of burnt offering? And why did the priest have to work so hard to minister the sacrifice? The point I am making here is that the remission of sins is not received with just words. Just because we say to God, "Lord, please forgive me. Let this sin of mine slide by," God does not turn a blind eye to our sins. God is the God of Truth, and therefore He cannot tolerate any sin. There are two things that the omniscient and omnipotent God cannot do. One is lying, and the other is sparing a sinner without any consequence. He even made His own Son bear the sins of the world and die on the Cross. Although God is the God of love, at the same time, He does not tolerate sin. That's because God is holy. And because of this the Lord took upon all our sins, was condemned for them in our place, died in our place, and rose from the dead again, all to enable us to receive the remission of sins. And it is by believing in this gospel that we are saved.

Many Christians offer their own prayers of repentance in vain, claiming that they have received the "gift of repentance," but what exactly is this gift of repentance? It's absolute nonsense. You must be on your guard against such lies. You ought to think rationally and ask yourself, "What sin have I now committed against God?"

When a sin offering was made, a sacrificial animal was killed, its kidneys were removed, and the kidneys along with the fat were burnt on the altar of burnt offering. What does this mean? The primary function of kidneys is filtering our blood of bad elements. We must think rationally about what it is that we have wronged God, realize it, and filter it out like the kidneys. We must also recognize that we cannot avoid but be condemned for our sins. And we must realize as well that our Lord was condemned for all our sins in our place. Only then can we receive the remission of sins.

It is very important for us to realize here that when the common people received the remission of sins, their sins could be remitted away because the female goat had born them and was sacrificed in lieu of the common people. We have to realize clearly here that this remission of sins was not obtained because the common people had knelt down and begged. The so-called "gift of repentance" and the "gift of tears" are all nothing more than made-up stories resulting from a corrupted Christianity. It's heart-wrenching to see people claiming to have received the gift of tears, but there is no reason for them to cry at all. In fact, when they come to church and cry, they are actually just venting out their frustration to the Lord after suffering some misfortune out in the world.

The remission of sins, however, is not received just by coming to church and crying a lot. Just because you shed tears, the Lord does not forgive your sins solely on this account. It's not possible even if you cry a river. The remission of sins can be received from the Lord only if the wages of sins is paid by death. Blood must be shed. But, it would be self-defeating if we were put to death. That is precisely why God had prepared our own propitiation instead of putting us to death. Having thus prepared our own sacrificial offering, God has made it possible for us to receive the remission of sins if only we would by faith pass our sins to this sacrificial offering through the laying on of hands. The sacrificial offering would then bear the condemnation of our sins and accomplish everything for us. It is by believing in this Truth that we reach our salvation. Unfortunately, today's Christianity has veered so far off from the Truth that it has turned itself into a superstition.

Nowadays many pastors consider their ministries as a simple occupation or referee. Like for example, a barber, when a pastor who has not been born again gives a sermon, he is just doing a job. The barber makes a living out of giving hair cuts, while a false pastor makes a living out of lying. The two are the same. Any pastor ministering without being born again is no different from a vendor in the market.

When Did Our Lord Bear Our Sins of the World?

Let us turn to Matthew 3:13-17 here: *"Then Jesus came from Galilee to John at the Jordan to be baptized by him. And John tried to prevent Him, saying, 'I need to be baptized by You, and are You coming to me?' But Jesus answered and said to him, 'Permit it to be so now, for thus it is fitting for us to fulfill all righteousness.' Then he allowed Him. When He had been baptized, Jesus came up immediately from the water; and behold, the heavens were opened to Him, and He saw the Spirit of God descending like a dove and alighting upon Him. And suddenly a voice came from heaven, saying, 'This is My beloved Son, in whom I am well pleased.'"* The word "then" at the beginning of the passage here refers to when Jesus turned 30. During the age of the Old Testament, a priest had to turn 30 before assuming his ministry. This is all recorded in the Book of Numbers. Like this, Jesus "then" came to John the Baptist, when He turned 30. And He commanded John the Baptist to baptize Him. John the Baptist then asked Jesus, "How could such a lowly man like me baptize You, when I should be baptized by You?" But Jesus said firmly, *"Permit it to be so now"*, that is, to baptize Him—and John the Baptist allowed Him.

Where Jesus said here, *"Permit it to be so now, for thus it is fitting for us to fulfill all righteousness,"* the words "all righteousness" is "δικαιοσυνην (dik-ah-yos-oo'-nayn)" in the original text, that is, in Greek. This means "the most appropriate," "the most right," or "the fairest." In other words, it was the most appropriate for John the Baptist to baptize Jesus. Why did Jesus want to be baptized by John the Baptist specifically? It's because John the Baptist was the representative of all mankind.

When we turn to Matthew 11:11-13, we see Jesus saying, *"Assuredly, I say to you, among those born of women there has not risen one greater than John the Baptist; but he who is least in the kingdom of heaven is greater than he. And from the days of John the Baptist until now the kingdom of heaven suffers violence, and the violent take it by force. For all the prophets and the law prophesied until John."* So, Jesus Himself made it clear that the representative of all mankind was no one other than John the Baptist. Before sending Jesus as promised, God had sent a representative of mankind who would minister as the last Old Testament high priest of the earth, and this man was John the Baptist. It is by being baptized by this John the Baptist that Jesus could bear all our sins. Jesus was saying to John the Baptist, "It is thus fitting for us to fulfill all righteousness. It is right for you to baptize Me, for Me to be baptized by you, and thus blot out everyone's sins and make atonement for them."

The God-established method by which the common people in the Old Testament could receive the remission of their sins was by laying their hands on an unblemished female goat and thereby passing their sins to it. In a similar way, in the age of the New Testament, Jesus Himself bore all the sins of everyone by being baptized by John the Baptist. That is how Jesus made atonement for us, by taking up all our sins and being condemned for them in our place. And that is what is meant by atonement for sin, and how God has made everyone sinless. Put differently, Jesus accepted all the sins of mankind by being baptized in the Jordan River. The Jordan River is about waist-deep, but this is where He was immersed when He received baptism.

When Jesus came to John the Baptist, He commanded him, saying, "You shall baptize Me." John the Baptist then said to Jesus, "Although I am the representative of mankind, are You not the Representative of the Kingdom of Heaven? So how could I even dare to baptize You?" To this, Jesus replied and said, "Permit it to be so. In this way, you shall pass the sins of the world to Me, and I shall accept them from you. This is the most fitting way to blot out everyone's sins. Did I not promise it in the Old Testament? So it must be done in this way." John the Baptist therefore laid both his hands on the head of Jesus, just like all high priests did in the past. This was the most appropriate way for the Lord to accept our sins.

No matter how hard we try, the sins that are inside us do not disappear. That is why our Lord came to this earth to blot out these sins, and He accepted them through John the Baptist in the most appropriate way. Having thus accepted our sins, the Lord was then crucified to death. It took Him three years to go the Cross since accepting our sins. The next day, after Jesus accepted all the sins of the world by being baptized, John the Baptist saw Jesus coming towards him again, he then bore witness of Him by saying, "Behold! The Lamb of God who takes away the sin of the world!" Having thus taken away the sins of the world, the Lord carried them to the Cross. Having accepted the sins of the world, He shouldered them all to the Cross. And there, He was condemned in the place of us the sinners.

Just as the unblemished female goat accepted the sins of the common people, shed its blood, and was put to death in their place, Jesus also accepted our sins, carried them to the Cross, and was condemned in our place. That is why the Lord said in John 19:30, *"It is finished!"* When Jesus passed away after saying this, the veil of the Sanctuary was ripped apart from the top to bottom. This symbolizes that Jesus had completely fulfilled the remission of sins, which is obtainable neither by crying nor by repenting, by coming to this earth, being baptized in the Jordan River, and shedding His blood to death on the Cross. The Lord has saved all those who believe with their hearts that He has blotting out all the sins of this world in this way, and He has made them His own people.

All of these things were done by the Lord, there is nothing that we did. It is absolutely impossible for anyone to be spared from condemnation as long as he is sinful. Neither crying nor repentance can accomplish this, as a hymn goes, "Crying can't deliver us. Tears can't make us sinless, nor can they send us to Heaven. Neither our own effort nor our own virtue can save us." However, our Lord has accomplished our salvation. He has saved us all and blotted out all our sins.

What about you then? Do you believe that there is nothing we have done for our salvation? What is there that human beings have done for salvation? Can you and I really avoid committing any sin just by trying hard? No, this is impossible. Of course, I'm not saying here that you should feel free to sin. Rather, my point is that we must remember that our Lord took away all the sins of the world. He bore the sins of the world in the most appropriate way, by being baptized. He accepted all the sins of the world precisely because we cannot help but sin until the day we die. He did this to make us whole, so that we would receive the remission of sins by faith.

Let me emphasize once again that there is nothing that we have done or deserved for this. We have received the remission of sins not because of anything of our own doing, but all because of what our Lord has done for us. It is also the Lord who has made us righteous. It is also the Lord who let us be born. It is also the Lord who has given us everlasting life. And it is also the Lord who has blessed us to enter Heaven. The fact that we are alive, that we can breathe, has all been made possible because the Lord has given us the air to breathe. Like this, there is nothing of our own doing. God is now admonishing us to preach this gospel and this love. He has entrusted us with the task of making it possible for everyone to receive the remission of sins, and He is telling us to spread this gospel.

The Lord is saying to us that He Himself has saved us, that He will send us to Heaven, that He has made us righteous, and that He has blessed us. All these things have been done by the Lord. There is nothing that we have done. It is all by the grace of the Lord that we have reached our salvation, received His blessings, become God's workers, and will go to the everlasting Kingdom. All of this is a gift from God. It is not something that we have received as a reward for our own effort. Everything has come by the grace of God. We have put on God's infinite love and grace. We are living in the presence of God by His love. I give all thanks and praise to our Lord for everything He has done for us! ✉

SERMON

9

You can download Rev. Paul C. Jong's Christian Books on iPhone, iPad, or Blackberry by going to Amazon's Kindle e-bookstore (www.amazon.com).

Sermon on
The Trespass Offering

< Leviticus 5:14-19 >

"Then the Lord spoke to Moses, saying: 'If a person commits a trespass, and sins unintentionally in regard to the holy things of the Lord, then he shall bring to the Lord as his trespass offering a ram without blemish from the flocks, with your valuation in shekels of silver according to the shekel of the sanctuary, as a trespass offering. And he shall make restitution for the harm that he has done in regard to the holy thing, and shall add one-fifth to it and give it to the priest. So the priest shall make atonement for him with the ram of the trespass offering, and it shall be forgiven him. If a person sins, and commits any of these things which are forbidden to be done by the commandments of the Lord, though he does not know it, yet he is guilty and shall bear his iniquity. And he shall bring to the priest a ram without blemish from the flock, with your valuation, as a trespass offering. So the priest shall make atonement for him regarding his ignorance in which he erred and did not know it, and it shall be forgiven him. It is a trespass offering; he has certainly trespassed against the Lord.'"

We Must Give the Trespass Offering to God

Today, I would like to share the Word with you regarding

the trespass offering. Unlike the burnt offering, the trespass offering required the people of God to add one-fifth to the restitution made for their offence. When the people of Israel sinned against God or man, they had to offer a sacrificial animal to make restitution for the sin they committed. Spiritually speaking, this trespass offering implies that we must not only make restitution for our sins, but also pay an additional price on top of the wages of these sins. God said here that we should add one-fifth to the restitution that we must make for our sins. In those days, the people Israel gave to God such offerings as burnt offerings, sin offerings, trespass offerings, thanksgiving offerings, and peace offerings, and this was the requirement for the trespass offering.

It's written in Leviticus 5:14-16: *"Then the LORD spoke to Moses, saying: 'If a person commits a trespass, and sins unintentionally in regard to the holy things of the LORD, then he shall bring to the LORD as his trespass offering a ram without blemish from the flocks, with your valuation in shekels of silver according to the shekel of the sanctuary, as a trespass offering. And he shall make restitution for the harm that he has done in regard to the holy thing, and shall add one-fifth to it and give it to the priest. So the priest shall make atonement for him with the ram of the trespass offering, and it shall be forgiven him.'"* As written here, the people of Israel during the age of the Old Testament had to add one-fifth to the restitution they made for their sins. The Scripture also tells us how the trespass offering ought to be given spiritually in the age of the New Testament, and by what kind of faith it ought to be offered. To find this out, we must first of all realize that all of us sin against both God and man all the time. Let me then explain to you what offering of faith such sinners must give to God.

When does anyone living on this earth commit a trespass? As the Word of God says, *"If a person commits a trespass, and sins unintentionally,"* and that means we commit sins while living in this world. When we sin against God, it starts from liking something else more than God. Liking something else more than God may not seem like a big deal at first, but it will inevitably lead us to commit a greater sin against God. We must therefore realize our faulty nature and admit our trespasses against God.

Even though we have been remitted from all our sins by believing in the gospel of the water and the Spirit, we are still prone to like the things of this earth. Such a phenomenon implies that even the believers in the gospel of the water and the Spirit may like something else more than God. They may like the things of the world just a little bit at first, but in time, they can come to serve and love them even more. And once they come to serve the things of the world, this constitutes a sin against God. Their hearts will then be darkened, they will drift further and further away from God, and instead of being joyous, they will always feel frustrated. God therefore told His people committing such sins to give a trespass offering by faith.

How do we actually behave? We sometimes come to like something else more than God and serve them, even though we know that this is wrong. Once we let this happen, we are bound to sin against God and drift away from Him further and further, despite the fact that God ought to be our first priority if we have truly received the remission of sins. That is why God is saying to you and me here to offer the trespass offering spiritually by faith.

As we the Christians carry on with our lives, we often end up serving something else more than God. We also come to like the things of the world more than God. What do you like môre, God or this world? There is no question that it's God. This is clear for all those who have received the remission of sins by believing in the gospel of the water and the Spirit. In contrast, almost all of those who have never been born again yet like this world. It's a matter of fact that the born-again love God more than anything else in their hearts, even though they may fail to live accordingly with their acts.

If you ever lose your heart's love for the God of righteousness, you must restore it fast through your faith in the gospel of the water and the Spirit without fail. It's all about how we bring the trespass offering to our Lord in this age. When the saints commit a trespass against God, they are to be remitted from their sins by offering a ram and giving one-fifth of its value to the priest. It's written, *"So the priest shall make atonement for him with the ram of the trespass offering."* In other words, the saints who commit trespasses are made clean once and for all by believing in the baptism our Lord Jesus Christ received from John the Baptist, and the blood He shed on the Cross.

Indeed, just as the people of Israel were cleansed by offering a sacrificial animal to God and adding one-fifth to this restitution for their sins, a trespasser's heart is made clean by believing that Jesus Christ has forever cleansed His saints by being baptized by John the Baptist, shedding His blood on the Cross, and rising from the dead again. As the Lord paid off the wages of all our trespasses more than sufficiently with His baptism and the shedding of His blood, His believers have been saved. As the priest gave such trespass offerings to God, His people were freed from all the sins of the world.

Our Fundamental Nature

Do we all sin against God or not? We all sin against God. As we carry on with our lives before God, we can see ourselves sinning in no time, sometimes without even realizing it ourselves for a while. This becomes clearer once we receive the remission of sins. When we like something else more than the Lord and fall head over heels for it, even if it has not harmed anyone yet, this in itself can darken our hearts. Strictly speaking, this is akin to worshiping a deity other than God. Like this, when we the saints commit a trespass, we must bring a trespass offering to God with our faith in Jesus Christ, who is more precious than our lives. The saints must always remember Jesus Christ, who has become the propitiation sacrifice for their trespass offering.

Todays' Scripture reading is applicable to people today who sin after believing in the gospel of the water and the Spirit. So, it's something that we should all know after receiving the remission of sins by believing in the righteousness of God. The trespass offering of the Old Testament reminds us of our knowledge and faith, that when Jesus Christ came to this earth, He bore all our sins once and for all through the baptism He received from John the Baptist, and He was condemned for all our sins with the blood He shed on the Cross as the wages of our sins. It teaches us to remember that the wages of our sins were paid with the righteousness of Jesus Christ, who is incomparably greater and more precious than us.

For us to give such a trespass offering to God, we must be cognizant of the fact that we sin against God all the time. The trespass offering is required when we commit sin against God; if we were capable of not sinning, then they would be no need for us to give such an offering or have such faith. But sometimes we like and serve something else more than God. Such sins are the sins that are committed by the righteous against God. We must therefore always admit to God the sins that we commit. This applies to every believer regardless of whether one's faith is great or small. Whenever we sin whatever it is, all of us ought to confess to God, "Lord, I have sinned against You. These are the sins that I have committed." Strictly speaking, the trespasses we commit are the sins that could not have been washed away were it for the righteousness of God.

This applies even when we commit a small sin against another human being. For instance, the Ten Commandments teach us to honor our parents, not to kill, not to steal, not to commit adultery, and so on. If we break any of these commandments, then this actually constitutes a sin. What kind of sins do we commit against God then? It is none other than the sin of idolatry, worshiping something else other than God. When we commit this sin, we are prone to think that it's not such a big deal, but in the end, this sin will lead us to stand against God down the road. Think about it more deeply. What would we have left if we liked something else more than God and drifted away from Him? We would just turn into idolaters. Given the fact that our Savior is God alone, if we like and serve something else more than God, we will end up turning into His enemies.

No matter what kinds of sins we commit, they are all trespasses. Therefore it is absolutely necessary for us to turn against these mistaken sins and cleanse our hearts. In other words, there is a need for us to bring a trespass offering to God spiritually. We are supposed to not only make restitution for our sins before God, but also to add one-fifth to it. Such offerings are made when we believe that the baptism of Jesus

Christ and the blood He shed on the Cross are far greater than our sins. This is the kind of faith held by the believers in the gospel of the water and the Spirit.

Let's say that we stole $50 from someone. According to the sacrificial system of the Old Testament, first of all we would have to give an unblemished ram to God as the price of this sin. Secondly, we would have to make restitution for the theft by not only paying $50, but adding one-fifth of this amount. What does this mean for us living in this age of the New Testament? It teaches us to think and believe that the righteousness of the holy God is greater than our sins. The sacrifice of the Lord is greater than our sins. In other words, the baptism the Lord which He received from John the Baptist and the blood He shed on the Cross are far greater than the wages of our sins. Therefore, we know and believe that the Lord's baptism and His blood on the Cross were more than sufficient to pay off all the wages of our sins, for He is greater than us. This is the faith implied by the trespass offering.

Look unto Jesus Christ, Our High Priest

It's written in today's Scripture reading, *"So the priest shall make atonement for him with the ram of the trespass offering, and it shall be forgiven him."* This passage implies that the Lord paid off all the wages of our sins more than sufficiently by being baptized and shedding His blood. We can bring burnt offerings to God daily by believing that our Lord forever bore all our everlasting sins by being baptized once.

Our Lord has made your heart and mine clean by giving us the gospel of the water and the Spirit. Can we then return to God to be made clean always? Yes. It's when we bring the trespass offering to God by believing in the gospel of the water and the Spirit. That's because the Lord has at once paid off all the wages of your sins and mine more than sufficiently by being baptized by John the Baptist and shedding His blood on the Cross while shouldering the sins of the world. By confessing our faith in the gospel of the water and the Spirit often, we can be made clean often.

The Lord does not want us to just list our sins, saying to Him, "Lord, I've committed this sin and that sin." Rather, the Lord wants to hear us confessing our faith in the gospel of the water and the Spirit, saying to Him, "Lord, I believe that You have cleansed me from all my sins once and for all through the water and the Spirit!" It's absolutely indispensable for us to remember that, and to believe with our hearts that the Lord bore all our sins and paid off all these wages which was more than sufficient. To wash such lowly beings like us from our sins, the holy Lord was baptized by John the Baptist and gave up His body, shedding His blood on the Cross, and thereby, paying off all the wages of our sins once and for all. For us to return to the holy God, there is no other way but to believe in the gospel of the water and the Spirit.

All of us commit sins, and the only way for us to return to God is coming to His presence by our faith in the gospel of the water and the Spirit. We can come to the presence of the holy God by believing that our Lord paid off all the wages of our sins which was more than sufficient, no matter what the wages might have been, with the baptism He received from John the Baptist and the blood He shed on the Cross. As the believers in the gospel of the water and the Spirit, we can love and worship God alone, the one and only true God. We can never approach the righteous God with a good conscience unless we know that our sins and their wages were all passed on to Jesus Christ. Is there anyone here who thinks, "I don't commit that many sins?" But you and I must know our true selves clearly, realizing that we are all sinners committing the wicked and depraved sin of worshiping something else other than God. We commit all kinds of sins while living in this world. And the everyday sins that we commit are, in some ways, understandable from our human standard. However, in God's sight, we must still be condemned for these sins.

My dear saints, just how many sins are we all committing, whether knowingly or unknowingly? Knowing how many shortcomings we have, while that is important, is not all that matters. Rather, we also need the knowledge that our Lord bore all the sins of this world once and for all by being baptized by John the Baptist, and that He paid off the wages of all our sins. In other words, no matter what kind of sin we commit against the Lord, what's truly important is to know and believe in the righteousness of God. It's absolutely indispensable for us to follow the Lord energetically with this faith.

Everyone will die sooner or later. Regardless of whether one worships an idol or not, everyone will die in the end. We the redeemed will also die at some point. All of us must therefore trust in the righteousness of God alone and follow it. It is only thanks to God that we can succeed and receive His blessings in our lives.

My dear saints, it's written in today's Scripture reading, *"So the priest shall make atonement for him with the ram of the trespass offering, and it shall be forgiven him" (Leviticus 5:16)*. What does it mean when the Scripture says here, *"So the priest shall make atonement for him?"* By the way what does the sin offering mean? Atonement was made when the sacrificial animal bore the sins of the people of Israel, and the way to accomplish this was through the laying on of hands. The sin offering was all about passing one's sins to the sacrificial animal, whereupon this animal bore the person's sins and died in his place. The wages of the sins of the people of Israel were paid off by the sacrificial animal in their place, and this was what the sin offering was all about.

When the Bible says here, *"So the priest shall make atonement for him,"* it means that the priest ministered to blot out the sins of this person. How did the priest then cleanse the people of Israel from their sins? The people of Israel laid their hands on their sacrificial animal before God, and the priest then offered this sacrificial animal to God, thereby cleansing away the people's sins more than sufficiently. However, the trespass offering required a higher price for the sins of the people than these ordinary offerings. In this age of the New Testament, God has made it possible for us to bring the trespass offering by believing in the gospel of the water and the Spirit. To save you and me from our sins, our Lord Jesus was baptized by John the Baptist, and at once paid off the wages of all our sins more than sufficiently on the Cross, just as it's written,

"So the priest shall make atonement for him with the ram of the trespass offering, and it shall be forgiven him." Who is our Priest here? It is Jesus Christ, who is the unblemished. Jesus Christ, the Son of God the holy Father, accepted our sins through His baptism and paid off all their wages on the Cross once and for all. Thanks to this work of salvation, my heart has been made sin free by believing in the gospel of the water and the Spirit. What about you then? Have you also been made clean by believing in the gospel of the water and the Spirit with your heart? Have you been cleansed from all your sins by faith? Or do you still think that the work of Jesus Christ was not enough to blot out your sins, even though He bore all your sins by being baptized by John the Baptist and was crucified to

death in your place?

Jesus Christ is the God who created the whole universe. God Himself had come to this earth to save mankind from sin. Having come to this earth incarnated in the flesh of man, the Lord took upon our sins by being baptized by John the Baptist and paid off all their wages more than sufficiently by being crucified. Jesus Christ bore the sins of mankind by being baptized and paid off all their wages more than sufficiently by shedding His blood. In doing so, the Lord has ensured that we the believers in the righteousness of God would lack nothing. No matter what sins we might have committed and what blemishes we might have, Jesus Christ was punished for all these sins more than sufficiently and washed them all away. By being baptized, Jesus Christ accepted all our sins and washed them away.

As our Lord Jesus Christ was baptized by John the Baptist and paid off the wages of our sins by being crucified, we the believers are compelled to praise God for His righteousness. By believing in the righteousness of God, we have come to live in God's grace of salvation. I give all my thanks to our God. I praise the Lord for blessing our saints and God's servants to live by faith in God's grace of salvation.

My dear saints, how else could we praise the righteousness of God in our lives and forever? Of course, it's all because of the righteousness of the Lord, who paid off the wages of our sins more than sufficiently. That's why we can praise God, by believing in His righteousness and our Savior. How else could we come to the presence of God and serve His righteousness alone in our lives? It's all because the Lord has paid off the wages of our sins more than sufficiently. It is because of the God-given gospel of the water and the Spirit that we can always serve the righteousness of the Lord alone and live in His presence. Like this, the Lord has paved the way for us to come to His presence. Just as He said, "I am the way," the Lord is indeed the way to everlasting life, the way to Heaven, and the way to the remission of sins. He has paved the way to life more than sufficiently, so that His people may follow Him.

Do You Want to Live out Your Faith and Save Other Souls Also?

If so, learn about the righteousness of God and believe in it. If you attain this knowledge of the righteousness of God and have faith in it, you will be able to follow the Lord wholly in your life. Although we often fall into weaknesses in times like these, we must remind ourselves that the Lord took away all our sins. It's absolutely important for us to be always cognizant of the fact that the Lord took away all our sins once and for all by being baptized and shedding His blood. As long as we believe in the righteousness of the Lord alone and follow it wholly, there is no need for us to worry about anything else. The Lord already paid off all the wages of our sins. If only we know this clearly and believe in it wholeheartedly, we can all live as the righteous forever.

The Scripture tells us to entrust all our burdens to the Lord. This means that God wants us to be able to follow the Lord's desire and will for us. The Lord wants us to live by trusting in the righteousness of God alone. He wants us carry out His righteous work alone by faith. Yet, we set our sights on the things of the world all too often. Whenever we sin like this, we should say to God, "Lord, You also took away this sin once and for all. Thank You!" Our duty is preaching the gospel of the water and the Spirit. We should not set our hearts on the things of the flesh as we like.

No matter what kind of sin we commit, the Lord has already washed away all our sins more than sufficiently and paid off their wages more than sufficiently. We ought to give the offering of thanksgiving to God by always believing in His righteousness. Believing in the righteousness of God, you and I must set our purpose in life on the glory of God. From now on, we ought to rely on the righteousness of God and work diligently to save other people's souls, rather than living just to establish our own righteousness. We must love the righteousness of God, follow it alone, and dedicate our lives in unity to the things that are pleasing to God. We must now put on the armor of the righteousness of God and live by faith in this righteousness.

In other words, we must now wage war for the salvation of people's souls. Like this, as you and I have received the remission of sins by believing in the gospel of the water and the Spirit, the gospel of God, we have become God's workers living for the spreading of His righteousness. We must wage a spiritual war against Satan. God has enabled us to fight the Devil as a well-disciplined army of faith.

Can we lead a godly life by relying on the righteousness of our flesh? No, we cannot live by relying on the righteousness of our flesh. It's absolutely indispensable for us to given our offerings to God by faith. When we were just babies, we were breastfed, but once we grew up, we ate what the grown-ups eat. Likewise, our faith in the Word of God must also grow in time. Twenty years have gone by since I first began my life of faith with you in God's Church. Over those 20 years, we were fed spiritual milk from the Word of God. From now on we ought to live by our faith in the righteousness of

God. Only if we do this can we carry out the righteous work as we carry on with our lives on this earth.

Our lives of faith should not be stuck at the same level day in and day out, year in and year out. Those who only seek the prosperity of their own flesh rather than running by trusting in the righteousness of God are bound to do foolish things. You and I ought to life with gratefulness, thanking our Lord for saving us once and for all from all the sins of this world which was more than sufficient through the gospel of the water and the Spirit. I give all my thanks to the Lord for being baptized by John the Baptist and paying off the wages of our sins.

In the Old Testament, the Lord wanted to lead the twelve tribes of Israel into the land of Canaan. After leading these descendants of Abraham into the land of Canaan, God then enabled them to conquer all the tribes that were already settled in that land. It was God's will for the people of Israel to enter into the land of Canaan and conquer all its habitants in order to occupy it. If Abraham's descendants did not enter into this land, and did not wage war against their enemies by faith, then clearly they could not have learnt to have faith in the righteousness of God. The Scripture writes that when the twelve tribes of Israel invaded the land of Canaan, they either conquered its habitants or dwelt with them. Why does the Bible leave such a record then? It is to reveal the righteousness of God. It was the will of God for the people of Israel to fight their enemies and conquer the land of Canaan completely. So the people of Israel had to conquer the land of Canaan, and once this was done, they had to continue to give to God all the sacrificial offerings that were pleasing to Him.

But what happened afterwards? They stopped offering sacrifices. When the people of Israel settled in the land of Canaan, at first they did give every sacrificial offering that God required from them, but eventually, they came to neglect this. What happened to the people of Israel when they started neglecting the sacrifices they were supposed to offer to God? Were their lives happy, or were they later enslaved? They were enslaved. As we carry on with our lives on this earth, we must always be mindful to offer spiritual sacrifices to God for the sake of those who are perishing for their sins. Here the spiritual offering is blotting out their sins with the gospel of the water and the Spirit. The Lord offered His body as our own sacrificial offering to remit away our sins. We ought to remember that the Lord has paid off the wages of our sins more than sufficiently through the gospel of the water and the Spirit. We ought to give God the offering of faith by believing in the gospel of the water and the Spirit and the righteousness of God. We ought to give this offering of faith to God for the souls that are perishing before Him also.

Indeed, you and I must always give the offering of faith to God for the salvation of other people's souls. Praising the righteousness of God from the depth of our hearts, we must wage a spiritual war, so that everyone may see the light of salvation. It is now time for us to shine the light on the whole world with the gospel of salvation. To do this, we must unite ourselves with God's Church while we remain in this world. If God's Church fails to meet its calling, the people of the world will all perish spiritually. We must therefore make the gospel of the water and the Spirit known throughout the whole world. We must spread our faith on this earth and wage our spiritual war. We must also live in unity with God's Church to proclaim His righteousness and serve it faithfully.

Do you know what it means to be one with God? It is to be one with the gospel of the righteousness of God, the gospel of the water and the Spirit. And it is to be one with the servants of the righteousness of God also. That is what is meant by true unity. To serve the righteousness of God, it is absolutely indispensable for us to live by faith in unity with God's Church. When the hearts of the people of God cease to believe in and rely on His righteousness, they can return and turn back into Satan's servants.

If one's heart and mind is not set on spreading God's gospel, then this means that the unity this person is seeing is of man, that is, he is living to serve an idol. You and I should never allow this to happen to us. Where should our focus be? It should be on the very hearts of those who are spreading the righteousness of God. We must follow God's righteousness, and taking this righteousness as our shield of faith, we must vanquish the darkness and save souls from sin. God has raised us up so that we would preach His righteousness. To this end, the Lord has given us God's Church and His servants. It is for this work that God allowed us to be born on this earth and find the gospel of the water and the Spirit. It is to make us carry out His righteous work that God has allowed us to remain on this earth.

However, if we do not set our hearts on preaching the gospel of the righteousness of God, then we will end up falling into the sin of idolatry in God's sight. When we come to commit the sin of idolatry and realize this, we must bring the offering of faith to God by relying on His righteousness. Although we have received the remission of sins by believing in the gospel of the water and the Spirit, we are still weak in many aspects. We should therefore not go out to the world while in such a state. On the other hand, no matter how weak we may be, as long as we remain in God's Church, His priests will minister righteous offerings for us whenever they are needed and guide us back to the righteous path. The Lord has paid off the wages of our sins more than sufficiently, and we ought to realize His righteousness through the gospel of the water and the Spirit, believe in it, and praise it by faith. We must devote ourselves to proclaiming this Truth throughout the whole world, that the Lord bore all our sins and blotted them all away.

My dear saints, are you grateful to the Lord for becoming our own propitiation of righteousness? As mere mortals with the flesh, what strength do we really have? What merit do we have? What power of the flesh do you have? We have none, nothing. We are so weak that even while walking, our eyes often end up drifting to stare at something that we shouldn't. For instance, when our brothers see a well shaped woman wearing a short skirt, they can't help but gawk at her legs. We are all such wretched sinners who cannot be saved from our sins unless we have the gospel of the water and the Spirit. Fundamentally, we are all inevitably bound to die for our sins.

Even though we have received the remission of sins by believing in the gospel of the water and the Spirit, we can still be tempted easily. How about the sisters in our Church? They are prone to get jealous of their neighbors, trying keep up with the Jones's. When their neighbors buy something new, such as furniture or a car, they want to buy it as well in envy. Our eyes of the flesh often see many lustful and beautiful things. There are so many things that look wonderful to our eyes. Men are also drawn to material things. Even if they don't always express it, they also like good things in life. That's because this is in the very nature of all human beings living on this earth. However, how should we the Christians live from now on? Believing that our Lord has blotted out our sins by the gospel of the water and the Spirit was more than sufficient, and we ought to live with our hearts united with the Lord.

For Us to Follow the Righteousness of the Lord Wholly, We Must Believe in His Righteousness Wholly and Preach It in Our Lives

Through His self-sacrifice, the Lord has paid off the wages of our sins more than sufficiently by being baptized and shedding His blood. Our Almighty Lord Himself has paid off all the wages of our sins completely once and for all by the baptism He received from John the Baptist and the blood He shed on the Cross. Had the Lord not paid off our wages like this with His sacrifice, how else could we have followed His righteousness? Do we have the faculty to follow the Lord completely? Do we have such an ability?. No, we don't.

The Offering Indispensable for Us

Let's turn to today's Scripture passage and read Leviticus 5:17-18 here: *"If a person sins, and commits any of these things which are forbidden to be done by the commandments of the LORD, though he does not know it, yet he is guilty and shall bear his iniquity. And he shall bring to the priest a ram without blemish from the flock, with your valuation, as a trespass offering. So the priest shall make atonement for him regarding his ignorance in which he erred and did not know it, and it shall be forgiven him."* What did the Lord say about our sins, even if they are committed unknowingly? He said that they are transgressions.

For instance, as I mentioned just a short while ago, if you saw a passing woman and thought to yourself without even realizing it yourself, "Wow, she is so attractive and sexy," this would constitute a sin that's committed without knowing. Did anyone plan for this woman to come your way? Did you know that the woman would cross paths with you? No, that's not the case. No one planned this, nor did you know that you would come across this woman. This is a sin that you committed subconsciously following the lust of your flesh, without even realizing it yourself. However, God said that even if you commit a sin unknowingly like this, you are still guilty. For all the people of God, the transgressions committed by them unknowingly still bring guilt to them and constitute sins. In other words, even if you sin unintentionally without any particular aim, it is clearly still a sin.

What did God then say you must do once you commit a sin like this? He said that once you commit any sin at all, regardless of whether intentionally or unintentionally, you must *"bring to the priest a ram without blemish from the flock, with your valuation, as a trespass offering."* But what has already happened to your sins? Even when it comes to the sins that you commit unknowingly, our Lord has already paid off their wages more than sufficiently with His own body, by being baptized personally by John the Baptist and shedding His own blood. The Lord has made restitution for all our sins with His baptism and His blood on the Cross. With the sacrifice He made and the righteousness of God, the Lord has blotted out any and all our sins more than sufficiently, regardless of whether they are committed intentionally or unintentionally. There is only one requirement for us to reach salvation, if only we do not deny that Jesus Christ is our Savior who has blotted out all our sins once and for all with the gospel of the water and the Spirit, if only we believe in this Truth, then you and I are more than able to be saved by faith no matter what kinds of sins we commit. Like this, the Lord has freed us from the sins of the world through the gospel of the water and the Spirit, so that we may escape from the punishment and condemnation of our sins, and our hearts may be made clean.

Jesus offered His own body as your propitiation, just as it's written, *"He shall bring to the priest a ram without blemish from the flock, with your valuation, as a trespass offering. So the priest shall make atonement for him regarding his ignorance in which he erred and did not know it, and it shall be forgiven him."* That the priest passed the people's sins to the sacrificial animal by laying his hands on its head, and thereby washed their sins away and made the animal bear their condemnation of sins in their place, implies that the remission of sins is received once and for all by all those who believe in the Truth of salvation. For all of who can't help but commit sins and be faulty, our Lord has paid off the wages of all our sins more than sufficiently and cleansed us all.

The offerings we bring to God are absolutely indispensable. Do we then have to keep on giving such offerings? Yes, we must continue to offer them. It's because the Lord has paid off all the wages of our sins more than sufficiently that we are now able to serve the righteous Lord. And we can also follow the righteous Lord by faith. We can praise Him for His righteousness. We can thank our Lord by faith. Precisely because the Lord has paid off the wages of our sins, we are now able to live forever and praise God in a sinless and clean state.

Let's turn to Leviticus 4:32-35 here: *"If he brings a lamb as his sin offering, he shall bring a female without blemish. Then he shall lay his hand on the head of the sin offering, and kill it as a sin offering at the place where they kill the burnt offering. The priest shall take some of the blood of the sin offering with his finger, put it on the horns of the altar of burnt offering, and pour all the remaining blood at the base of the altar. He shall remove all its fat, as the fat of the lamb is removed from the sacrifice of the peace offering. Then the priest shall burn it on the altar, according to the offerings made by fire to the LORD. So the priest shall make atonement for his sin that he has committed, and it shall be forgiven him."*

The word "atonement" here means "shouldering sins." That the sin offering was sacrificed to make atonement for a sinner means that the sacrificial animal bore the sinner's iniquities in his place. Who then is the sin offering that bore our sins in our place? It is none other than Jesus Christ, the Lord of the water and the Spirit. Indeed, it is Jesus Christ who bore all our sins in our stead, including the sins that we commit unknowingly through the baptism He received from John the Baptist and the blood He shed on the Cross. He is the One who accepted and shouldered all our sins. That is why we say that the Lord became our own propitiation for all our sins by accepting them through His baptism. This is the very work of salvation done by Jesus Christ, our own sacrificial offering. It is Jesus Christ who shouldered all our sins once and for all. It is He who bore all our sins in our stead.

Given this, do we the believers in this gospel of the water and the Spirit then have any sin still left with us? No, of course not. Has your heart been made clean then? Have all the sins committed by you been passed on to Jesus Christ? Yes, they have. Therefore, all of us who believe in the gospel of the righteousness of God through Jesus Christ have no more sin. Now that we have become sinless, does this then mean that you should not sin anymore? While we should indeed strive not to sin, because we are all human, we can't help but commit transgressions even after receiving the remission of sins.

Think about it. If we were capable of not sinning, then there would have been no need for the Lord bear the sins of the world by being baptized by John the Baptist. Because we still have our flesh, we still have many shortcomings, and therefore we can't help but continue to sin. That is precisely why the Lord has saved us from all the sins of this world once and for all by being baptized by John the Baptist and bearing each and every sin on Himself. He was then crucified to death, shedding His precious blood on the Cross. Words cannot express just how grateful I am that the Lord became our own propitiation to blot out all our sins. I am so thankful that the Lord Himself became our trespass offering for our sake. Truthfully, God Himself took upon all our sins once and for all through His baptism, and He bore all the condemnation of our sins that we should have borne. The Lord bore not only all our sins but also all their punishment once and for all in our place.

The trespass offering is all about this sacrifice the Lord made for us. The smell of the sacrificial offering burning on the Altar of Burnt Offering was a sweet aroma to God, one that satisfied Him. The people of this world perished because they did not give such an offering. Even for us the believers in the gospel of the water and the Spirit, we may also be ruined spiritually if we fail to give such an offering of faith.

Do you know just how those who do not have the gospel of the water and the Spirit have gone astray? It is not just their acts that have gone astray, rather, the very gospel they believe in is wrong. Their failure to believe in and follow the gospel of the water and the Spirit is their biggest mistake, as is their refusal to be one with the righteousness of God. Although we the believers in the gospel of the water and the Spirit have no sin regardless of how many sins we commit mistakenly, this is not the case for anyone who does not believe in the righteousness of God. So how could such people not be condemned for their sins? The one sin whose remission cannot be received from God is the sin of not believing in the gospel of the water and the Spirit. Trusting only in the righteousness of the Lord and the salvation He has brought to us, all of us must believe in the baptism the Lord received from John the Baptist to bear the sins of the world, and the blood He shed on the Cross, so that we may have nothing to do with any sin anymore.

Our hearts are so hopelessly wicked that unless we have faith in the righteousness of God, we cannot be saved from all our sins. We must therefore hoist up the righteousness of the Lord and run to the end of the world. Trusting in the righteousness of God, we must run in unity with His Church. When your Church leaders say something to you, don't just ignore them and leave them to their own devices. Instead, listen to their words with trust. If you at least listen to the servants of God by trusting them, you will come to think about what it is that you can do for God's work and how you can do your part. Like this, carrying out the gospel work of the water and the Spirit with each of us taking up our respective tasks is what it means to be one with the righteousness of God in unity. If we otherwise fail to be in unity with the righteousness of God, then none other than this is idolatry. It is akin to worshiping something else other than God.

The people of Israel gave the offering of faith to God, and they also waged a spiritual war. Out of a grateful heart we also ought to give burnt offerings, trespass offerings, and sin offerings to God in His Church. And we ought to have the arms of faith ready to wage our spiritual war. Our workers must prepare these arms of faith in God's Church, ready to fight their spiritual war as His faithful saints. They must be wholly united with one another for the righteousness of the Lord. The Lord told us not to worry about what to eat, what to drink, or what to wear. Give it a try yourself. Try actually living for the gospel by faith and see what will happen. All your needs will be met as a matter of course. You will have nothing more to worry about.

The sins of mankind must be judged without fail. All of us ought to be thinking long and hard about what we can do for the Lord and how we can serve Him and in what ways we can. Don't you want to live like this before the Lord, who has blotted out all your sins more than sufficiently? I am sure that you would all like to live like this. But, are you hesitant of what it is that you should do and how? Then I ask you to listen closely to what your Church leaders are saying to you, what they are urging you to do in their sermons, and what their heartfelt desire is for you. And I ask you to serve God together with your Church leaders every step of the way. None other than this is what it means to serve God, serve the gospel, and live for the Lord. This is how you wage your spiritual war.

If you really are God's saint, then it's only a matter of course that you ought to wage your spiritual war and give your trespass offerings to God. Why do we keep falling into sin? Why do we succumb to our weaknesses? It's because we do not give the trespass offering to God exactly as we should, and also because we do not follow His righteousness spiritually. We keep falling into our weaknesses because we still have not united ourselves with the Lord definitively. So, my fellow believers, I urge you to trust in our Lord who became our own trespass offering, believe in the righteous of the Lord who took upon and paid off all the wages of our sins more than sufficiently, and run to Him by this faith. I ask you to live by trusting in the righteousness of God alone. Just as the Lord said, *"The just shall live by faith,"* I urge you to be victorious by your faith in the righteousness of God.

Rise up by putting your faith in the righteousness of God. No matter what your circumstances are, seek the will of God, ask His servants for it, and lead your life united with the gospel of the water and the Spirit as much as possible. You will then live a victorious life without fail. Our God's help and guidance will follow you in everything you do and wherever you go, whether at your home, at your workplace, or at the Church, in both body and spirit. The indescribable kindness and goodness of God will be with you forever. We must also remember this always. Do not follow the Lord all on your own. You must follow Him with your heart united with Him clearly and concisely. Unless you are in unity like this with Him, you will stumble. You will keep on stumbling and falling.

When you first participate in the righteous work, it may seem as if something is amiss and the work doesn't suit your personality well, but if you stick to it, it will all come together eventually. God's work may not seem suitable to you at first only because you have been too accustomed to sinning, but once you do it often enough by getting used to it, you will find that it suits you just fine. Think about a thief. It's very difficult for a hardened thief to do what is right for the first time, but once the thief does it often enough, he will find it more suitable than stealing.

Among the people sitting here who have received the remission of sins by believing in the gospel of the water and the Spirit, is there anyone who is still living according to one's own wishes? Raise your hand if you are such a person. If there are such brothers and sisters here, I urge them all to give the trespass offering at this hour. I ask them to serve the Lord by faith. Now then, do you really believe in the Lord, and that He has paid off all the wages of your sins more than sufficiently? The Lord has indeed paid off all the wages of our sins more than sufficiently. I give all my praise to the Lord for this. I ask you to walk with the Lord. Do you find it difficult? Then ask your Church leaders for prayer and guidance. And start with small baby steps. Do you feel you are not cut out for God's work? Keep at it until it becomes second nature to you. If you feel God's work is suitable to your liking, then suit yourself to the Lord's liking. Your personality will then be changed to suit the Lord for sure.

Of all the people calling themselves Christians, the most foolish are those who believe according to their own wishes without knowing the gospel of the water and the Spirit. The Church leaders never say anything that is harmful to the saints. Of course, you may not understand what they are saying at first. But once you obey their instruction and follow in their footsteps, you will eventually come to realize their intention. And the Lord will help such saints. None other than this is the kind of life that all the people of God ought to lead.

Jesus Christ said that He is the way. Since the Lord said that He is the way, all that we have to do is just follow this way. Walking ahead of us, Jesus has already paved the way for us. All that remains for us to do is realize that this is the way God has set for us and walk on this path. It's my sincerest hope and prayer that you would all experience such guidance of the Lord. I admonish you all to give it a try by exercising your faith. Give it a go and begin walking with the Lord. You will then surely see the work of the Lord unfolding right before your eyes in your own experience.

Cast aside your own wisdom and knowledge, and rely on the Lord alone. He will then guide you personally. He will make you happy. Don't try to do everything well at first; instead, do just one thing well to begin with. Everything will then come together. I thank the Lord for giving us the trespass offering. Our Lord has blotted out all our sins more than sufficiently, so I ask you trust in this sacrifice until the day you stand in His presence, believe in Him, and praise Him in your life. Hallelujah! ✉

SERMON

10

You can download Rev. Paul C. Jong's Christian Books on iPhone, iPad, or Blackberry by going to Amazon's Kindle e-bookstore (www.amazon.com).

How to Ruminate on the Word of God in Our Lives

< Leviticus 11:1-12 >

"Now the Lord spoke to Moses and Aaron, saying to them, 'Speak to the children of Israel, saying, "These are the animals which you may eat among all the animals that are on the earth: Among the animals, whatever divides the hoof, having cloven hooves and chewing the cud—that you may eat. Nevertheless these you shall not eat among those that chew the cud or those that have cloven hooves: the camel, because it chews the cud but does not have cloven hooves, is unclean to you; the rock hyrax, because it chews the cud but does not have cloven hooves, is unclean to you; the hare, because it chews the cud but does not have cloven hooves, is unclean to you; and the swine, though it divides the hoof, having cloven hooves, yet does not chew the cud, is unclean to you. Their flesh you shall not eat, and their carcasses you shall not touch. They are unclean to you. These you may eat of all that are in the water: whatever in the water has fins and scales, whether in the seas or in the rivers—that you may eat. But all in the seas or in the rivers that do not have fins and scales, all that move in the water or any living thing which is in the water, they are an abomination to you. They shall be an abomination to you; you shall not eat their flesh, but you shall regard their carcasses as an abomination. Whatever in the water does not have fins or scales—that shall be an abomination to you.""'

Today, I would like us to examine the life led by the Christians who have been born again by believing in the gospel of the water and the Spirit. Through the clean and unclean animals distinguished here in Leviticus chapter 1, God is through them teaching us important spiritual lessons. It's written, *"Now the LORD spoke to Moses and Aaron, saying to them, 'Speak to the children of Israel, saying, "These are the animals which you may eat among all the animals that are on the earth: Among the animals, whatever divides the hoof, having cloven hooves and chewing the cud—that you may eat. Nevertheless these you shall not eat among those that chew the cud or those that have cloven hooves: the camel, because it chews the cud but does not have cloven hooves, is unclean to you"'"* (Leviticus 11:1-4). In this passage, God is telling us the true Christians how we ought to live. Spoken specifically to us who believe in the gospel of the water and the Spirit today, this Word teaches us an absolutely indispensable spiritual truth for every walk of our lives.

The Spiritual Meaning of the Clean Animals

What were the clean animals that the people of Israel allowed to eat? God said here first of all, *"Among the animals, whatever divides the hoof, having cloven hooves and chewing the cud—that you may eat."* While this was applicable to the people of Israel in actual practice, spiritually speaking, it is also applicable to us. In the Bible, we can find more animals that were defined as clean other than cattle or sheep. But, as we know very well, cattle and the sheep were used for bringing sin offerings to God. God was telling His people to eat such cattle or sheep that chewed the cud, and, had cloven hooves.

Spiritually speaking, the animals that chew the cud here refer to spiritual food, while the cloven hooves imply that the saints ought to lead their lives of faith apart from the world.

As we know, a cow has four compartments in its stomach. The largest chamber is where the food is initially softened, separated into layers of solids and liquids, and the solids are regurgitated and chewed again, a process known as rumination. This is why the Lord said that we the believers in the gospel of the water and the Spirit are ruminants. In today's Scripture passage, in other words, God is telling us the believers in the gospel of the water and the Spirit to ruminate on His Word always and at all times.

Who is leading such a ruminant life of faith in the age of the New Testament? These people are none other than those who believe in the gospel of the water and the Spirit and who ruminate on this gospel Word all the time. It's very important for us to grasp here that in this age, God is pleased to accept the faith of those who believe in the gospel Word of the water and the Spirit, and who ruminate upon it by faith. In other words, the people of faith accepted by God are those who know how to ruminate on the Word of the righteousness of God by faith.

It's absolutely indispensable for us the believers in the gospel of the water and the Spirit to ruminate on the Word of God. As the believers in the gospel of the water and the Spirit, our lives of faith do not end with our salvation from sin, but rather, we are going forwards by always ruminating on the Word of God by faith. The Word that we ought to ruminate on continually is the gospel Word of the water and the Spirit that has blotted out our sins once and for all. This gospel Word of the water and the Spirit is the Truth that every sinner must know and believe. When our Lord came to this earth, He bore all the iniquities of the human race through the baptism He received from John the Baptist, and because of this, He had be condemned for the sins of the world on the Cross while shouldering them. Having thus received baptism from John the Baptist and died on the Cross, our Lord then rose from the dead in three days, and is now forever sitting at the right hand of the throne of God the Father. As we carry on with our lives on this earth, whenever our hearts and bodies fall into weaknesses, we can renew our lives thanks to this faith in the God-given gospel Word of the water and the Spirit the Lord.

Therefore, we must trust in the gospel Word of the water and the Spirit our Lord has given to us, and live by always ruminating on this Word by faith, for the Lord has enabled us to renew our souls by ruminating on the Word of God whenever we fall into the weaknesses of the flesh. Having made us receive the remission of sins by believing in the gospel of the water and the Spirit wholeheartedly, the Lord is renewing us at all times by making us ruminate on the gospel Word of the water and the Spirit in our lives. This is because this Word of salvation cleanses us whenever our blemishes are exposed. It's because our Lord has blotted out all our sins by being baptized and shedding His blood on the Cross. That is why the Lord is telling us to ruminate on the gospel of the water and the Spirit. And that is how the Lord is renewing our souls so that we can find new strength. In short, we the righteous must lead such a life of faith.

There were many more animals in Israel other than the ones that were allowed to be eaten. But God did say to the people of Israel that they could eat all such animals indiscriminately. The edible animals were set aside for them. Such animals had to chew the cud first of all, and secondly, they had to have cloven hooves. However, God also said that even if an animal had cloven hooves, it should not be eaten if it did not chew the cud. It's very important for all of us to remember this.

What Animals Chewed the Cud but Did Not Have Cloven Hooves?

It's written in Leviticus 11:4, *"Nevertheless these you shall not eat among those that chew the cud or those that have cloven hooves: the camel, because it chews the cud but does not have cloven hooves, is unclean to you."* Spiritually speaking, the animals that do not have cloven hooves here refer to the lives of those who lead an improper life. It's absolutely important for us to realize this, which ought to be the motto in our lives: When God prohibited the people of Israel from eating any animal that chewed the cud but did not have cloven hooves, He was warning us about those who do not serve the righteousness of God despite having receiving the remission of sins by believing in the gospel of the water and the Spirit. Put differently, God is telling us to not only have faith in His Word but also live for His righteousness.

Despite this clear teaching, we will find some believers in the gospel of the water and the Spirit who are not serving the righteousness of God by faith in their lives. Today's Scripture passage is warning us about such people who are living amongst us in the world rather than living by faith in the righteousness of God, and, being united with His Church. These people must therefore be awakened and begin to serve the righteousness of God in their lives even now. God is saying to us that even amongst the believers in the gospel of the water and the Spirit, we should not be in fellowship with anyone who does not ruminate on this gospel. We must remember that God told us to not only believe in His Word of righteousness but also to continue to lead our lives of faith apart from the world. God wants the believers in the gospel of the water and the Spirit to live out their faith in His righteousness alone. With today's Scripture reading from the Old Testament, the Lord is showing His will to us who are living in the age of the New Testament.

The Righteous Should Not Live a Fleshly Life

When we turn to Leviticus 11:7-8, we see God saying, *"The swine, though it divides the hoof, having cloven hooves, yet does not chew the cud, is unclean to you. Their flesh you shall not eat, and their carcasses you shall not touch. They are unclean to you."* Everyone knows about the swine, right? Like cattle, pigs also have cloven hooves. Unlike cattle, however, pigs do not have multiple chambers in their stomach to chew the cud. A cow can chew the cud because it has several compartments in its stomach. A pig, in contrast, does not have a stomach that allows it to chew the cud, although it has cloven hooves.

The pig here refers to those who are not leading a life of faith, and these are the ones who still do not know the God-given gospel Truth of the water and the Spirit that constitutes the righteousness of God. In other words, God is speaking about those whose souls have not been born again here. Those who still do not know the gospel of the water and the Spirit cannot ruminate on the Word of God even if they want to. One can ruminate on the Word of God only if he has the gospel Word of the water and the Spirit in his heart. This is made possible only by the Holy Spirit. However, it is possible for people to lead a life of faith that pretends to ruminate on the Word of God. Even such people can go to church, pray and worship God piously. They can also give donations, tithes, pray to God daily, and serve Him in their everyday life.

In some ways, in their outside appearances it may even look as though they are leading a more pious life of faith than those who know and believe in the gospel Word of the water and the Spirit. This is because the foot of a pig is clearly divided with cloven hooves. The outside appearance of the feet of a cow and those of a pig look the same. However, this does not mean that the cow and the pig are the same. Likewise, just because people believe in Jesus, does not mean that they have the true faith. On the contrary, the Lord disapproves the life of faith led by such people who neither know nor believe in the gospel of the water and the Spirit.

The Righteous Living in the Age of the New Testament Must Ruminate on the Word of God Always

God loves us human beings so much that He has blotted out all the sins of this world once and for all with the gospel Truth of the water and the Spirit. However, as we carry on with our lives in this world, we cannot help but continue to sin out of our weaknesses. It is therefore extremely important for us the righteous to ruminate on the gospel of the water and the Spirit in our lives. How do we do this then? The righteous admit their transgression to God whenever their weaknesses are exposed, and they ruminate in the God-given gospel Truth of the water and the Spirit by faith. Only when we do so can we continue on with our lives of faith. We must therefore ruminate on the gospel of the water and the Spirit, God's Word of salvation, every day by faith. It is by doing this that we can be healed from our wounds of iniquities and get the nourishment necessary to our new lives.

However, those who have not been born again out of their ignorance of the gospel of the water and the Spirit cannot ruminate on this Word of salvation by faith. Sinners who do not know the righteousness of God cannot ruminate on His Word because there is no knowledge of the righteousness of God in their hearts, they cannot ruminate on this righteousness of God even if they want to. How can such people who have not been born again ruminate on the Word of God? They cannot do this unless they repent and believe in the gospel of the water and the Spirit. Yet, because these people think mistakenly that God has failed to blot out all their sins, they are incapable of ruminating on the gospel of the water and the Spirit by faith, the God-given Truth of salvation.

They think that although God has blotted out their original sin, He is yet to blot out the personal sins they are committing now, and as a result, they are beholden by their own fleshly notion that offering prayers of repentance is absolutely indispensable. This is all because their hearts lack the Word of God to ruminate on in the first place. That is why they are living as sinners every day even though they believe in Jesus as their Savior. Like this, because those who are ignorant of the gospel of the water and the Spirit do not have the Word of God in their hearts, and because their faith is corrupted and has become a mere religion, they cannot ruminate on God's Word even if they wanted to. Their faith is therefore all in vain even as they keep on saying to God, "Lord, although You have saved me, I have sinned again now. Since I have sinned, I am once again a sinner. Even though You have blotted out my sins up to yesterday, today, I am a sinner once again."

For this reason, all those who have not been born again must be washed from their sins once and for all by believing in the gospel of the water and the Spirit. Otherwise, they will turn themselves into pigs spiritually. To keep its life, a pig must eat constantly nearly every waking moment, day in and day out. Like such pigs, those who do not know the gospel of the water and the Spirit even as they profess to believe in Jesus as their Savior have no choice but to feed on the food of death rather than the food of life. In contrast, the righteous can ruminate on the Word of God properly, and their faith is fundamentally different from the rest. The righteous always feed on the gospel of the water and the Spirit by faith, regurgitating the Word of God that's in their hearts and ruminating on it by faith every moment.

Our Lord told us that He has blotted out all the sins of mankind once and for all with the gospel of the water and the Spirit. The gospel of the water and the Spirit is the Truth of salvation, and having accepted this gospel into our hearts by believing in the God-given Word, we must ruminate on it always. As we the righteous believers in the gospel of the water and the Spirit carry on with our lives on this earth, whenever our weaknesses are exposed, and whenever we are in need, we regurgitate from our hearts and ruminate on the Word that the Lord has blotted out all our sins once and for all with the gospel of the water and the Spirit. That is how we receive God's blessings. As those who have become righteous in the Lord's sight, when we ruminate on the gospel of the water and the Spirit once again and mediate over its profound meaning, we come to thank God for His grace once more. This is the faith of those who believe in the gospel of the water and the

Spirit, and the distinct life of faith led by them. Such a faith, and such a ruminant life, are what the life of faith is all about for the righteous.

God said here to Moses and Aaron, as well as all the people of Israel, "Of the animals on these animals, you shall eat only those who chew the cud and have cloven hooves. You shall not eat any other animal." God also said that no animal should be eaten if it does not meet either of the two criteria. Although this Word of God teaches us about the life of the righteous, at the same time, it also teaches sinners about the true faith.

What Is and Who Are Acceptable to God?

The animals accepted by God are those that chew the cud and have cloven hooves. It's such animals that God accepts, and these are the animals that His people eat. Those who have not been born again say, "Although I have been remitted from all my past sins, when it comes to the sins that I commit now in the present, I must obtain their remission every day." This, however, is something that is said only by those who cannot ruminate. The very fact that one cannot ruminate indicates that one is a sinner. Therefore, the notion that one must receive the remission of sins on a daily basis is a completely flawed belief before God. It's a belief that makes no sense either when reflected upon the Old Testament.

Our Lord said in 1 John 1:9, *"If we confess our sins, He is faithful and just to forgive us our sins and to cleanse us from all unrighteousness."* What does this verse really mean? It means that because the Lord already bore all ours sins by being baptized by John the Baptist, we should confess our sins by believing in this Truth. In other words, God has already blotted out all the sins of the world once and for all with the gospel of the water and the Spirit, eradicating all the sins ever committed by each and every one of us. Indeed, God has made you and me His very own people who can ruminate on the gospel of the water and the Spirit. Despite this, however, in their ignorance of the gospel of the water and the Spirit, some people still try to receive the remission of their sins by repenting over and over again. Just because we beg for the Lord's forgiveness on our own, can God forgive our sins every day without the gospel of the water and the Spirit? No, this is not possible.

If it's true that we have to obtain the forgiveness of our daily sins every day, then the Lord would have to say to us day in and day out, "Ok, I am forgiving your sins." If this were the case then He would have no time other than doing this. And the Truth that the Lord has blotted out our sins once and for all with the gospel of the water and the Spirit would be the untruth. The Lord is now seated and resting in the Kingdom of Heaven. He has completed His work by blotted out all our sins perfectly once and for all with the gospel of the water and the Spirit.

How are those who have not been born again leading their lives? They are unable to ruminate on the Word of God in their lives. They flip-flop constantly between being the righteous one moment and sinners the next as easily as they change clothes, thinking that they are made righteous the moment they repent, but turn into sinners the moment they sin again. But has God really blotted out our sins through such ignominious prayers of repentance? Would the Lord save us just from our original sin and then say to us, "Since you've made a mistake again, you are a sinner again"? No, of course not. When we believe in His Word, God seals our hearts with the Holy Spirit right away. This means that once we receive the remission of sins by faith, it is forever.

Yet despite this, countless Christians are engaged in various spiritual movements all in vain. There are so many movements nowadays, from the "Mizpah repentance movement" to the "awareness movement," the "discipleship movement," and so on. But is anyone made God's child just by taking part in any of these movements? Are one's sins blotted out in this way? Do people become God's children by participating in such religious movements? Is anyone made God's child just by taking part in these repentance movements? If this were the case, then we would all have to repent every day. However, there is no record in the Scripture that says, "You will become one of God's own people if you participate in the repentance movement."

The Word of the remission of sins is God's clear promise, and the notion that the remission of sins must be received every day makes absolutely no sense at all. Because the Lord has already blotted out all our sins perfectly, because He has eradicated each and every sin once and for all, whenever we fall short of His glory, we are to ruminate on this Word of God, reaffirm that God has indeed blotted out all our sins, and thank Him for it once again. This is the everyday life led by the believers in the gospel of the water and the Spirit.

We the believers in the gospel of the water and the Spirit must ruminate on the Word of God by faith. We must regurgitate the gospel of the water and the Spirit that's in our hearts and chew on it again. The Scripture says that no animal that does not chew the cud should ever be eaten. Do this then apply to only the people of Israel? No, that is not the case. Every Word in the Old Testament is also spoken to us living in the age of the New Testament. All this Word is God's Word of promise for mankind.

God promised that He would blot out all the sins of mankind by sending His Son, the Messiah, saying, *"Though your sins are like scarlet, they shall be as white as snow; though they are red like crimson, they shall be as wool" (Isaiah 1:18)*. And when the time came, God sent Jesus Christ to this earth, transferred all the sins of the entire human race to His Son, and thereby blotted out all our sins. Furthermore, God also said that He would accept only those who receive the remission of sins into their hearts by believing in this Word of God, and who ruminate on it. The opposite side of this coin is that God will never accept anyone who does not believe in His Word and cannot ruminate on it.

The Word of God written in the Pentateuch is all about the remission of sins. If this is the case, then we can say that now in this present age of the New Testament, all the Christian sinners who do not believe in the Word of God according to the gospel of the water and the Spirit have not been born again yet. Even though countless Christians claim to be leading a life of faith and say that they have been born again, in reality, they are not the born-again, for they are incapable of ruminating on the gospel of the water and the Spirit, the Word of God. Although they have cloven hooves, they cannot chew the cud as they do not have such a ruminant stomach.

Those who have not been born again through the gospel of the water and the Spirit are like a pig in their flesh. They are satisfied if believing in Jesus would make them rich. Material prosperity at the present is all that matters to them even as they profess to believe in Jesus. If they are healthy and prosperous, they say everything is just fine. Even if they end up in hell down the road, they are satisfied as long as their businesses thrive and they become rich now. But what will happen to them when they die after living like this? Unless they are born again as someone who can ruminate on the Word of God, they will all end up in hell. It's very important for us to realize the will of God hidden in His Word.

This Word of God is not something that is relevant just for us. Rather, it applies to each and every human being. God said that He will never accept any animal that does not chew the cud. What about you and me then? Are we ruminating on the Word of God? It's absolutely important for us ruminate on God's Word. This means regurgitating the Word whenever we need it and ruminating on it so that it would become our flesh and blood. We have been saved by realizing with our minds that our Lord has blotted out all our sins once and for all with the water and the Spirit, and by believing in this with our hearts. Although we have been saved from all our sins, the shortcomings of the flesh still remain in our everyday lives. It's precisely such times when we must ruminate on the Word that the Lord has blotted out our everyday transgressions also. In other words, we must ruminate by faith on the Truth that the Lord has blotted out once and for all each and every sin that we commit out of our weaknesses in our everyday lives.

Even though you and I believe in the gospel of the water and the Spirit, do we still not have many shortcomings, and do we still not commit transgressions on a daily basis despite having received the remission of sins? Indeed, all of us sin every day. It's precisely because we sin like this that we must once again pull out the gospel of the water and the Spirit and reaffirm the fact that the Lord has blotted out all our sins once and for all. That is how we can enjoy freedom in our hearts and escape from the condemnation of sins. Like this, the righteous must ruminate on the Word of God every day. It is by our faith in the gospel of the water and the Spirit that we can lead a new life. God has turned us the righteous into such people who ruminate on His Word, and for this, I give all my thanks to God. Even though we the righteous are weak, by ruminating on the Word of God, we have become the saints fit for God's acceptable.

It Is Not by Not Sinning That We Are Made Righteous

It is not because we have not sinned that we have become righteous. Rather, we have become completely clean animals, that is, saints—in God's sight even though we still sin because we believe in the Word that the Lord has already blotted out all our sins, and we ruminate on this faith whenever we succumb to our weaknesses. That the righteous ruminate on the Word of God is so important for us the Christians that it cannot be emphasized enough. If the righteous were to beg God to forgive them everytime they sin while living out their lives on the earth, then they would be no different from a pig. They would be the same as the swine that cannot chew the cud despite having cloven hooves. God commanded the people of Israel not eat any pigs meat. God did not accept any swine for a burnt offering either. God said clearly that the swine is unclean. So, even now, the people of Israel do not eat any pork. It's an insult to invite Jewish people and serve pork to them. Although they eat lamb, goat meat, and beef, they never eat pork even to this day.

Although the swine has cloven hooves, because it cannot chew the cud, it could not be offered to God. It's absolutely important for us to realize that no matter how zealously one might lead his life of faith and follow the will of God, if this person has not been born again, then such a life is deemed invalid. It's a completely useless life. The Scripture addresses this point so clearly and unambiguously that it is completely unbiblical to claim that one can be remitted from his daily sins by repenting every day without being born again. Can we even repent from all the sins that we ever commit? No, this is not possible. We struggle with sin even after being born again, so how can anyone who has not even been born again think their own prayers of repentance would take care of all their sins?

Is there a day when a pig is ever clean? Can it stay clean even for a single day? Of course, there are times when the pig pen is cleaned, shoveling out the filthy excrements and washing the pen with detergents. But what happens in just half a day when the pig is put back into the pen? It gets all filthy in its own excrement in no time. So there is not a day when a pig pen is clean. The same is true for those who have not been born again. No matter how hard they try to lead their lives with cloven hooves, that is, try to live in holiness—there is not a day when they are clean. A cattle pen is as dirty as a pig pen, but a cow is fundamentally different from a pig. The cow also produces excrements. But unlike the swine, the cow chews the cud. That's why God accepted the cow but not the swine.

We the righteous also commit wrongdoings before God. However, because we the righteous know how to ruminate on the Word of God, God still accepts us wholly as His clean saints. It's because we ruminate on the Word of God that we are clean. Without ruminating like this, the righteous can never become clean. But, what do those who have not been born again say? Despite the fact that they have not even been born again and cannot ruminate on the Word of God properly, they say that they can receive the remission of sins by repenting every day. This is a completely preposterous claim that makes absolutely no sense at all.

The Christian life is all about ruminating on the Word of God. The righteous have been freed from all their sins by ruminating on the Word of God, and it is also by ruminating on every Word of God that they get new nourishments for their lives. This is why God's Church speaks so often about this rumination. Although this issue is addressed on a daily basis, it is refreshing to hear it every day. The born-again also follow the will of God clearly, just as the hoof is divided. Dividing the hoof here means taking a clear, unequivocal position of faith. Although the righteous still have many shortcomings, they still unite with the born-again Church, listen to the Word of God, and seek the will of God that's pleasing to Him. Like this, the born-again live apart from the world in a clear separation. In contrast, those who have not been born again cannot follow the will of God. Because they feel insecure when they are brought to the born-again Church, they are incapable of following the will of God wholly.

Although the righteous still have inadequacies, they know what the will of God is, and they also have the heartfelt desire to live according to this will that's pleasing to God. The Holy Spirit dwelling in their hearts then is joyful. The Holy Spirit in the hearts of the born-again wants them to live a life that's pleasing to God. No matter how full of shortcomings we may be our outside appearances, we have the Holy Spirit living in our hearts. When Abel and Cain brought an offering to God, the Bible writes that Abel offered the firstborn of his flock and their fat. When the burnt offering of the Old Testament was made, the flesh of the sacrificial animal had to be cut into pieces without fail. With its whole body cut, unclean parts such as entrails were removed and thrown out, while the kidneys and the fat covering the liver, that is, the fat covering the entrails—were removed without fail. This fat was not thrown out, but instead was burnt on the altar invariably.

The fat here refers to none other than the Holy Spirit. His Holy Spirit is inside us the born-again righteous. Even though our flesh has many shortcomings, because of this Holy Spirit, we have the desire to live a life that's pleasing to God. It is because we have the Holy Spirit that we are leading the life of cloven hooves. In other words, we are leading a distinctly holy life and following God in our everyday lives. Only the righteous live such a life. Of course, sinners can also try to live a godly life. But they do so only to fill their own personal ambitions, to establish their own righteousness. The righteous are different. The righteous deny themselves and follow only the will of God even if it does not match their preferences, not because they want to establish their own righteousness, but because it is what God wants from them, and because it is pleasing to God. This is the everyday life led by the born-again.

"These You May Eat of All That Are in the Water"

Let's turn to the Word of God again, *"These you may eat of all that are in the water: whatever in the water has fins and scales, whether in the seas or in the rivers—that you may eat. But all in the seas or in the rivers that do not have fins and scales, all that move in the water or any living thing which is in the water, they are an abomination to you. They shall be an abomination to you; you shall not eat their flesh, but you shall regard their carcasses as an abomination. Whatever in the water does not have fins or scales—that shall be an abomination to you"* (Leviticus 11:9-12). God said here, any fish that does not have scales must not be eaten. He was saying in effect, "Of all that are on the earth, eat only those that chew the cud and have cloven hooves. Next, of all that swim in the water, eat only those that have scales."

Why did God say here to eat the fish that have scales while prohibiting the fish that do not have scales? Whatever fish that does not have scales, such as eels and mudfish, hide itself in the ground with its head stuck in the mud. Here, the fish that have scales refer to those who are leading a proper life of faith. God also spoke about what can be eaten and what cannot be eaten of all the birds in the sky. This also teaches us the righteous believers in the gospel of the water and the Spirit to live by faith. God is saying here that He does not approve anyone who does not live by faith. When it comes to the lives of the born-again saints, whom does God approve? God approves those who live by faith. God is saying here that not all have faith (2 Thessalonians 3:2), and this it is something that only the righteous possess.

Indeed, only the righteous live out their faith in this way. They alone live on this earth by trusting in God. Even among the righteous, God does not approve just anyone who does not live by faith. This means God does not approve the life of anyone who just pretends to follow and obey Him. God accepts only those who chew the cud, have cloven hooves, and have scales. What does this all mean? It means God approves only those who live out their faith. Even if you chew the cud and have cloven hooves, that is, even if you have been born again—if you do not live out your faith like this, then it is all in vain. You are approved by God and used for His work only if you live out your faith. It's absolutely important for us the righteous to use our faith. The fish that do not have scales go anywhere and hole themselves behind rocks and in the mud. In contrast, the fish that have scales cannot bury themselves away like this. Why is this so? It's because their scales move whenever they swim. If the scaled fish bury themselves away in the mud, the mud will lodge between the scales and they will not be able to breathe through their gills. Any fish that has scales cannot survive buried in the mud.

We must live by faith. Even if our faith is as small as a mustard seed, we the born-again must still live by this faith. We the Christians must realize that it is only right for us to live by faith, and indeed live by this faith. We must rise to every challenge by faith. Even if it looks formidable, we must still rise to the challenge by trusting in God with all our hearts. Only then can we achieve our goals. And it is then that God approves us for the life of faith we are now leading. He will give us an even greater faith and bless us to live by this faith. However, there are many people who are not living by faith despite having been born again. Thinking that they can take care of themselves with what they now have without asking for God's help, they refuse to exercise their faith at all, saying to God, "Lord, I am so thankful that You have remitted away all my sins and blotted them out. So what more could I possibly ask from You? I will take care of myself like I always have." Thinking like this, they do not exercise their faith before the Lord. Whenever they face a problem, they just rely on their own resources to address it. So they have no reason to live by faith.

God told us the born-again to eat only of the fish that have scales. But, even if a fish has scales, how many scales would it really have. Most fish have tiny scales. Fish like goldfish have such small sales that if you were to descale them with a knife, the scales will come out like fine white particles. The scaled fish are tasty. I know a few things about fish because I lived by the ocean for a long time. Some of you might know a few fish species that are strong and have sturdy scales. These fish taste the best. Some fish, like snapper, have scales that are very sharp. I've caught a few snappers while fishing. After descaling them and filleting them, I've had them as sashimi. They taste unlike any other fish. Another fish called spotty belly greenling is also easy to catch, and this fish has scales also. But its scales are very fragile, so much so that it would slip if you grab it with your hand. The snapper, in contrast, has such sturdy fins that they can cut your hand. But, snapper / sashimi tastes the best. Its taste is totaly different from any other fish.

It's true that all of us the righteous have been born again equally. Although we all have shortcomings and cannot live by faith 100%, if we rise to our challenge by trusting in the Word of God, and walk and live by faith, God will approve us for living out our faith like this. And God will entrust His work to such saints and fulfill His will through them. In contrast, the will of God cannot be entrusted to any sinner who is not living by faith. Why is this so? It's because such people do everything on their own by relying on their own human means and efforts, because they have buried their heads in the mud and have no scales; and so are incapable of fulfilling the will of God properly.

The Scripture clearly says that only the fish with scales should be eaten. It's said that the Seventh-Day Adventists never eat any fish that has no scales. Many people here like squid, but the Adventists would never touch it. I'll be more than happy to take and eat all the squid they don't want. Jokes aside, God is not saying here in today's Scripture passage that we should literally not eat any fish without scales. Rather, God is telling us to soar by faith before Him, and to live by faith in His sight. In other words, God is teaching us the righteous how we ought to live spiritually through these verses of Scripture.

Although the righteous may not exercise their faith that much at the beginning, the more faith grows in them, the more they listen to the Word of God, and the more hardship they face, they more they will come to rely on their faith, saying to God, "Lord, please do this for me. What is pleasing to You? What is Your will?" Like this, the righteous whose hooves have been divided exercise their faith and walk in the direction that is pleasing to God. They walk in this direction even if it looks like it's leading them to ruins. But, needless to say, they will never be ruined actually, as long as they live by faith. The lives of the righteous saints are all about ruminating on the Word of God, following His will, and living by faith. Only the righteous, our God's own people, can live such a life. God will then approve such lives of the righteous in joy. However, there are many animals that God prohibited us from eating. He spoke of these things all in reference to sinners. Those who are slimy and without scales like the mudfish do not live by faith. What is happening to the churches around us nowadays? The competition for church membership is so fierce that they are trying their best to poach the congregation from one another.

You've all seen tiny little churches in your neighborhood. There are many churches that have only a handful of adult members and many children. It's said that in Korea, over 10,000 new churches are opened up in just a year. Of these 10,000 newly opened churches, 7,000 churches usually throw the towel in and close down. Why are so many new churches closing down so soon? It's because they are not financially viable. Nowadays, you need a lot of money to keep a church open. For instance, you have to pay the rent and other utilities, and in these days the rent is not cheap even for a church.

So, when someone opens a new church, he makes a budget for the next two, three years, and invests tens of thousands of dollars thinking that he will come out ahead if he can attract enough members over this time period. However, if the newly opened church fails to attract enough members within this window period, the church has to close down as it cannot sustain these financial losses. As mentioned already, out of 10,000 new churches that open up every year, 7,000 churches end up shutting down. Even among the surviving 7,000 churches, only about ten of them are sustainable while the rest of them have a bleak long-term prospect. Churches are closed down when they run out of money and cannot raise any more financial resources. This is not what faith is all about. Yet, this is the reality faced by today's Christianity.

That's why so many spiritual movements have been launched across Christian communities, calling for a godly life or pleading for some other cause. Of course, such movements are not bad in of themselves. However, before taking part in such a movement, one must first receive the remission of all his sins. Before even opening a church, one must first of all obtain the complete remission of all his sins from God.

The Lives of the Righteous Are All about Faith

Those who lead their lives of faith properly carry out God's work by faith even if they have nothing of their own. They live their everyday lives by trusting in God, and they rise to the challenge of His work by believing that God Himself will save souls. God will then indeed save them ultimately. As long as we preach the Word of God by faith, the souls that hear us will be saved without fail. This is possible because we are the righteous. Even if the whole world says that the Church of the righteous is wrong, the righteous stand upright by their faith and live without any shame. It's all because they have faith. It's all because God is making them live like this. And it's because they trust in God. But, what would happen if we had no faith? We would tremble in fear the moment someone says anything bad about us. We tremble only because we lack faith.

However, if we believe that this is the path God has set for us, follow His will and live by this faith, and trust that God will fulfill everything for us, then what is there for us to fear? God said, *"The just shall live by faith" (Romans 1:17).* The Scripture should not be changed according to one's own interpretation. Nowhere in the Bible is it written that sinners shall live by faith. It says clearly that *"the just shall live by faith."* Indeed, only the righteous live by faith. Only the righteous can exercise their faith and only they can live out their faith. No sinner can ever live by faith. Are we then going to change this passage into saying, "Sinners shall live by faith"? Sinners may change it like this, but the Scripture can never be altered no matter how hard they try. Whoever the Scripture says is righteous is righteous, whoever the Scripture says is a sinner is a sinner, and this can never change.

What kind of life are we the righteous leading? It is a life that's led with conviction and boldness, ruminating on the Truth that even though we have many shortcomings while living on this earth, the Lord has remitted away all our sins once and for all. Secondly, we follow the will of God despite our shortcomings. The will of God is clear to us, and we follow this will steadfastly even though we all are inadequate in ourselves. Thirdly, although we might have great faith, or our faith may instead be as small as a mustard seed, we must still live by faith, trusting that God will do everything for us and meet all our needs. None other than this is the life led by the righteous. This is the life led by the true saints. And it is also your life and mine.

In contrast, how is the life of faith led by those who have not been born again yet, who are like the eels? Their lives are as smooth as butter. Those who have not been again, that is, those who do not know Jesus—live a life that's slippery like an oily eel on wet grass. Even though the faith of the righteous may be as small as a mustard seed, they still look toward God and live by this faith. And God said clearly that He approves only those who live by faith like this.

Therefore, all of us the righteous must live by faith. No matter who, anyone who does not live by faith will perish. Such people will all be rejected by God. We must not only learn to have faith, but we must also exercise this faith. Every chick has a pair of wings, but it cannot use them yet. It hops around on its two feet. It walks like this because it does not know that it has wings. However, when a chick jumps from a place that's too high for it, it opens up its wings without even realizing it. It can't fly, of course, but it still opens its wings. It will fall even after flapping its wings, but it still uses the wings it has. By flapping its wings, the likelihood of injury is reduced. When in danger, even a chick uses its wings. The same principle applies to us also. We exercise our faith when we encounter something dangerous. We are like the chick flapping its wings.

Do you now understand what kind of life we are meant to live? No one who has not been born again can ever live by faith. Nothing will change this, not even if they are given artificial wings. But the righteous are different. Because they have faith, they must live by this faith. Only then can they escape destruction. This evening's sermon is all about the life led by the righteous.

What is this life of the righteous all about? Firstly, it is all about ruminating on the Word of God. Secondly, it is all about following the will of God. And lastly, it is all about living by faith. Those who ruminate on the Word of God spring forth the redemption of the Lord. As they believe in the Lord who has come by the water, the blood, and the Spirit, they give rise to the gospel proclaiming that the Lord has blotted out all their sins. This true Word of the Lord and faith springs forth from them. So they ruminate on the Lord, saying to Him, "Lord, even though I am full of shortcomings, You have made me whole. Though I am inadequate, You are prefect. That's why I have been made righteous, by believing in You, Lord." The life that we are leading as the righteous is all about such ruminations. As you ruminate on the Word of God, I ask you to also ask those who have not been again yet if they are able to ruminate as you do. If anyone criticizes you for not repenting from your sins, then say to such a person, "Do you ruminate on the Word of God? Are you even able to ruminate?"

It's very important for us to speak about this issue to those around us. As I look at you and ponder, I am absolutely convinced that you are here in this place because you have all ruminated on the Word of God. None of you could have come here unless you have ruminated. Think about it. Could you be sitting here if your heart was still sinful? Although you may still have many shortcomings, because you ruminate on the Word of God, that is, you remind yourself that the Lord has blotted out all your sins despite your shortcomings—you can still come here, praise God, pray to Him, and be one with Him. If you are incapable of ruminating on the Word of God, then you could not be sitting here.

The same is true for me also. It's only because I have ruminated on the Word of God that I have been able to live to this day. I would have perished a long time ago if I couldn't ruminate. What about you then? Is this not also true for you? If you had not ruminated on the Word of God, then you would have also fallen into despair and perished already. It is because our rumination that we the righteous have carried on with our lives to this day. And we will continue to ruminate on the Word of God. Why? It's because in God's sight, the righteous are His cattle, His sheep, His own people, and His saints that are acceptable to Him. That is why we must continue to ruminate on God's Word. Moreover, although we the righteous arc inadequate on our own, because we have clearly cloven hooves, we continue to follow the will of God.

Those who have been born again by believing in the gospel of the water and the Spirit never seek the interest of their own flesh. The more their faith matures and grows, the more they seek the interest of God alone. They do not care about themselves no matter what hardship they face. Knowing that the glory of God is far more important, they follow the Lord completely. They lower themselves to the bottom while exalting God to the highest. Like this, the born-again live by faith alone. All of us are God's people. We are the saints who ruminate on the Word of God. We are the people who follow the will of God. God has given us the righteous such faith, so that we may carry on with our lives in this world by faith and lead a godly life in both body and soul. Therefore, it's absolutely indispensable for us to exercise this faith.

We the righteous must acknowledge God in all things, and we must also live by trusting in God always. God has saved you and me perfectly, so that we would be able to get all our wishes and needs answered by God for the rest of our lives. God accepts the faith of the righteous and answers all their prayers, and God has given such wonderful blessings to none other than you and me, His very own people. It is therefore imperative for you to exercise your faith. Even if you have not been able to live by faith until now, it is never too late. From now on, you must use your faith. You must exercise your faith and see for yourself how God's blessings will start flowing your way, for the everyday life of the born-again is all about faith, one that stands clearly set apart from the world. ✉

SERMON

11

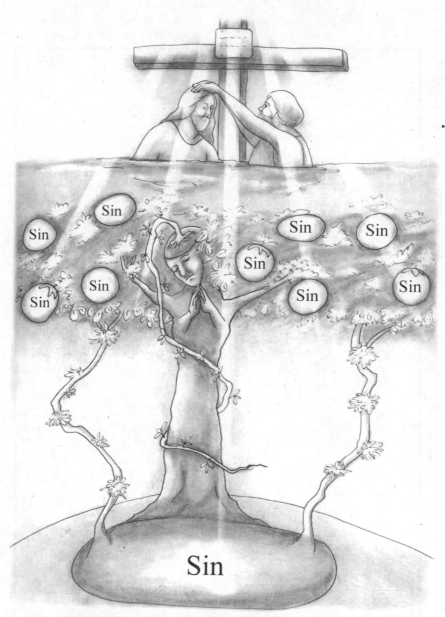

Sin

Human Beings
Are Fundamentally
A Brood of Sin

< Leviticus 13:1-15 >

"And the LORD spoke to Moses and Aaron, saying: 'When a man has on the skin of his body a swelling, a scab, or a bright spot, and it becomes on the skin of his body like a leprous sore, then he shall be brought to Aaron the priest or to one of his sons the priests. The priest shall examine the sore on the skin of the body; and if the hair on the sore has turned white, and the sore appears to be deeper than the skin of his body, it is a leprous sore. Then the priest shall examine him, and pronounce him unclean. But if the bright spot is white on the skin of his body, and does not appear to be deeper than the skin, and its hair has not turned white, then the priest shall isolate the one who has the sore seven days. And the priest shall examine him on the seventh day; and indeed if the sore appears to be as it was, and the sore has not spread on the skin, then the priest shall isolate him another seven days. Then the priest shall examine him again on the seventh day; and indeed if the sore has faded, and the sore has not spread on the skin, then the priest shall pronounce him clean; it is only a scab, and he shall wash his clothes and be clean. But if the scab should at all spread over the skin, after he has been seen by the priest for his cleansing, he shall be seen by the priest again. And if the priest sees that the scab has indeed spread on the skin, then the priest shall pronounce him unclean. It is leprosy. When the leprous sore is on a person, then he shall be brought to the priest. And the priest shall examine him; and indeed if the swelling on the skin is white, and it has turned the hair white, and there is a spot of raw flesh in the swelling, it is an old leprosy on the skin of his body. The priest shall pronounce him unclean, and shall not isolate him, for he is unclean. And if leprosy breaks out all over the skin, and the leprosy covers all the skin of the one who has the sore, from his head to his foot, wherever the priest looks, then the priest shall consider; and indeed if the leprosy has covered all his body, he shall pronounce him clean who has the sore. It has all turned white. He is clean. But when raw flesh appears on him, he shall be unclean. And the priest shall examine the raw flesh and pronounce him to be unclean; for the raw flesh is unclean. It is leprosy.'"

Warm greetings to all of you. Today's Scripture passage is drawn from Leviticus chapter 13, which speaks about diagnosing physical leprosy, but I would also like to address spiritual leprosy. Before I explain this spiritual leprosy in detail, however, it's necessary to explain physical leprosy. It's written in today's Scripture passage that if someone had a swelling, a scab, or a bright spot on his skin, he should be thought as a potential leper; therefore, whenever such signs developed, this person had be taken to a priest first, and the priest had to examine him. Every illness requires a correct diagnosis before anything else. That's why anyone suspected of leprosy had to be taken to a priest first. This implies that when it comes to spiritual matters as well, a correct diagnosis of one's sins is also indispensable.

What the Bible Says about Leprosy

The Bible says, *"If the bright spot is white on the skin of his body, and does not appear to be deeper than the skin, and its hair has not turned white, then the priest shall isolate the one who has the sore seven days" (Leviticus 13:4).* Put differently, anyone suspected of having leprosy was quarantined first. If the sore had spread when the priest examined the patient after seven days of isolation, the priest had to declare him unclean. The physical leprosy mentioned in today's Scripture passage also entails a spiritual message, that is, it refers to the exposure of the sins of the human heart. Everyone has committed sin before God, and when people commit sin repeatedly, they can be described as spiritual lepers.

Human beings are Adam's descendants. As a result, everyone was born with a sinful nature, and therefore everyone commits countless sins while living in this world. No one can help but commit sin. Although some people repent from their repeated sins and resolve themselves to never commit sin again, because all human beings were fundamentally born into this world with sinful natures, they can't avoid sin just because they are determined not to do so. To expunge the sinful nature from mankind, the human heart, which is at the fundamental master of every person, it must be changed first and foremost. For this to come about, one must be washed clean from sins by believing in the gospel of the water and the Spirit that has become the righteousness of the Lord, and the Holy Spirit must, then, from that moment become the master of that heart.

Once this happens to you, you will begin focusing on carrying out the work of God, and therefore you will commit fewer sins. When we commit sin, we know that it's wrong. Despite this awareness, however, our human nature is such that we cannot help but commit sin. People not only commit sin by themselves, but they also inflict harm on others, and they themselves live the rest of their lives in guilt. The Bible says that this is because everyone was fundamentally born as a seed of sin. It's such people whom our Lord calls "unclean." People commit sin in their lives precisely because they were all born with sinful nature.

Even when they try not to commit sin, they keep on sinning time after time, and this is because they do not know the righteousness of Jesus Christ, the way to receive the remission of sins. This can be explained by the fact that their hearts are still not indwelt by the Holy Spirit. In the Bible, if someone had a sore that was deeper than his normal skin, he was considered to have leprosy. This refers to the sins of the human heart, which are fundamentally deeper than outward sins. If one has an evil heart, common sense dictates that it would be exposed eventually. It's obviously wrong for us to commit sin, but this is because we have sinful desires in our hearts. This teaches us that we were born with fundamentally sinful natures, and that these sins are committed by none other than ourselves. Put differently, this follows the same logic as a leper's body rotting away due to the presence of leprosy bacteria. When someone accumulates sin like this, it will eventually kill him. This is the nature of sin.

God does not call us "unclean" or "sinners" on account of just a couple of sins that we might have committed. Whom does God then call a sinner? Fundamentally, God points out the descendants of Adam as sinners. Even if we try not to commit sin against God, because our hearts have sinful nature, we can't help but commit the same sin repeatedly. Spiritually speaking, it is such people who are called spiritual lepers. As the Lord said, the evil thoughts that proceed from the human heart, that is, murder, jealousy, conflict, theft, blasphemy, fornication, pride, and foolishness—are the very sins of mankind. Human beings commit sin repeatedly in their lives precisely because of such sinful natures, and that is why God calls them sinners.

Our God Calls Sinners Those Who Repeatedly Commit Sin Like This

God doesn't call us human beings sinners without any reason. Far from it, God wants to examine and diagnose us correctly. Why are we then called sinners before God? It's because we were all born as sinners. It is not as though we commit sin just once in our lifetime. Just like leprosy spreading all over the skin, sin continues to spread around in our everyday lives. When one is young, he/she commits minor sins. But the older one gets, the more he/she accumulates repeated sins, and the weight of these sins keeps on growing. Eventually, one turns into a pile of sins, doing nothing but committing sin for the rest of his/her life. Our Lord had such people in His mind when He spoke of those who still have not been saved.

Referring to everyone, the Book of Romans says, *"Through one man sin entered the world, and death through sin, and thus death spread to all men" (Romans 5:12)*. This means that we had become sinners from the moment we were born precisely because we had inherited the sinful nature from our forefathers. The Bible therefore says that we cannot help but commit sin throughout our lifetime. When the Bible speaks of sinners, it is speaking about none other than you and me, we who were born with such sinful natures that make it impossible for us not to commit sin.

As such, no one can help but commit sin. Let me explain this by drawing an analogy to an apple tree. Can an apple tree bear pears or persimmons? Can the apple tree avoid bearing apples, just because it doesn't want to bear them? No, of course not! An apple tree cannot help but bear apples for this is its very nature. It's bound to blossom when the spring comes, and it's bound to bear apples in the fall.

Like this, just as an apple tree bears apples, so are human beings born with their parents' sinful nature inherited in them, and therefore they cannot help but commit all kinds of sins. As such, every type of sin, whether it is committed in one's heart or outwardly with one's act, is still a sin. Once born, human beings are destined to continue to commit sin until their very last breath. We were conceived as sinners in our mothers' wombs, and we were born in sin. David realized this and confessed in Psalm 51:5, *"In sin my mother conceived me."* David is saying here that when his mother conceived him, he was conceived and born in sin and iniquity. From whom, then, did our parents inherit sin? They inherited it from their own parents and so on. In short, all of us were born into this world as a brood of sin.

We Are Sinners Because We Inherited Every Sin from Our Forefathers

The root of our sins is traced back to our grandparents and beyond, all the way to Adam and Eve. In other words, we are sinners because Adam and Eve, the ancestors of our human race, committed sin, and we have inherited this sinful nature as their descendants. Our forefathers sinned against God because they fell into the Devil's temptation. Sin entered them because they did not believe in the Word of God. After their fall, they bore many children, and these children inherited their sins and they passed them all the way down to us. Since the children have inherited the sins of their father and mother, isn't it only natural for them to act in the same way as their parents? Indeed, they end up committing the same sins. Even when the children are not taught about the sins committed by their parents of the flesh, they still commit the same sins. This is why there is a saying, "Like father, like son."

As such, because we humans have inherited the sins of our forefathers, it is impossible for us not to commit sin in our lives even if we want to. In the days of the Old Testament, when one had a swelling or a bright spot on his skin, he had to be examined by a priest and isolated for seven days. If he was okay when reexamined after seven days, he was declared clean, but if the sore had spread over the skin, he was declared unclean, that is, a sinner. This implies that we don't just commit sin once or twice, but we sin continuously time after time. That is why all human beings are called sinners.

The Word of God Is Very Different from Man's Thoughts

It's written in today's Scripture passage, *"If leprosy breaks out all over the skin, and the leprosy covers all the skin of the one who has the sore, from his head to his foot, wherever the priest looks, then the priest shall consider; and indeed if the leprosy has covered all his body, he shall pronounce him clean who has the sore. It has all turned white. He is clean"* (Leviticus 13:12-13). We can see from this passage that it is actually those who continue to commit sin that can receive the remission of sins. However, in the earlier passage, it was said that someone who had a minor outbreak of leprosy should be declared "unclean." What did God say in the passage that we just read then? He said, *"If leprosy breaks out all over the skin, and the leprosy covers all the skin of the one who has the sore, from his head to his foot, wherever the priest looks, then the priest shall consider; and indeed if the leprosy has covered all his body, he shall pronounce him clean who has the sore."* The word "clean" here implies spiritual purity.

In some ways, this may seem paradoxical. But it still is the Word of God. The Bible says here that those who think they commit only a few sins are actually the ones who are unclean. Is this who we are, thinking that we commit sin once in a blue moon, all unintentionally? How do such people consider themselves? They don't think of themselves as sinners bound to hell. Instead, they think to themselves, "Well, actually I think I am quite clean. I can avoid sin if I just give some more effort. Although it's true that I still commit sin, I can still avoid the kinds of sins committed by others." What will the Lord say then? Will He say that these people are clean, or will He declare them unclean? He will declare them unclean. Yet despite this, everyone thinks of himself virtuous.

In contrast, when it comes to those whose leprosy has spread all over the whole body, God declares them to be clean. If leprosy had spread all over the body, from the head to the toes, then the priest actually said, "You are not just slightly leprous, but you are completely leprous. You have then become clean." This may seem to be puzzling, but you have to grasp its spiritual meaning here. God said this because He gives the remission of sins to those who are completely sinful. Put differently, while everyone commits sin before God, those who say that they are just slightly sinful will remain sinners unable to put on the grace of the remission of sins. And such people who think that they are only "slightly sinful" do not accept their true depiction even when a priest of God tells them that they are exceedingly sinful and therefore are destined to hell. In their own minds, they think that they will never go to hell for their sins.

In contrast, some people do recognize their sinfulness and are actually tormented by it, realizing that they have committed so many sins repeatedly. These people keep committing more sins to cover their earlier sins. They know that they can't help but commit sin because they are too weak, and so some of them commit even more sins out of despair, thinking to themselves, "I'm already ruined, and so I might as well commit more sins." How do these people think of themselves before God? Such people know clearly that they are sinners.

You need to realize here that such an exceedingly sinful person is none other than yourself. Shouldn't you then confess to God, "Lord, I am a sinner committing sin all the time. Please save me from my sins?" Wouldn't God then give the gospel of the water and the Spirit to such people and cleanse them once and for all? It's the believers in the gospel of the water and the Spirit whom God declares to be clean and pure. This means that in the age of the New Testament, if anyone admits before God and the Law that he is a sinner, recognizes that he is destined to hell according to the Word of God, and begs the Lord to save him from all his sins, the Lord will wash away all his sins once and for all with the gospel of the water and the Spirit and make him as white as snow.

However, those who do not know the Word of the Lord think that they haven't committed that many sins, and therefore they don't think that they deserve to go to hell. Some people think mistakenly that all that they have to do is just fix a few minor flaws. But such people can never believe in the gospel of the water and the Spirit and hear God declaring them to be clean. Those who claim before God to be just slightly sinful and ignore His Word cannot be approved as clean people. Only those who know fully well that they are completely sinful before God can receive, by faith, the grace of the remission of sins manifested in the gospel of the water and the Spirit.

Let me make it clear to you that only those who recognize that they can't help but continue to commit sin as they had done all their lives can believe in the gospel of the water and the Spirit given by the Lord and thereby receive the remission of sins. Every sinner must confess the following and ask God's help: "Lord, this is who I really am. I am by nature nothing but a pile of sins. Please save such a sinner like me from all my sins." When a sinner prays like this, the Lord will blot out all his sins, for this is the reason why He has given the gospel of the water and the Spirit. The Lord will say to him that He has washed away all his sins with the gospel of the water and the Spirit and made him as white as snow.

It's such people who can grasp the righteousness of God and thus receive the remission of sins by faith. What are we humans before God? Fundamentally, every human being is a pile of sins before God. Everyone born in this world commits so many sins both before God and man. Let's then ponder on our own weaknesses once again and examine the Word of true salvation. To do this, let us turn to Mark chapter 7 to first understand how every human being is a sinner by nature: *"And He said, 'What comes out of a man, that defiles a man. For from within, out of the heart of men, proceed evil thoughts, adulteries, fornications, murders, thefts, covetousness, wickedness, deceit, lewdness, an evil eye, blasphemy, pride, foolishness. All these evil things come from within and defile a man" (Mark 7:20-23).*

How Many Sins Are in the Heart of a Man?

How do you feel now that you've read what Jesus said about the sins of mankind? It's said here that there are twelve sins proceeding from the human heart. There are twelve months in a year. Likewise, there are twelve kinds of human sins. We are bound to commit such sins repeatedly until the day we die. These are the sins that we ourselves commit. We commit these sins repeatedly—thefts today, wickedness tomorrow, evil thoughts the next day, deceit the following day, fornications the day after, adulteries the next day, murders the following day, and so forth, repeating the cycle time after time. These are the sins that we commit continuously day after day, month after month, and year after year.

It is in human nature to commit sin repeatedly like this, day in and day out, trying out different sins just for the sake of novelty. All of us commit iniquities constantly every day. Human beings are destined to sin until the day they die. That one is bound to commit sin throughout his entire lifetime is not about someone else, but it applies to ourselves.

What kind of fruit does an apple tree bear throughout the course of its life? It bears nothing but apples, even if this is not what it wants. Does any apple tree say to itself, "I don't want to bear any apples. I hate them! They are so heavy on my branches and they take up all my nutrients?" But even if an apple tree says this, what can it do? It can't help but bear apples again the following year. Even if the tree doesn't want to bear any apples because they are too heavy, it will bear apples once again. Having come into existence as an apple tree, it is only natural for the tree to bear apples throughout the course of its life regardless of whether it likes it or not. Likewise, everyone is born with sin, and therefore no one can help but practice evil whether one likes it or not. Human beings practice evil precisely because they were born with sinful nature—the evil thoughts, fornications, murders, jealousy, and conflicts that proceed from the heart of man. When such sinful nature is provoked in our hearts, it bears sinful fruits, sometimes manifesting as transgressions.

I once visited a leprosarium, a village set apart inhabited by a group of lepers. There, I saw an extremely beautiful woman. She was a cosmetics saleswoman. But she had such wonderful skin. So I starred at her for a long time, but later on I found out that she was also suffering from leprosy. Yet her skin was so smooth and clean, like a white gem. This woman was a not a chronic patient with a full outbreak of leprosy, but she had a dormant case. Despite her disease, her skin was so smooth that it was more refined than most ordinary women that we come across. It was so beautiful that I couldn't just pass her by. I even thought to myself, "Have I ever seen a woman with such beautiful skin? I wonder what cosmetics she is using. She has such nice skin."

We Were Spiritual Lepers

It's said that when one is infected with leprosy, the skin actually gets better for a while. When leprosy infects someone, it progresses silently for three years without the patient realizing it, and it takes another three years before symptoms become severe enough for others to find out. So one can hide leprosy for up to three years since finding it out himself. It's possible to hide the symptoms—for instance, by putting bandages over sores and using artificial eyelashes. After six years go by since the first infection, the skin begins to turn smooth. When one is infected with leprosy, at first the skin actually looks more beautiful than ordinary people's skin.

Like this, in the eyes of sinners, people's transgressions look wonderful. Take a look at people committing sin openly without any hesitation. Take a look at people making money by committing sin. They look so wonderful. They even look so glitzy.

When we continue to commit sin before God, the whole body, from the head to the toes, is marked with the remnants of our transgressions. That is our nature as human beings. It's easy for us to just pick one offence and think to ourselves, "This is all that I've done wrong before God. That is my sole mistake." However, God sees us committing sin all our lives, and He says that we are constantly sinning. As such people, we are lepers before God. When we stand before God, we must realize that our transgressions are not limited to just small mistakes, but our thoughts, words, acts, hearts—indeed, our everything—are completely wrong.

In God's sight, it is therefore inevitable for us to commit countless sins until the day we die. There is no spot that's clean in our lives, and we are destined to fill them with nothing but transgressions until the day we stand before God. That is our destiny as human beings. And this is why we human have nothing to boast of before God, other than our faith in the righteousness of Jesus. We have nothing to show off except the gospel of the water and the Spirit that we believe in. We were all nothing but piles of sins before God. We were all inexorably destined to hell for our sins. Yet despite this, despite the fact all of us were bound to hell for our sins, our Lord has saved such people like us once and for all through the gospel of the water and the Spirit. We don't really appreciate just how insufficient we are before God. I can't emphasize this point enough. We should not have any sin before God. Yet the evil things in our hearts are bound to come out sooner or later, and that is precisely why we must believe in the gospel of the water and the Spirit.

My message for today is that everyone is a pile of sins. We human beings cannot help but commit sin before God throughout our entire lifetime until our death. Not a day goes by without committing any sin. That we are spiritual lepers in God's sight means this; We must realize that we ourselves are piles of sins, and we must receive the remission of sins by believing in the gospel of the water and the Spirit, for the Lord said that if leprosy has spread from the head to the soles of the feet, He will declare this person to be completely clean. If we instead say to God, "I am only this much of a sinner," it will be next to impossible for us to receive the true remission of sins. God says to such people that they are unclean. The secret of the remission of sins lies with the mercy of God, which is bestowed on those bound to hell for their sins. The same is true when it comes to the way for us to receive the remission of sins by believing in the gospel of the water and the Spirit. Our remission of sins is the blessing of faith that God has bestowed on us through the gospel of the water and the Spirit.

To all those who cannot hide their sins from God, and therefore confess themselves as sinners and ask for His mercy, God will give them the gospel of the water and the Spirit, make them believe in this true gospel, and thus declare them to be clean. That's because God is the God of mercy. Therefore, having sent His own Son to this earth, God cleanses such complete sinners, the lepers of the soul, through the gospel of the water and the Spirit. However, as I mentioned before, even if some people have committed only minor sins before God, and therefore have much to say to Him, claiming that while they are sinners, they are neither completely sinful nor destined to hell, they cannot help but be cast into hell for their pride.

My fellow believers, everyone in God's sight is nothing but a pile of sins. No one can help but commit sin. However, some people can still receive the remission of sins, while others are going straight to hell. This all depends on whether or not one receives the remission of sins by believing in the God-given gospel of the water and the Spirit. The saved reached their salvation by realizing that they were bound to hell, asking for God's mercy, and believing that the Lord had given them His own flesh and blood and delivered them from all their sins through the gospel of the water and the Spirit.

For those who are otherwise deluded into thinking that they have committed only minor sins before God, and therefore believe that they can become good people if they just try a bit harder, nothing but destruction awaits. In other words, these people will be cast into hell for not believing in what the Lord has done for all sinners. Did you and I really commit just a few sins before God? Did you really commit just a couple of sins in your life? No, of course not. Moreover, all of us will continue to commit sin in the future. This is so self-evident. Before our Lord, those who are saved from their sins by faith are those who know that they are completely sinful, recognizing and acknowledging themselves, "I have no virtue at all. I am always insufficient, and there is nothing that is not evil in my acts and thoughts. All that I have is shortcomings. Without the Lord, I can't avoid but be cast into hell." Only such people can be saved from sin by believing in the righteousness of God.

Our human existence is such that we simply cannot be saved from our sins just by correcting a few mistakes before God. From our very birth, we were nothing more than piles of sins. It is in our human nature to commit sin until the day we die. In short, we are spiritual lepers. When one is infected with the physical illness of leprosy, you will develop sores all over your body, your flesh will rot away, and you may eventually even lose your eyelashes, your nose, and your ears. But what about someone whose heart has gone astray? Does someone like this, whose heart is misplaced, appear healthy in God's sight? No, of course not. In God's eyes, it is a far more serious illness for the heart to go astray than for the body to fall ill. In other words, it is better for you to have physical leprosy than spiritual leprosy.

If you hate someone to death in your heart, then in God's sight you've already broken His Word commanding you not to commit murder. When your heart harbors such murderous hatred, sooner or later it will be manifested in action and you may even end up committing murder. This is exactly what is meant by having a heart that's gone astray before God, and it is this heart that leads you to commit the sin of murder. Because of such sins that we commit personally, and because we were born with sin from our very birth, we are destined to hell unless we are remitted from these sins. All of us must realize that we are lepers before God. We must grasp fully that we are nothing but piles of sins. And I ask you all to believe that our Lord has saved even such people like us once and for all through the gospel of the water and the Spirit. And from now on, I ask you to give all thanks and glory to the Lord in your life. ✉

SERMON

12

The Law

You can download Rev. Paul C. Jong's Christian Books on iPhone, iPad, or Blackberry by going to Amazon's Kindle e-bookstore (www.amazon.com).

How Is Our True Reflection?

< Leviticus 13:1-23 >
"And the LORD spoke to Moses and Aaron, saying:
'When a man has on the skin of his body a swelling, a scab,
or a bright spot, and it becomes on the skin of his body like
a leprous sore, then he shall be brought to Aaron the priest
or to one of his sons the priests. The priest shall examine
the sore on the skin of the body; and if the hair on the sore
has turned white, and the sore appears to be deeper than
the skin of his body, it is a leprous sore. Then the priest
shall examine him, and pronounce him unclean. But if the
bright spot is white on the skin of his body, and does not
appear to be deeper than the skin, and its hair has not
turned white, then the priest shall isolate the one who has
the sore seven days. And the priest shall examine him on
the seventh day; and indeed if the sore appears to be as it
was, and the sore has not spread on the skin, then the priest
shall isolate him another seven days. Then the priest shall
examine him again on the seventh day; and indeed if the
sore has faded, and the sore has not spread on the skin,
then the priest shall pronounce him clean; it is only a scab,
and he shall wash his clothes and be clean. But if the scab
should at all spread over the skin, after he has been seen by
the priest for his cleansing, he shall be seen by the priest
again. And if the priest sees that the scab has indeed spread
on the skin, then the priest shall pronounce him unclean. It
is leprosy. When the leprous sore is on a person, then he

shall be brought to the priest. And the priest shall examine him; and indeed if the swelling on the skin is white, and it has turned the hair white, and there is a spot of raw flesh in the swelling, it is an old leprosy on the skin of his body. The priest shall pronounce him unclean, and shall not isolate him, for he is unclean. And if leprosy breaks out all over the skin, and the leprosy covers all the skin of the one who has the sore, from his head to his foot, wherever the priest looks, then the priest shall consider; and indeed if the leprosy has covered all his body, he shall pronounce him clean who has the sore. It has all turned white. He is clean. But when raw flesh appears on him, he shall be unclean. And the priest shall examine the raw flesh and pronounce him to be unclean; for the raw flesh is unclean. It is leprosy. Or if the raw flesh changes and turns white again, he shall come to the priest. And the priest shall examine him; and indeed if the sore has turned white, then the priest shall pronounce him clean who has the sore. He is clean. If the body develops a boil in the skin, and it is healed, and in the place of the boil there comes a white swelling or a bright spot, reddish-white, then it shall be shown to the priest; and if, when the priest sees it, it indeed appears deeper than the skin, and its hair has turned white, the priest shall pronounce him unclean. It is a leprous sore which has broken out of the boil. But if the priest examines it, and indeed there are no white hairs in it, and it is not deeper than the skin, but has faded, then the priest shall isolate him seven days; and if it should at all spread over the skin, then the priest shall pronounce him unclean. It is a leprous sore. But if the bright spot stays in one place, and has not spread, it is the scar of the boil; and the priest shall pronounce him clean.'"

I hope everyone had a good dinner. The Church of Seoul has been treating me with such sumptuous meals that if I stay here for too long, I will end up gaining a lot of weight. The pastor, his wife, and the congregation here have all been very nice to me, and thanks to them, I have been leading this revival meeting with creature comforts.

When we turn to the Book of Leviticus, we see something peculiar about how the priests examined lepers. The priests of the Old Testament and the priests in this present age of the New Testament are both spiritual physicians, ensuring the health of the children of God. In particular, the spiritual priests in the age of the New Testament are those who preach the gospel of the water and the Spirit.

How Leprosy Was Examined

Today's Scripture describes how the priests of the Old Testament diagnosed people's illness of sin. It's written, *"And the Lord spoke to Moses and Aaron, saying: 'When a man has on the skin of his body a swelling, a scab, or a bright spot, and it becomes on the skin of his body like a leprous sore, then he shall be brought to Aaron the priest or to one of his sons the priests. The priest shall examine the sore on the skin of the body'"* (Leviticus 13:1-3). As it says here, when an Israelite had a sore that looked leprous, he had to first show it to a priest. The priest then examined the man's sore and made a diagnosis, as it's written, *"The priest shall examine the sore on the skin of the body; and if the hair on the sore has turned white, and the sore appears to be deeper than the skin of his body, it is a leprous sore. Then the priest shall examine him, and pronounce him unclean"* (Leviticus 13:3). If it was ascertained that the man had leprosy, then he was taken to a leper colony on the outskirts of the city.

In Korea, there is a small island called Sorokdo, which is widely known as a leprosarium. The government established a leper colony on that island and sent leprosy patients to it who are quarantined from the rest of the population, so as to prevent the spread of this contagious disease. In the same vein, if an Israelite suspected of having leprosy was diagnosed by the priest to indeed suffer from that disease, then he had to be separated from everyone including his own family. So, the people of Israel took this disease very seriously. Because the people of Israel were serving the holy God, no one who had leprosy could live amongst them. The reason for this was because the Israelites had to be separated from uncleanness. As a result, leprosy was considered to be the most serious disease in Israel. So, whenever the people of Israel noticed some type of trouble on their skin, it was common for them to wonder if it was not a symptom of leprosy.

If a skin sore did not heal easily and it persisted, it usually indicated a serious problem. A leprosy patient's skin is different from the skin of a healthy person. To draw an analogy, leprous skin is like the skin of a persimmon that fell from the tree and turned soft on the ground. When an unripe persimmon falls from the tree, its skin begins to soften, and mold begins to grow inside to rot it away. Similar things happen also when someone is infected with leprosy and its symptoms begin to show in the skin. Sores and scabs appear, and the skin begins to rot away.

In Korea also, there was a time when leprosy was widespread and the disease was taken very seriously. Leprosy patients used to be quarantined from the rest of the society including their family. No doubt the patients were extremely traumatized by this, making them wonder why they were born in this world and feeling utterly desolate about their situation. Leprosy used to be very prevalent in the old days. Nowadays, leprosy is said to be treatable if discovered early. But that was not the case in the past. There was no treatment for it, nor was there any way to hide it as its symptoms showed up glaringly for everyone to see. Anyone who came down with leprosy had to be separated from the family and could no longer have a social life. This separation from the rest of society, cut off from any normal social interaction, was one of the greatest sufferings faced by leprosy patients.

Spiritually speaking, lepers refer to sinners who are facing condemnation for their sins. Anyone who has any sin in God's sight must be washed clean from this sin, and if the person fails to do this in the living years, he must be cast into hell. This applies to your family also. Although we will go to Heaven since we have received the remission of sins by believing in the righteousness of Jesus Christ, your family members who still have not been remitted from their sins will end up in hell. With the gospel of the water and the Spirit, God has washed away all the sins that we commit while living on this earth. Whoever believes in this gospel will therefore receive the remission of sins and go to Heaven, but sinners who do not believe in this gospel will face the punishment of hell forever. That is why lepers had to show their disease to the priest and get a treatment for it.

Let's See Who Is Diagnosed As a Leper

It's written in Leviticus 13:8-13: *"And if the priest sees that the scab has indeed spread on the skin, then the priest shall pronounce him unclean. It is leprosy. When the leprous sore is on a person, then he shall be brought to the priest. And the priest shall examine him; and indeed if the swelling on the skin is white, and it has turned the hair white, and there is a spot of raw flesh in the swelling, it is an old leprosy on the skin of his body. The priest shall pronounce him unclean, and shall not isolate him, for he is unclean. And if leprosy breaks out all over the skin, and the leprosy covers all the skin of the one who has the sore, from his head to his foot, wherever the priest looks, then the priest shall consider; and indeed if the leprosy has covered all his body, he shall pronounce him clean who has the sore. It has all turned white. He is clean."* Leprosy is a disease that spreads slowly throughout the whole body. When one is infected with leprosy, the external symptoms appear as skin lesions which cannot be healed by any topical treatment as the leprosy pathogen is resistant to such treatments. Left untreated without specific medication, the lesions will eventually spread all over the body and cause serious skin deformities.

Spiritually speaking, someone whose heart has sin is like someone who is infected with leprosy. It is through such sinners that every sin has spread throughout this earth in every nook and cranny. Those who are infected by this disease of sin cannot avoid sinning even if they try. That's because human beings, born in iniquity, are bound to commit sin habitually and endlessly throughout their lives. Spiritually speaking, they are infected with the disease of sin. Just as the leprosy pathogen spreads and devours the skin of the patient, for those whose hearts are sinful, so does the disease of sin spread and devour them spiritually.

God says that everyone was born with iniquity from the moment they are born from the mother's womb. What, then, is this spiritual leprosy everyone has? This leprosy is the sin that is found in each and every human heart. God says that as a brood of evildoers by our natures, we are the spiritual lepers. God is asking us, "What is your life all about? What is Heaven? Who are sinners? What is the consequence for those who believe in the gospel of the water and the Spirit?"

The Fundamental Nature of Human Beings

Let's now turn to Psalm 51:5-6 in the Old Testament:
"Behold, I was brought forth in iniquity,
And in sin my mother conceived me.
Behold, You desire truth in the inward parts,
And in the hidden part You will make me to know wisdom."

How does the Bible explain our basic nature in God's sight? As it's written in the Word of God, every human being is a pile of sin. Human beings were nothing more than piles of sins the moment they were born from their mothers' wombs. So, if we are asked about the fundamental nature of human beings, our answer will be that they were born as piles of sins from their mothers' wombs. David is saying here that everyone was conceived in sin and brought forth in iniquity. That everyone was conceived in sin means that by nature, everyone was born with such wicked desires as murder, theft, jealousy, and foolishness inherited from one's father and mother.

In other words, we human beings became sinners because we inherited the sins that Adam and Eve, our forefathers had. We were all born as a brood of iniquity from our very birth. We are a brood of evildoers. It is not just our flesh that we inherited from our parents, but we have also inherited a sinful heart. That's why the Bible says, *"For as by one man's disobedience many were made sinners" (Romans 5:19)*. It's because Adam and Eve sinned against God that all of us came to have sin in our hearts. Put differently, it's because of the fall of the first man that we were all born as a brood of evildoers.

The Sins of the Human Heart

Let's turn to the Word of God again to see what kind of sins the human heart has. It's written in Mark 7:20-23: *"And He said, 'What comes out of a man, that defiles a man. For from within, out of the heart of men, proceed evil thoughts, adulteries, fornications, murders, thefts, covetousness, wickedness, deceit, lewdness, an evil eye, blasphemy, pride, foolishness. All these evil things come from within and defile a man."*

Because we are human, evil thoughts pour out of our hearts relentlessly no matter how much we resolve ourselves not to do anything bad anymore. For instance, we can't stop but gawk at tragic events. When there is a house fire, we like to watch the house burning. When we hear in the news about some disastrous accident out in the sea that took away 300 lives, we feel sorry for the victims at first, but no sooner than this do we start wondering if there ever has been a worse accident. Everyone's thoughts are evil like this. We are drawn to sensationalism, even if it involved 300 who deid tragically. In short, everyone was born with the evil desire to sin from their very birth. It is precisely because human being have wicked thoughts and immoral desires in their hearts that they do wicked and immoral things wherever they go.

The problem, of course, is that every sinner is followed by

the wrath of God. This is God's justice. However, the salvation that has come by the righteousness of God has already eradicated all sins. That's because the Lord came to this earth incarnated in the flesh of man, bore all the sins of this world by being baptized by John the Baptist, was crucified to death while shouldering these sins, and rose from the dead again. If we know and believe in this Truth, we are saved from all our sins once and for all. We the believers in the gospel of the water and the Spirit are no longer sinners as we used to be in the past. This is because our hearts are indwelt by the gospel Truth of the water and the Spirit. Therefore, we the redeemed no longer find it pleasant to sin in this world. Most people find it pleasing to live according to their immoral hearts, but this is not the case for the righteous ones.

This had not been so in the past. We didn't know that we were actually sinners doing nothing but sinning against God. We used to think highly of ourselves, wondering what sin we ever committed. Thinking that whatever we did was out of our basic instincts, we did not even know that such things constituted grave sins in God's sight. However, when we reflected upon ourselves and on the God-given Ten Commandments, we could realize that we were in fact sinners. Giving us the Ten Commandments, God had told us not to murder, not to commit adultery, and not to steal. But, even while committing such sins, we did not know that we were sinners. Afterwards, when we realized that God would pour His wrath out on sinners, we came to recognize that we were indeed sinners.

By their very nature, human beings are a brood of evildoers and selfish beings. People's thoughts are so evil that they prefer everyone else to fail than succeed, except when it comes to their own family members or loved ones. They can't stand it when someone else is prosperous. If a fire breaks out in someone else's house, they wish for the house to be completely burnt down. That's how evil human beings are. Do you think I am exaggerating here? But let's look deep inside us. Isn't it true that we would feel at least somewhat disappointed if the fire is put out too soon? We can't help but wish for more because that's in our human nature. While we might worry about the fire spreading to our own houses, but on the one hand, we get so much excitement out of watching someone else's house burn down.

Like this, what proceeds out of the human heart is nothing but evil thoughts, and unless God pointed out our sins, we wouldn't have even realized that we were piles of sins. I also had such sins, and it was only after I found the righteousness of Jesus that I could realize my true self. I had thought that I should live my life without any shame, and I had believed that this was how I had lived, but all this time, I didn't know that I was in fact nothing but a pile of sins in God's sight.

Evil Thoughts Begets Sin

Just like leprosy spreading throughout the whole body, one's sins eventually devours your whole soul. Just as anything alive grows, so do the evil thoughts of human beings grow. As iniquity spread like this, wherever human beings go, they end up bearing the fruit of sin. They cannot help but commit all kinds of sins day in and day out. Throughout their entire lifetime spanning 70-80 years, human beings do nothing but commit one sin after another. That's why the Bible says that human beings are a brood of evildoers. In short, human beings are so evil that they all deserve to fall into hell, unless of course they know and believe in the righteousness of Jesus. This is the most serious problem confronting everyone who is living with sin.

However, God has bestowed His mercy on such people like us, and He is waiting patiently for each of us to be saved. Unlike us human beings, who are incapable of forgiving anyone who offends us repeatedly, God is merciful, and even now He is saying to us, "Return to the gospel of the water and the Spirit. You are a spiritual leper. Return to Me, and I will heal you of your disease." The Lord Himself has prepared our salvation with the righteousness of God.

The Lord said, *"What comes out of a man, that defiles a man. For from within, out of the heart of men, proceed evil thoughts, adulteries, fornications, murders, thefts, covetousness, wickedness, deceit, lewdness, an evil eye, blasphemy, pride, foolishness. All these evil things come from within and defile a man" (Mark 7:21-23).* God looks direct at people's souls rather than their outward appearances. The same is true for the priests. During the days of the Old Testament, it was the priests who examined for leprosy, and if the sore had spread, then it was considered to be leprosy. It was also diagnosed as leprosy if the sore appeared to be deeper than the skin, or the hair on the sore turned white. This meant that even if the symptoms had not spread through the whole body, leprosy was still pronounced as leprosy. Like this, even if someone has not sinned with his acts yet, if his heart is sinful and he still has not received the remission of sins from God, then this person is a sinner. The leprosy pathogens can remain dormant in the body without showing any symptoms, but eventually, symptoms will begin to appear. In the same vein, anyone who has a sinful heart - is always a sinner.

The people of this world do not call anyone a sinner over

the sins that this person has in his heart. They call someone a sinner only when the sins in his heart are acted upon outwardly, that is, when one commits a definite and concrete sin. Through the Law, God commanded us not to commit adultery and not to murder. However, from the perspective of human beings, there is no one who can keep all the commandments of God. Like the girl in the red shoes fairy tale, we do nothing but what has told us not to do. God told us not to have any other gods before Him, but what have we human begins done? We have created all kinds of false gods. Some people even claim that everyone and everything is divine. The same disobedience is found when it comes to the norms that we are supposed to follow in our relationship with one another. Even though God clearly told us to honor our parents, we don't do so. Many people even think of their parents as someone to be used for their own gains, and they regard their aging parents as an annoying burden. Too many people nowadays just keep on taking from their parents rather than giving, and far from honoring their parents, they even abuse them in their old age.

The Lord also told us not to steal, but we are so prone to do what the Lord told us not to do. It's because human beings were born as a brood of iniquity that they are incapable of doing anything virtuous even if they want to. Because their hearts are filled with nothing but sin, they cannot do anything else but sin. This is their very human nature. They sin whenever and wherever they go. Of course, countless people want to do good, thinking to themselves, "I should act virtuously," but no one is capable of this. Some people even cry over their failure, wondering, "I've read about all these great people who led such a virtuous life. I want to be a good and decent person like them also. Why am I then so wretched?" Although human beings have an evil heart, they also have, on the other side, the desire to seek goodness. However, they are incapable of practicing the virtues that they desire, while they can't help but practice the wickedness that they do not want. That is why human beings are a brood of evildoers by their fundamental nature. The seed of human beings is such that we were all born as a brood of evildoers. That's what the Word of God in the Scripture says, so this is the truth even if we don't like hearing it.

Let's Pay Close Attention to What the Book of Isaiah Says about the Sins of Mankind

Let's turn to Isaiah 1:2-4,
"Hear, O heavens, and give ear, O earth!
For the LORD has spoken:
"I have nourished and brought up children,
And they have rebelled against Me;
The ox knows its owner
And the donkey its master's crib;
But Israel does not know,
My people do not consider.
Alas, sinful nation,
A people laden with iniquity,
A brood of evildoers,
Children who are corrupters!
They have forsaken the LORD,
They have provoked to anger
The Holy One of Israel,
They have turned away backward."
This is what God said through the Prophet Isaiah. When God lamented about a *"sinful nation, a people laden with*

iniquity, a brood of evildoers, children who are corrupters,"
He was speaking about not just the people of Israel but all of us.
Our forefathers became sinners because they did not believe in
the Word of God, and as they passed down their sins to us, we
were also born in sinfulness. We are therefore a brood of
evildoers in God's sight. And we are a people laden with
iniquity. When we look at just our acts, how many virtues do
we really have? While it is noble for human beings to try to do
good, in reality this is just hypocrisy in God's eyes. In other
words, people try to do good because they are fundamentally
evil, in order to hide this wickedness. Some people do virtuous
deeds expecting some sort of compensation in return, thinking
to themselves, "What good things should I do get rewarded? If
I do something good, like giving some money to that beggar I
see, I'm sure God will see this and reward me for it."

What is hypocrisy? In Chinese character, the word
hypocrisy is written as a combination of two characters, one
denoting "false" and another denoting "goodness." So in this
case, hypocrisy means "false goodness." It applies to someone
who is not virtuous acting as though he is virtuous. For
instance, making a donation to an orphanage is in itself a good
deed, but if the donor did this with the ulterior motive of hiding
his own wickedness or making a name for himself, then this is
practicing false goodness. The same goes when it comes
donating to a scholarship fund to help poor students. While in
itself this is a good deed, if one does it while expecting
something in return from God, then it is hypocrisy. Many,
many people practice hypocrisy in order to hide their own
wickedness.

Let's say that someone committed a fraud and embezzled
$3 million. Let's also say that this person donated $500,000 to
a scholarship fund of this money. What happened to the

remaining $2.5 million? It went straight into that man's pocket. But, the newspapers make a big deal out of his donation of half a million dollars while not saying anything about how he got that money. So the man is portrayed as a very good person for donating half a million dollars of his ill-gotten gain. None other than this is what is meant by hypocrisy. What did the man actually do? He had embezzled millions of dollars. He was a criminal who had taken someone else's money without working for it. Yet, such people are highly respected in society. Like this, human beings are hypocritical to the core.

Those who truly practice goodness are those who have received the remission of sins by believing in the gospel of the water and the Spirit and who are living for this gospel. A life that serves the gospel of righteousness before God, a life that obeys God's commandments without seeking one's selfish gains, is the life that practices true goodness.

When everyone's heart is filled with evil desires like this, how can we say that human beings are good? When God examines the hearts of people today, He will see that they are filled with nothing but iniquity. These sins in the heart eventually all flow out and spread around. Sometimes people sin in their hearts alone, but other times they sin with their flesh. Born with iniquities, people put into action all these iniquities while living in this world, and while at first they may commit only small sins, eventually, everyone ends up committing grave sins. That is why God said that everyone is a sinner, a brood of evildoers.

Before we believe in the gospel of the water and the Spirit, we must first of all realize that we are sinners bound to hell in God's sight. To do so, we must have the Law of God in our hearts. God has given His Law to all of us, which is composed of 613 commandments including the Ten Commandments:

"You shall not have any other gods before Me. You shall not make a carved image for yourself and bow down before it. You shall not take the name of God in vain. You shall keep the Sabbath holy. You shall honor your parents. You shall not kill. You shall not commit adultery. You shall not steal. You shall not bear false witness. You shall not covet your neighbor's wife or belongings." When we accept this Law of God into our hearts, we can then realize just how wicked we are before the Law of God and what a brood of evildoers we all are.

Without the Law, it is not possible for us to realize that we ourselves are sinners on our own. It other words, it is only when we reflect ourselves upon the Law of God that we are exposed as sinners. Based on one's own standard, everyone has some excuse to justify his behavior, and therefore no one will admit by himself that he is a sinner bound to hell. Those who say to God that they only have tiny sins also think at the same time that they have a great deal of goodness. So they think that while they might have committed small sins, they have done much more benevolent things. But such thoughts are totally wrong.

No sin of mankind, no matter how small, can ever escape from God's just judgment. Yet, people come up with all kinds of excuses for themselves, trying to make up for their sins with their hypocritical acts of goodness. This is precisely what is meant by the righteousness of mankind. But you must realize here that the righteousness of mankind is like a filthy rag in God's sight. Hanging onto one's own human righteousness before God is like playing peekaboo. It's like a pile of manure saying to God that it doesn't smell and it's clean. God is holy, just, and completely sinless. His heart is holy, just as His acts are holy and just. Given this, how could human beings, who are nothing more than piles of sins, seek God's approval by hiding their filthy sins and sprucing up just their façade? Even if they protest to God, saying, "But Lord, I have done so many good things," is their fundamental nature changed at all? No, of course not. God will just say to such people, "What's so holy about you when you are filled with filthiness? You are a sinner. You have failed to obey My Word!"

Therefore, when we human beings stand before the Law of God, we are completely exposed as sinners. And we realize just how worthless we really are, devoid of any merit of or own at all. Like this, when human beings stand before God, it's inevitable for their own human righteousness to be completely broken down. Even the believers in the gospel of the water and the Spirit, when they reflect themselves upon God, amount to nothing except for serving the righteousness of God. If we only know the God-given statutes and Law, if we only know God's commandments, and if we only know that God is the righteous and is the just Judge, then we would realize that we are nothing, and we would also recognize what a wonderful grace it is that God has saved such sinners from all sins through the gospel of the water and the Spirit. The only reason why people still claim to have some righteousness of their own is because they still have not seen their true selves before God.

The Fallacy of Self-Righteousness

If you are self-righteous thinking highly of yourself, then it is the evidence of the fact you still have not come forward to the holy God with honesty. Try approaching God with honesty and see if it's still possible for you to be self-righteous before God. Anyone who is full of self-righteousness must first realize just how filthy his own righteousness is. It is to bring about this realization that God allows so much suffering to people. There are countless people in this world committing all kinds of sins. Why does God tolerate them then? Why does He spare their lives? In other words, why does God not punish them instead? God does this in order to let everyone know His righteousness and bestow true salvation.

However, many people still suffer while living in this world because they neither know nor believe in the gospel of the water and the Spirit that constitutes the righteousness of God. It's very important for us to recognize here that we are no different from such people. We also have done nothing virtuous before God. It's just that God allows hardship to such people in order to wake them up to the fact that they must acknowledge the righteousness of God and to receive the remission of sins.

Anyone who is self-righteous cannot help but suffer even more. And if such people insist on their own righteousness until the end, then they cannot avoid but face the just judgment of God. Those who are exceedingly self-righteous are beyond salvage even for God, and these are the people who are trying to go to Heaven by sanctifying themselves. Even God can't do anything for such people. These are the people who say, "I have been remitted from my original sin by receiving Jesus. From now on I will get the remission of my personal sins by offering prayers of repentance every day, and in that way I will go to the Kingdom of Heaven."

Following the abominable doctrine of incremental sanctification, they claim that as long as they continue to sanctify themselves throughout their lifetime, they will be completely free from their sins by the time they reach death. Those living such a misguided life of faith cannot be helped even by God. In contrast, those who know their own shortcomings believe that it is only by their faith in the righteousness of God that they can go to Kingdom of Heaven. The foolish, however, think that they will go to Heaven on their own merit.

The self-righteous cannot avoid but be cast into hell. Now then, do you have any merit before God? Step forward if you think you are meritorious. If you still think you have at least some merit, let's turn to the Word of God right away to see if you are right. Before we turn to anywhere else, remember what the Bible says about sin: *"The wages of sin is death" (Romans 6:23).* Let's turn to Exodus 20:3 and read, *"You shall have no other gods before Me."* You might protest and say that you really believe only in God. But do you really believe only in God? Have you really served God alone?

Let's see. You need money for our livelihood. Let's say that you are being recruited by another company offering you a higher salary. But the owner of that company doesn't like the fact that you are a Christian. So the business owner asks you to skip worship service a couple of times a week, and in return promises to pay you an extra $3,000 a month. Would you not be tempted by this offer? You are bound to be tempted for sure. Nowadays, we are living in a world where money has become a god, as are people. The things of this world have turned into gods. Is there anyone who doesn't like money? Even Christians don't like it if God is an obstruction interfering with their moneymaking schemes and ventures. Is there then really anyone who does not worship any other gods but God? No, Christians nowadays claim to worship God with just words, while in fact they worship money. Can you then say confidently that you have worshiped only God despite this? Are you really sure that you have not worshiped an idol?

If someone worships money more than God like this, then

is this person guilty of sin or not? Of course he is guilty. God said that anyone who has even the smallest sin will be cast into hell. He said in Romans 6:23, *"For the wages of sin is death, but the gift of God is eternal life in Christ Jesus our Lord."* This means that if you have any sin at all, no matter how tiny, you will be thrown into hell. This is God's law. It is by believing lawfully that we receive the remission of sins. If we do not believe lawfully, we will be cast into hell. To receive the remission of sins by believing lawfully we must believe in two things. Firstly, we must believe in the Law, and secondly, we must believe in the law of grace. If we know these two laws and believe accordingly, we can all reach salvation.

The Destruction Awaiting the Self-Righteous

Let me repeat again, anyone who is self-righteous will be destroyed. Some people in this world say that they are so decent that they don't even need the law, but they are all wrong to think like this. How do such people actually behave by claiming that they have no need for the Law of God? While pretending to be upright but are somehow disadvantaged, or whenever they see any gain for themselves, they sin while others are not looking. Is there anyone here who has never, ever taken anything from anyone else without permission, not even once? I am sure you have all taken something from someone else without permission, even if it's just a donut or a cookie.

Those who say that they can live without the Law of God are actually the worst of all sinners, since they think so highly of themselves that they don't even see any need to receive the remission of sins. Imagine what a disastrous blunder it would have been if we had thought like these people. We would not have believed in the gospel of the water and the Spirit, nor would we have received the remission of sins. But God is watching us all the time. He sees every sin we ever commit, and He has them all recorded in the Book of Deeds. God says in Psalm 139:2, *"You know my sitting down and my rising up; You understand my thought afar off."*

If we live without relying on the righteousness of God, we will all be caught in the trap of sin only to end up in hell. It's like a fish swimming around merrily having no clue that it is about to be trapped in the net. The fish doesn't go into the net knowing that it's a trap. It just swims as it always has, but once caught in the net, it can never escape. Like this, human beings also get caught in the trap of sin to fall into hell. It's because they fall into sin that they are cast into hell. Can any human being born in this world never commit any sin at all, not even once? No, of course not. It's absolutely impossible! Yet, so many people are so self-righteous that they think they are actually good people. Such self-righteous people can't help but stand against the righteousness of God, and as a result, they cannot avoid but face death. If you are such a self-righteous person, I urge you to admit to God as soon as possible that you are a sinner, believe in the gospel of the water and the Spirit, and thereby be saved from our sins. You can find the light only if you first confess that you are a sinner.

I see that some of you are starring at the floor, afraid that I might ask about your sins again. I won't ask you about your sins anymore. But, I do urge you once again to confess your heart to God. If God asks you whether you have sin or not, confess yourself. You can then be saved from all your sins by believing in the gospel of the water and the Spirit. However, if you say that you are not sure whether you are a sinner or not, or if you insist on hanging onto your own self-righteousness rather than relying on the righteousness of God, you will just provoke God's wrath. God allows such stubborn self-righteous people to turn themselves into evildoers. He lets them fall into the sin of standing against the righteousness of God on their own.

God rules over the life and death of all human beings. You must grasp this here. Everyone has one type of weakness or another unique to each person. Some people are weak when it comes to the opposite sex, while others are weak when it comes to money. So it's impossible for human beings not to fall into sin. God knows all about this condition of ours. No matter how strong you might be, unless you rely on the righteousness of God, you have no choice but face hell, but by then, no amount of regret or excuses will be of any use. Unless you rely on and believe in the righteousness of God, the sins you have committed will never disappear.

God writes our sins in His Book of Judgment, as well as in the tablets of our hearts. When we turn to Jeremiah 17:1, we see God saying, *"The sin of Judah is written with a pen of iron; with the point of a diamond it is engraved on the tablet of their heart, and on the horns of your altars."* This means God writes each and every sin we ever commit on the tablets of our hearts. So, once our sins are written in our hearts, we are reminded of them continuously. And we keep on coming up with excuses. Whether lying in the bed or sitting at the dinner table, our guilty consciences reminds us of our sins constantly, and to ease our consciences, we blame others for them, saying to ourselves that we would not have sinned were it not for that other person. Although we claim to be innocent like this, deep inside us, our consciences tells us that we are guilty. This happens because our own righteousness is struggling with the

Law of God inside us.

The Most Serious of All Diseases Is the Disease of Sin

Just as one of the most serious and repulsive physical illnesses is leprosy, the most terrible and repulsive spiritual disease of all is the disease of sin in the human heart. The sin in the human heart is what causes the most repulsive disease. It's these sins in the heart that engulf us with an unbearable stench, make us unable to fulfill our proper role as human beings, and holds us back from others. None other than sin is what makes human beings lose their humanity.

Human beings were originally created in the likeness of the image of God, and therefore they are the most beautiful of all the creatures made by God. However, although human beings were created as such wonderful beings originally, if they have sin, they can degenerate into dreadful beings that are so wretched and shameful. It's the sins of mankind that make human beings so depraved. Sin makes them worthless and turns them into human garbage. It is the sins that are in one's human heart and his sinful acts that turn him into trash. However, even such people can still be delivered from all these wretched conditions if only they receive the remission of sins. Therefore, the greatest gift for mankind is the fact that Jesus Christ has blotted out all sins. It is with this knowledge that we must believe in Jesus.

Let's turn to Leviticus 13:12-13, *"And if leprosy breaks out all over the skin, and the leprosy covers all the skin of the one who has the sore, from his head to his foot, wherever the priest looks, then the priest shall consider; and indeed if the leprosy has covered all his body, he shall pronounce him clean who has the sore. It has all turned white. He is clean."*

Anyone who has not received the remission of sins is in a sinful state. Born as a sinner, everyone remains a sinner unless one receives the remission of sins. How can such a sinner be saved then? The way to salvation is described here in verses 13-14 *"And if leprosy breaks out all over the skin, and the leprosy covers all the skin of the one who has the sore, from his head to his foot, wherever the priest looks, then the priest shall consider; and indeed if the leprosy has covered all his body, he shall pronounce him clean who has the sore. It has all turned white. He is clean."*

You might be wondering here how it's possible to say that one is clean when leprosy has spread all over his body. Given the fact that even a small sore in a difficult-to-see part of the body can be construed as a sign of leprosy, how is it possible to say that someone whose whole body is covered by the symptoms of leprosy is clean? The Biblical standard is different from our human standard. Through the Scripture, God is now speaking about how the remission of sins is received. What this passage teaches is that human beings are saved by God if they recognize that they have no righteousness before Him, admit that they have done nothing right when reflected upon the Word of the Law, and acknowledge that they cannot avoid but face death, confessing, "Lord, I deserve to be cast into hell. I have done absolutely nothing right."

A sinner who admits only part of his sinfulness cannot be saved. In the same vein, God said that if leprosy covered all the skin of a person to turn it white, from the head to the sole of the feet, then this person was clean. This means that God saves such people and makes them perfect by blotting out all the sins of their entire lifetime, just as leprosy is healed. This is the

Word of God. God saves a person who admits fully that he is a complete sinner, not someone who admits his sinfulness only partially. A complete sinner is someone who admits to God that he has failed to obey and follow His Word, that he has stood against God, and that he is inevitably bound to hell, and who asks God to save such a sinner like himself. When one fully recognizes himself as a complete sinner, then such a person can be saved by God.

Some of us who have received the remission of sins may be tempted to think, "I have sinned, but it's no big deal if I don't sin again. Thank You Lord for remitting away all my sins." Those who think like this, however, are not really that grateful to God. It implies that now that Jesus has saved them and remitted away all their sins, they think they don't need Him anymore. In other words, they think that since they have already received the remission of sins, there is no need to walk with Jesus anymore, nor any need to abide in the Church. While such people have received the remission of sins, they feel like they are being restrained by Jesus and don't like this. Since they know that Jesus has blotted out all their sins, they don't see any need for Him anymore, so they go their own way and think that they will just see Jesus again down the road in Heaven. If this is not an utterly ungrateful thought, what else could it be? Far from entering Heaven, such people will surely end up in the everlasting hell fires, for they are guaranteed to betray the righteousness of Jesus Christ without fail.

Let's turn to Hebrews 6:1-8, *"Therefore, leaving the discussion of the elementary principles of Christ, let us go on to perfection, not laying again the foundation of repentance from dead works and of faith toward God, of the doctrine of baptisms, of laying on of hands, of resurrection of the dead, and of eternal judgment. And this we will do if God permits.*

For it is impossible for those who were once enlightened, and have tasted the heavenly gift, and have become partakers of the Holy Spirit, and have tasted the good word of God and the powers of the age to come, if they fall away, to renew them again to repentance, since they crucify again for themselves the Son of God, and put Him to an open shame. For the earth which drinks in the rain that often comes upon it, and bears herbs useful for those by whom it is cultivated, receives blessing from God; but if it bears thorns and briers, it is rejected and near to being cursed, whose end is to be burned."

I have seen how some people do not come to God's Church even after receiving the remission of sins by believing in the gospel of the water and the Spirit. Whenever I see such people, I wonder about what will happen to them in the end. Will I really be able to see them again in Heaven? I don't think this is a question that I can answer myself with any certainty. Why does the Scripture issue such a dire warning then? What would happen to you if you were to leave the Church, stop preaching the gospel of the water and the Spirit, and live among the people of the world? If you let this happen, you will once again fall into the gravest of all sins. You will also come to hate God's servants, for while these servants of God are righteous, you will be living in sin.

Those who belong to darkness do not like the light, the two oppose each other. As they dislike the light, their hearts turn evil. And in time, they come to hate the servants of righteousness and stand against them. This happens not because they themselves decide that this is what they are going to do, but rather because they are seized by darkness and therefore do not like the light. Those of darkness do not like the righteous. As a result, even if such people received the remission of sins at one point, in the end, they cannot bear any fruit of righteousness desired by God.

Therefore, the born-again righteous must never ever leave God's Church to go on their way no matter what. To carry out the righteous work of God, there must be the prayer warriors who pray to God for this work first of all, and there must be those who are united with the righteousness of God. Only then can we pool our strengths together and carry out God's righteous work in this way. The Lord says that the Holy Spirit will continue to dwell in the righteous who never leave His Church and He will walk amongst them (2 Corinthians 6:16).

It's written in the passage we just read from Hebrews 6:1-2: *"Therefore, leaving the discussion of the elementary principles of Christ, let us go on to perfection, not laying again the foundation of repentance from dead works and of faith toward God, of the doctrine of baptisms, of laying on of hands, of resurrection of the dead, and of eternal judgment."* Here, the Scripture is speaking of none other than our faith in the gospel of the water and the Spirit. As God told us to go on to perfection, all that we have to do is believe in the gospel of the water and the Spirit and walk accordingly. It's also written here, *"And this we will do if God permits. For it is impossible for those who were once enlightened, and have tasted the heavenly gift, and have become partakers of the Holy Spirit."* This passage tells us that we the saved are indwelt by the Holy Spirit. That's why our hearts are always at peace and joyful.

However, the Bible continues to say, *"And having tasted the good word of God and the powers of the age to come, if they fall away, to renew them again to repentance, since they crucify again for themselves the Son of God, and put Him to an open shame. For the earth which drinks in the rain that often comes upon it, and bears herbs useful for those by whom it is cultivated, receives blessing from God; but if it bears thorns and briers, it is rejected and near to being cursed, whose end is to be burned."* What does God mean by saying this?

What will happen to those who do not unite with God's Church even after being born again by believing in the gospel of the water and the Spirit? These people have partaken in the work of the Spirit of God at one time. And they have tasted of the heavenly gift. They have, in other words, received the remission of sins. Yet their faith has been corrupted. These people are then more like the people of the world than the holy family in God's Church. The Lord is saying here that they cannot be renewed again to repentance. Even after believing in the righteousness of Jesus, such people still like what they hear from those who have not been born again. They are attracted to the claim that the remission of sins can be received by offering their own prayers of repentance every day. What explains this? It's because their acts are filthy.

For such people's to be cleansed, they must return and again believe in the gospel of the water and the Spirit and get their hearts healed. Even we the born-again believers in the gospel of the water and the Spirit still sin while living on this earth. However, when we listen to the Word of God in His Church, praise Him, and share fellowship with one another, we can see from our own experiences how our injured hearts are healed. On the other hand, if we don't get our our injured hearts healed caused from our everyday lives in this world, and we allow them rot away, then we cannot say to God with a good conscience that we are the righteous. Although we have received the remission of sins by believing in the gospel of the water and the Spirit, but if we go out into this world and live as Satan's slaves, then our hearts will become hardened. This can happen to those who have received the remission of sins who have come to realize the righteousness of God when they actually heard the gospel of the water and the Spirit with their ears, unless they live apart as the servants of righteousness. This is what God is saying to those who betray His righteousness.

Indeed the Scripture says, *"For the earth which drinks in the rain that often comes upon it, and bears herbs useful for those by whom it is cultivated, receives blessing from God; but if it bears thorns and briers, it is rejected and near to being cursed, whose end is to be burned" (Hebrews 6:7-8).* This means that God will sort out the wicked from the righteous and throw the wicked into the consuming fire. If God had not given us this Word of warning, we would not have known the end of those who betray the righteousness of God.

I am absolutely certain that if someone has sincerely been truly born again by believing in the gospel of the water and the Spirit, they will abide in God's Church. If this person instead abides in the world and follows Satan, then his heart, which had been made righteous, will once again be defiled. Some of you might have felt this already from experience. If anyone lets his heart fall into the world to be dragged down by it, his heart will turn wicked; and if anyone unites with the world and with its religious practitioners, he will end up turning into God's enemy, and standing against the righteousness of the Lord. And those who do not believe in the righteousness of God even after hearing it will be burnt in the end.

It's written in Exodus 30:10, *"And Aaron shall make atonement upon its horns once a year with the blood of the sin offering of atonement; once a year he shall make atonement upon it throughout your generations. It is most holy to the LORD."* We ought to thank the Lord with our prayers for bearing all our sins, and we ought to come to the presence of God with such faith and conviction. So then, how could we ever ask God to wash away our sins everyday?

At the time when the Epistles to the Hebrews was written, which we just read a moment ago, Rome had put in place a policy to scatter the Jews around the world. As a result, the Jews were scattered in abroad in many foreign countries. They were persecuted everywhere they went, and in particularly, those who believed in Jesus were persecuted heavily, with many of them being killed. Enduring such terrible persecution, they hid themselves in the mountains and in caves, but in time many of them came to betray Jesus. This is what worried the writer of the Epistle to the Hebrews.

Just as there were many believers who fell into the world and ended up betraying Jesus despite receiving the remission of sins in those days, in this age and time also, there will be many people who will end up betraying Jesus. Such people will abandon Jesus and worship a false god just to seek the prosperity of their flesh. And they will start persecuting those who believe in Jesus. They will start saying, "How can Jesus be the Son of God?" When the redeemed fall from grace, they turn even more wicked than those who do not know Jesus at all. That is why the Lord said, *"Salt is good; but if the salt has lost its flavor, how shall it be seasoned? It is neither fit for the land nor for the dunghill, but men throw it out" (Luke 14:34-35).* The Lord drew an analogy to salt to teach us that if we fall from His grace, we will turn into completely worthless beings, useless for the Kingdom of God and this world alike. I take each and every step very carefully. I feel as though the Apostle Paul was speaking for me when he said he was afraid that while he would save others by preaching the gospel, he himself would become disqualified.

My fellow believers, although our salvation has come by the grace of God, reaching our salvation is not the end of all.

Rather, it is even more important to keep this salvation as we carry on with our lives. Now that we have received the most precious heart from God, it is absolutely indispensable for us to keep this heart. If you lose this heart, we will have nothing left.

If you turn to 2 Kings chapter 6, you will see an account of cannibalism where two women ate their own children. War had broken out between Syria and Israel, and while Syria was besieging Samaria, there was such a great famine in the land that two women, desperate for food, agreed to eat their own children. They had agreed to eat one woman's son one day, then the other woman's son the next day. But a quarrel broke out between the two women regarding the eating of one woman's son, for the other woman hid her own son. The king of Israel stumbled upon the two women fighting, and one of the women pleaded to him, saying, "We are so hungrey and starving that we had agreed to eat each other's son. Yesterday we ate my son, and today we are supposed to eat the other woman's son. But she has hidden her son and is refusing to hand him over." How do you suppose the king felt upon hearing this? He needed food to address the plight of his people, but even though he was the king, there was nothing he could do. So, falling into despair, the king tore his clothes and wailed.

This account shows us just how evil human beings can be when they are desperate enough. Human beings are such wicked beings that the parents can devour their own children and likewise, the children towards their own parents. It has become a common occurrence to hear in the news about how some depraved person killed their own parents for money, or let their aging and sick parents starve to death just because they considered them burdensome. Such atrocious stories have become so common nowadays that they are not even that shocking anymore. Do you then still think human beings are good? Far from it, the wickedness of mankind knows no bounds. And in the end, you and I are also such wicked beings. We are also capable of devouring our own children if we are desperate enough.

How about you then? Does your heart have faith in the gospel Word of the water and the Spirit? If you don't have this faith, you are a sinner. You must then receive the remission of sins by faith. A sinner is someone who, when reflecting upon the Word of God, cannot live according to this Word. The remission of sins, on the other hand, is received once and for all to be enjoyed forever. It is not something that you receive multiple times or gradually over time. Just as someone whose whole body was covered in leprosy was pronounced clean, if you admit fully to God that you are a complete sinner, then you will be saved by God. Knowing this, I urge you to be saved from all your sins by believing in the gospel of the water and the Spirit, and to live a life that glorifies God. ⊠

SERMON

13

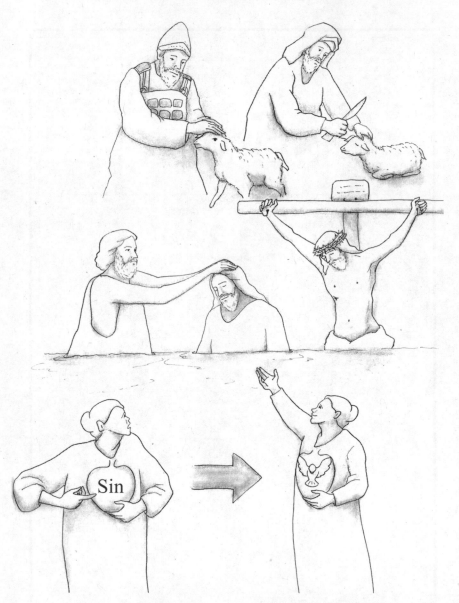

You can download Rev. Paul C. Jong's Christian Books on
iPhone, iPad, or Blackberry by going to Amazon's Kindle
e-bookstore (www.amazon.com).

The Lord Has Saved Those Who Are Inadequate

< Leviticus 13:18-28 >

"If the body develops a boil in the skin, and it is healed, and in the place of the boil there comes a white swelling or a bright spot, reddish-white, then it shall be shown to the priest; and if, when the priest sees it, it indeed appears deeper than the skin, and its hair has turned white, the priest shall pronounce him unclean. It is a leprous sore which has broken out of the boil. But if the priest examines it, and indeed there are no white hairs in it, and it is not deeper than the skin, but has faded, then the priest shall isolate him seven days; and if it should at all spread over the skin, then the priest shall pronounce him unclean. It is a leprous sore. But if the bright spot stays in one place, and has not spread, it is the scar of the boil; and the priest shall pronounce him clean. Or if the body receives a burn on its skin by fire, and the raw flesh of the burn becomes a bright spot, reddish-white or white, then the priest shall examine it; and indeed if the hair of the bright spot has turned white, and it appears deeper than the skin, it is leprosy broken out in the burn. Therefore the priest shall pronounce him unclean. It is a leprous sore. But if the priest examines it, and indeed there are no white hairs in the bright spot, and it is not deeper than the skin, but has faded, then the priest shall isolate him seven days. And the priest shall examine him on the seventh day. If it has at all spread over the skin, then the priest shall pronounce him unclean. It is a leprous sore. But if the bright spot stays in one place, and has not spread on the skin, but has faded, it is a swelling from the burn. The priest shall pronounce him clean, for it is the scar from the burn."

Diagnosing Leprosy

Today's Scripture reading comes from Leviticus chapter 13. It describes how to diagnose leprosy. Leviticus 13:18-20 says, *"If the body develops a boil in the skin, and it is healed, and in the place of the boil there comes a white swelling or a bright spot, reddish-white, then it shall be shown to the priest; and if, when the priest sees it, it indeed appears deeper than the skin, and its hair has turned white, the priest shall pronounce him unclean. It is a leprous sore which has broken out of the boil."*

Most of the people listening to the Word of God here today are probably city folks. I also have lived only in cities, so I can't say that I know much about rural life. Once, around the time I graduated from elementary school, I visited my brother's home in the countryside. There were many persimmon trees, and the people in the town were fond of them. Today's Scripture passage reminds me of these persimmons. When a persimmon falls from the tree, it's usually hard at first. In time, however, it begins to ripen and turn soft. Once the persimmon turns soft enough, people eat what's inside while discarding the skin. Sometimes, if there are too many persimmons that have fallen from the trees, they are gathered up and pickled with salt to be eaten later.

A persimmon usually changes its outside color over time. Eventually, tiny white hairs begin to form on the skin, like cotton balls. These are probably mold, formed when the persimmon begins to rot. Today, we are studying the Word of God how leprosy was diagnosed then.

In the age of the Old Testament, the priests were given the task of diagnosing the people of God for leprosy. If someone was diagnosed with leprosy, this person was driven out of the city and quarantined away from the rest of the population. One way they diagnose leprosy in Israel was as follows: When someone burned his skin and a sore appeared on that wound, diagnosis was made depending on whether or not the sore spread around the skin or not. If the sore did not spread around the skin, then leprosy was ruled out. But if that sore had spread around and was deeper than the skin, then leprosy was suspected. And if white swellings or reddish spots developed or spread, then the person was diagnosed with leprosy. In other words, if the skin began to develop uneven sores and these rotting sores spread around the skin, like a rotting persimmon, then the person was diagnosed with leprosy and was quarantined. Such lepers were normally driven out of the camp.

Although leprosy can spread to the whole body, at first, it's usually localized appearing on a certain part of the body. It's said that leprosy can even show up as baldness. Of course, this does not mean by inheritance you have gone bald, you have leprosy. There is a pastor in our gathering today who is rather thin on top, but he shouldn't be worried about this. The bald leper that the Scripture speaks of does not refer to such a person with few or no hairs on his head.

So, even if you are bald, you have nothing to do with the leprosy the Scripture is describing here. Leprosy was diagnosed when someone had sores that were deeper than the skin, and these sores were oozing and spreading around the body. However, the Scripture says rather counter-intuitively that if leprosy covered the whole body, then this person was pronounced clean, even though he was diagnosed with leprosy.

When we read this Word of God, we are reminded of how our Lord came to this earth to save sinners and delivered them from all their sins through the gospel of the water and the Spirit. It's important for us to remember, however, that even though the Lord came to this earth as the Savior of sinners, He has perfectly saved only those who have fully admitted themselves completely as sinners and were bound to hell. From today's Scripture passage describing how leprosy was diagnosed, we need to realize what the Lord is saying here to us about the sins that are in the human heart. Spiritually speaking, who then are the lepers? The spiritual lepers are those who do not know the gospel of the water and the Spirit and have not received the remission of sins.

General Naaman's Leprosy

When we turn to 2 Kings chapter 5, we read about General Naaman. It's written here that Naaman was the commander of the army of Syria, but he was also suffering from this dread disease of leprosy. Even though he was the commander of the entire army of a nation and highly respected for the many things he had done for his country, but because he was a leper, he could not find true happiness. Outwardly, he was rich, successful and powerful. As a solder, he was a great man of duty, but as a leper, he must have felt very sorry not only to himself but also to his family. General Naaman was ashamed of his leprosy, and his life was not very happy either.

However, he heard good news from his wife's slave, a young Hebrew girl working in his house. This young girl, a captive from the land of Israel, was serving Naaman's wife. When the girl found out that General Naaman was suffering from leprosy, she told his wife that if he went to Israel and saw a servant of God named Elisah, he would be healed from leprosy.

As you all know, in those ancient days leprosy was known as an incurable disease. Leprosy covers the victims' skin with sores and leads the whole body to rot away. At that time, it was considered to be a fatal disease.

In fact, there were other diseases that were as incurable and fatal as leprosy was in the days of the Old Testament, but spiritually speaking, what is the fatal disease that claims every victim's life? It is none other than the "diseases of sin." What kills and ruins everyone forever? It is the sins of mankind. It's very important for you to realize here that if anyone lives with a sinful heart, this person must face condemnation for his sins.

It's not anything else but the disease of sin that ruins one's soul. If there is one disease that kills everyone, it is none other than the disease of sin that afflicts everyone from the day one is born in this world. All human beings have sin from the day they are born in this world, and therefore unless they are washed clean from these sins, they will perish forever.

Because everyone has this dreaded thing called sin, everyone must face the punishment of that sin as the result. All human beings are born as sinners in God's sight, and they all live with these sins. It is therefore absolutely indispensable for everyone to realize their sinfulness before God. And people must also realize that regardless of whether or not they recognize God and His law, they were all born with sins, and therefore these sins will lead them to death. It is like the flesh of General Naaman rotting away because of his leprosy. Even though he was the commander of the army of Syria and the greatest hero of that nation, he was bound to lose his everything due to his leprosy. Like this, everyone is facing ruin because of their sins. What is killing everyone is the sins that people have. It is this dread sickness of sin that is killing human beings.

Leprosy Is Like the Sins of Mankind

The symptoms of leprosy do not appear right away, lying dormant. It's said that it can take up to three years for a leprosy patient to realize that he has the disease, and another three years for others to find it out. So, should the leprosy patient wish to hide his disease, he can do this anywhere from six to nine years. After this, the symptoms become so widespread that it's no longer feasible to hide it. Another characteristic of leprosy is that while its symptoms begin to appear in a specific, localized part of the body, eventually, the disease spreads over the entire body. As leprosy spreads over the whole body, it can result into severe disfigurement that sometimes leads the patient to lose body parts such as ears, fingers, toes, and so forth.

As you can see, leprosy is one of the most feared diseases that wrecks havoc on the patient. The Scripture sometimes speaks of leprosy as an analogy to the sins of mankind. Spiritually speaking, leprosy is like the sins that are in the human heart. During the age of the Old Testament, leprosy was widespread and whoever became affected with this disease perished from it eventually. In the same vein, whoever has any sin in the heart will ultimately reach death and destruction.

As the descendants of Adam, we were all born with sins. That's why the Lord said in Mark 7:21-22, what proceeds from the heart of man is what defiles him, *"For from within, out of the heart of men, proceed evil thoughts, adulteries, fornications, murders, thefts, covetousness, wickedness, deceit, lewdness, an evil eye, blasphemy, pride, foolishness."* Everyone is born into this world with such sins, there is no escape.

However, we see many people arguing otherwise to deny this Truth spoken by the Word of God. Regardless, God said clearly that from the moment human beings were conceived in the wombs of their mothers, they were all born with sins. Everyone was thus born into this world with such evil thoughts and attributes. In fact, not only were we all born with such wicked attributes in our hearts, but we also bear nothing but evil fruit throughout our entire lifetime. All of us were born into this world with these attributes of sin. We inherited from our parents all the evil attributes of sin. So, by their fundamental nature, all human beings were born into this world with an evil heart. All of us were therefore born into this world with every conceivable wickedness. That is why we keep on committing the same sins over and over again while living in this world. It's for this reason that everyone sins time after time until the day one dies.

Our thoughts are as evil as our acts. From the day we were born to the day we die, we have nothing but evil thoughts. Everyone's heart is filled with such evil desires as fornication, theft, murder, adultery, covetousness, wickedness, deceit, lewdness, an evil eye, pride, and foolishness, How about you then? Don't you also have such wicked desires? Of course you do. Not only were all of us born with such evil thoughts and desires, but we also act them out in our lives. Some of you might then wonder, "A lot of people don't actually do wicked things, so how can you explain this?" There is a reason for this. Although everyone in this world was born with such wickedness, people do not act it out freely because there are secular laws against them. So, when someone acts out his evil desires in a way that breaks the law, this person is punished under that law, which serves as a deterrent to restrain them from acting out their evil desires.

The problem, however, is that many people still do not realize that they have wicked desires in their hearts. When the Apostle Paul stood before the mirror of the Law of God and saw himself, he lamented over just how wicked his heart was. People are really self-righteous only because they do not know the function of the Law of God. It is so saddening to see so many people not realizing that they were all born as the brood of sin who commit sins from the day they were born from the wombs of their mothers to the day they die.

Most people do not realize their sinful nature even when they reach their teens and older. Nowadays kids grow up so fast that by the time they reach middle school, they can easily manifest their sinfulness. When people come to learn and understand the Word of God, they can quickly realize that they are evildoers, but we see that many people live without reaching this understanding. Although we can hide our hearts to a certain extent, by the time we reach puberty, we come to realize that we have all kinds of evil thoughts in our hearts. But, what's even more important is to agree with God when He says that everyone is born and lives with such wickedness as evil thoughts, murderous desires, adulterous lust, covetousness, theft, lewdness, foolishness, and so forth. So, we know from the Word of God that we ourselves are filled with the desire to commit such sins.

Everyone's heart is full of such impulsive desires, but people are very careful and secretive with their acts because they are afraid of the secular law and punishment that would follow if they acted out those desires. So, most people act out their wickedness only infrequently. The problem, however, is that they are still unaware of the fact that they have such wickednesses, and as a result they continue to deceive themselves into thinking that they are good people. In reality, they are living in darkness. This world is full of such confused people.

Because so many people are unaware of their sinfulness, when they see themselves committing all kinds of sins, they are shocked to see this and fear themselves. As a result, some people reproach themselves and grieve over their sinfulness, lamenting over the sins they committed. However, even as they reproach themselves for sinning, many of them still do not realize their true selves. On the contrary, with the passing of time, they end up committing even more sins and rationalizing themselves by blaming others, rather than realizing that it is in their human nature to sin like this. Eventually, they come to live without any awareness of their evil selves. In contrast to the Scripture, the secular educational system teaches that human beings are good by nature, and that everyone is therefore capable of living virtuously. Secular educators claim that if only people are given enough ethical education, they can all lead a morally upright life by their nature.

Countless people in this world think mistakenly that human beings are good by nature, but in reality, everyone sins constantly in his life because everyone was born with evil thoughts. It's absolutely indispensable for you to recognize this. Because the secular educational system teaches that everyone is born as a good person by nature, people can't admit their sinfulness even when they see themselves sinning. We see so many people being deceived by themselves and the fallacious deceitful teachings of the world. As a result, countless people come to struggle so much with themselves and suffer a great deal over their wickedness. Not knowing how to solve the problem of their sins, they therefore turn to the many diverse religious leaders in the world.

It's because these people do not know what to do about their sins that they rely on the religions of this world and these leaders. When we look at such religious leaders, we see that they try to discipline themselves not to commit any sin, in an effort to become a god themselves. Buddhism, for instance, teaches its many followers to become a god themselves. That's what Buddhists believe, and accordingly, they try to make themselves divine through their own human efforts.

However, no one can transcend oneself to become a god. What Buddhism teaches is simply impossible, for no human being can ever overcome its wickedness. Buddhism also speaks of 108 earthly desires, also known as defilements. It teaches that human beings face 108 earthly desires, and to overcome all these defilements, one must reach Nirvana. This, however, is totally impossible. It's nothing more than empty words, for the only way Buddhists can escape from their 108 earthly desires is death. In contrast, God teaches us that our hearts are washed from all our sins by believing in the gospel of the water and the Spirit.

There has not been a single person on the earth who has ever escaped from his sins through his own efforts. Some religious practitioners worship their ancestors. Saying that their ancestors are helping them, they claim that if they venerate their ancestors and do many good deeds, they will go to Heaven. They are fond of speaking of the so-called "moral path," teaching that one must cultivate oneself morally. Following this teaching, many people try to do good and kind to others, but it's all useless, as they only see themselves being hardened even more by their sins.

When we turn to Genesis chapter 1, we see God creating

man, starting with the sentence that says, *"In the beginning God created the heavens and the earth."* We also see God speaking to us human beings, explaining to us how we came to have sin, and why we can't help but sin in our lives. From the very beginning, God is explaining to us with what kinds of sins we were all born with in this world. He is telling us that everyone sins because everyone was born with a sinful heart. Like leprosy spreading over the whole body, the sins of mankind rule over every single person's entire life. Because all people inherited a sinful heart from their ancestors from the day they were born, they cannot help but sin all the time.

We Must Believe in the Righteousness of the Lord That Makes Us Sinless

Jesus said that He came to save such sinners from all their sins. He said to His disciples, "I did not come to call the righteous, but sinners." And He also said, "A physician is needed by someone who is ill. A healthy person has no need for a physician." Our Lord told us that He is our Savior. All human beings living in this world inherited sins from their parents from the day they were born. If this were not the case, then no one would need to find Jesus Christ the Savior, nor would anyone need to believe in Him. Put differently, if you were someone who commits no sin at all while living in this world, then there would be no need for you to seek Jesus Christ and believe in this Savior.

In contrast, if you recognize that you were born with sins, then you would be compelled to look for Jesus Christ and believe in His righteousness. Otherwise, you are inevitable bound to perish for your sins of not believing in the righteousness of God with your heart. Such people who recognize their sinfulness cannot help but look for Jesus Christ. The righteousness of God applies without fail to all those who realize clearly that they themselves are sinners before not only the ethics and morals of man, but also the commandments of God.

Because of the fall of the forefathers of mankind, all human beings became sinners. Because of one man Adam, everyone became a sinner and inherited Adam's sins. That is why, spiritually speaking, everyone is like a leper. Everyone, in other words, is a sinner before God.

Therefore, Jesus the Savior is absolutely indispensable to us to heal us from the disease of all our sins. Jesus Christ is the only Savior who can save us His people from all our sins. Every sinner without doubt, needs Jesus, and it is by believing in His righteousness that we are saved. All human beings must therefore know and believe in the righteousness of Jesus, and that is why they must all believe in the gospel of the water and the Spirit. Unless people receive healing from their sick souls which are laden with sins, they will end up reaching death. That's because the Lord said to us that "the wages of sins is death."

Having created us with dust and the breath of life, the Lord came to this earth incarnated in the flesh of man to save us personally when we fell into sin. He was then baptized by John the Baptist, shed His blood on the Cross, rose from the dead again, and has thereby become our Savior once and for all. Jesus was born in a small town called Bethlehem. We must believe that when Jesus Christ turned 30 years of age, He remitted away all our sins. We must believe in the gospel of the water and the Spirit without fail, the Truth of salvation through which Jesus has delivered us from the sins of the world. Since you and I were born as sinners, it's absolutely indispensable for us to realize the righteousness of God and believe in it. Jesus came to this earth as the Savior of mankind by coming to look for us. All of us were sinners, and that is precisely why it was necessary for Jesus to come looking for us. We must therefore believe in the righteousness of Jesus as our salvation.

Before Jesus came to this earth, there was a servant sent by God the Father beforehand. This servant of God is John the Baptist who baptized Jesus in the Jordan River. John the Baptist was God's servant who passed all the sins of this world to Jesus once and for all by baptizing Him. Wearing camel skin for clothes, John the Baptist shouted out in the wilderness to the people of Israel to repent. This man's daily food was honey, water, and wild fruits and plants. He shared fellowship with God in the wilderness while waiting for his time. Calling the people of Israel "a brood of vipers," he shouted out to them to repent. He preached to them to turn around from their idolatry. He also said, "Whoever does not repent will perish, for the ax is laid to the root of the tree. Just as tree is cut down and thrown into the fire, whoever does not repent will be destroyed."

Referring to John the Baptist, Jesus said that he came "in the way of righteousness." However, many people did not know that John the Baptist was the one whom Jesus was speaking of, who had come in the way of righteousness. When John the Baptist baptized Jesus Christ in the Jordan River, Jesus could wash away our sins by accepting the sins of this world once and for all. By baptizing Jesus Christ, John the Baptist could pass the sins of this world to Jesus Christ. In other words, because John the Baptist passed all the sins of everyone to Jesus Christ, this act made it possible to turn everyone who believes in this Truth sinless. John the Baptist's had come to pass the sins of this world to Jesus Christ through baptism, so that those who believe can become God's own children.

However, many people refused to believe this. The Pharisees in those days did not believe that John the Baptist had come to do this work. Many people in those days did not know that John the Baptist was the one who would fulfill the way of righteousness together with Jesus. Even though he walked on this way of righteousness by baptizing Jesus and passing all the sins of mankind to Him, people still did not believe. Who, then, believed this at the time? It was none other than tax collectors and the prostitutes.

To blot out everyone's sins, God sent John the Baptist and Jesus Christ to this earth. God wanted everyone to know the righteousness of Jesus and become a child of God. So God sent John the Baptist to pass everyone's sins to Jesus by baptizing Him so that He may make whoever believes in this Truth righteous. Sadly, many people did not believe in this gospel of salvation.

Who on this earth believed in the righteousness of Jesus Christ then? Those who had no righteousness of their own believed in it. Who really believed in the baptism Jesus received from John the Baptist? This baptism meant that Jesus Christ bore all our sins. Who then believed in this baptism? Who truly realized this Truth and reached salvation? Only those who recognized their sins and acknowledged God and His law were saved from their sins. In other words, only those who admitted that they themselves were spiritual lepers reached their salvation by believing in the gospel of the water and the Spirit which constitutes the righteousness of God.

In the days of Jesus, the Pharisees and the scribes did not believe in the role of John the Baptist, nor did they believe in Jesus Christ as their Savior. These people thought that although they did commit sins, but only committed very minor sins. Is this how you think also? Do we really sin just once in a while? Do you also think that we only commit small sins? Of course not! Leprosy causes otherwise healthy skin to slowly rot away, and this rot spreads around relentlessly. The same is true when it comes to sin.

Unless we believe in the righteousness of Jesus Christ, it's inevitable for us to be bound by our sins and continue to commit one transgression after another until we are ultimately ruined. No human being can help but sin repeatedly, and all must face the just condemnation for their sins in the end. That is why so many people are heading straight to hell, owing to their sin of not believing in the righteousness of Jesus Christ. Just as leprosy causes the whole body to rot away, the sins that are committed by everyone is causing one's soul and body to fall ill and perish.

Jesus said that it was tax collectors and prostitutes who believed that John the Baptist had come in the way of righteousness. This means that only those who really knew their shortcomings believed in the way of righteousness. You all know what prostitutes do, don't you? Since these people sinned openly, they must have also known very well that they themselves were filthy sinners before God.

John the Baptist testified repeatedly that he had passed the sins of the world to Jesus by baptizing Him. When John the Baptist baptized Jesus in the Jordan River, he passed all the sins of this world to Jesus and satisfied the condition for Jesus to bear the condemnation of these sins. Just as the people of Israel passed their sins to a sacrificial offering by laying their hands on its head during the age of the Old Testament, and in the age of the New Testament, all the sins of the world were passed on to Jesus Christ once and for all when John the

Baptist baptized Him in the Jordan River.

Many sinners including the tax collectors and the prostitutes believed that this Jesus testified by John the Baptist was indeed the Son of God, and that He had borne the sins of this world through His baptism. They believed that their Savior was Jesus who had come by the water and the Spirit. They believed in the Savior who had delivered them from all their sins once and for all. Such people whose sins were exposed outwardly were saved by believing in the righteousness of God.

There is another important fact that you should know here, and it is that those who did not realize their sinful selves despite sinning with their hearts, and, hiding them away, could not accept the righteousness of God, even though they themselves were facing the punishment of sins. We believe that John the Baptist came in the way of righteousness, and that Jesus has made us the believers in the gospel of the water and the Spirit sinless by accepting our sins once and for all through the baptism He received from John the Baptist. We cannot be saved from our sins unless we believe in the righteousness of God. We must realize that John the Baptist came in the way of righteousness. This way of righteousness proclaims that unless we believe that Jesus bore all our sins and has become our Savior, we cannot be saved from our sins.

Those Who Are Chosen by God and Those Who Are Not

The Scripture says that there are people chosen by God, and there are people who are not. Jesus explained this by using a parable. And this parable went as follows. Long ago, a certain king held a wedding feast for his son and invited many people throughout the whole kingdom. But, the invited all declined to come. Some of them said they couldn't come because they had to buy a bull; others said they couldn't come because they had some business to take care of; some declined the invitation saying they had to get married; and others said they couldn't come because they had to meet someone. When the king's servants returned to him and informed him that no one was coming to the wedding feast, the king told the servants to go out to the streets and invite whoever they saw.

So, the servants went out and brought as many people as would come, many of whom had no social status to speak of. Once these people arrived, the city gate was closed and the wedding feast began. As the wedding ceremony proceeded, the guests celebrated it with music, drinking and eating, and dancing. However, when the king looked around the guests enjoying themselves at the feast, he saw a man who was not wearing a wedding garment.

The problem was that no guest could come to the king's wedding ceremony wearing just any attire. Every guest had to wear a certain prepared wedding garment fit for the royal wedding without fail. Yet, there was this man who was attending this ceremony without having changed into the prepared wedding garments. The king asked this man why he was not wearing a wedding garment, but the man was speechless. The king then ordered his servants to bind the man's hands and feet and throw him out.

Using this parable, the Lord said that many are called, but few are chosen. This world is full of people professing to believe in Jesus. Although countless people nowadays believe in Jesus, but, many are called—few are chosen. What does it mean to be chosen? Jesus said here that many are called, but few are chosen. Whom has God chosen then? When we turn to

Ephesians 1:4, we see the Scripture saying, *"Just as He chose us in Him before the foundation of the world."* Whom did God the Father choose in Christ before the foundation of the world then? Did He choose the scribes? Or did He choose the prostitutes and the tax collectors? Exactly whom did God choose? God the Father chose the prostitutes and the tax collectors in Jesus Christ. Spiritually speaking, then, who exactly are the ones chosen by God?

To save sinners from the sins of the world, God the Father sent Jesus Christ to this earth, and by making Him bear the sins of this world through His baptism, He has solved away the problem of their sins. That is why God the Father said that He chose them in Jesus Christ. Who are the chosen? Who are the people chosen in Christ before the foundation of the world?

Speaking of Elijah in the Epistle to the Romans, the Apostle Paul described what happened when Elijah the servant of God, after fighting a battle of faith against 850 prophets of Baal by himself, heard King Ahab's wife Jezebel swearing that she would kill Elijah. Jezebel had sworn that if she had not killed Elijah by the next morning, she would end her own life. It was no less than the queen of Israel who swore that she would kill the Prophet Elijah.

Although the Prophet Elijah was bold enough when he stood against 850 prophets of Baal by himself, but when he heard this infamous Queen Jezebel was bent on killing him, he became fearful and fled with his servant. Fleeing into the endless desert, he soon became tired and rested under a large tree. That tree was a broom tree. Exhausted, Elijah collapsed under the broom tree and laid down wishing he would just die. He entrust himself completely to God, saying, "Lord, I have fought my battle of faith against 850 prophets of Baal. But now, Jezebel is out to kill me. I'm so weary that I don't want to live any longer. Take my life right now, Lord." However, God sent an angel to Elijah to comfort him and to strengthen him. The angel touched Elijah and brought him food and water so that he could regain his strength. On the strength of this food provided by the angel, Elijah was able to recover and move forward again.

After eating and drinking the food and the water the angel had brought, Elijah regained his strength, and on this strength he went all the way to Horeb where God had directed him to go. There, he went entered a cave. And while inside the cave, he began to hear a loud noise like thunder. Amidst this thundering sound, the Prophet Elijah's ears could not hear the Word of God. Then he heard the wind blowing savagely outside the cave. But the voice of God was not there either. When it all became quiet and calm, Elijah heard a very small, still voice. God began speaking to him with a whispering voice.

God asked him, "What are you doing here hiding?" He answered, "Lord, all Your servants in Israel are dead. I alone am the only one left. Your prophets were all killed by the sword or were starved to death. I am the only one left, and now they seek to take my life too." God then said to Elijah clearly, "I have reserved 7,000 men whom you do not know about. These 7,000 men have not bowed before Baal. You may think you are alone, but I have reserved 7,000 men." The Word of God says in Romans 11:5, *"Even so then, at this present time there is a remnant according to the election of grace. And if by grace, then it is no longer of works."* In other words, just as God had reserved 7,000 men for Elijah, even at this present there are those chosen according to the election of grace.

The word grace here means God's gift. It refers to the gift of salvation that God has given to us through the righteousness of Jesus Christ. The Son of God came to this earth to save us sinners from our sins. The Lord Himself came to heal spiritual lepers. And having come to heal us the spiritual lepers, God has indeed healed us.

We are healed from our spiritual leprosy by believing that the Lord bore all the sins of the world by being baptized by John the Baptist in the Jordan River. The Lord has healed us from all our sins once and for all with the gospel of the water and the Sprit. Jesus bore our leprosy and all its sores and wounds, and He has healed us completely. Through the baptism He received from John the Baptist, Jesus took upon all our sins and died on the Cross for us. He has ended the condemnation of all sins.

That is how God the Father chose us in Jesus Christ through the gospel of the water and the Spirit. Having invited countless people in Jesus Christ through the gospel of the water and the Spirit, God the Father chose those who truly believed. Whom did God choose specifically among all these people? He chose the sinners who had no righteousness of their own, and who admitted to God, "Lord, I am indeed suffering from the spiritual leprosy of sin. I deserve to be condemned and put to death for my sins by Your just judgment. I have this dread disease of sin. The sins that I have committed, the sins that are inside me, are killing me. I deserve to be destroyed for my sins. I am bound to hell." Like this, those who know their sins and need the righteousness of Jesus desperately are those who can receive the salvation offered by Jesus. It is to such people whom God the Father has saved once and for all in His Son through the gospel of the water and the Spirit.

My fellow believers, God chose you and me in Jesus Christ, in His salvation, because we recognized and admitted our sins like this. It is us whom God chose for salvation. He has saved us as His elect. It's very important for us to realize here that it is not because of our own righteousness or goodness that God the Father chose us in His Son Jesus Christ before the foundation of the world. On the contrary, it is because we are completely worthless and full of shortcomings before God that we were chosen on account of our faith in the gospel of the water and the Spirit. Because we cannot help but sin all the time out of our shortcomings and weaknesses, we would be heading straight to hell if God left us to our own devices. That's why God chose us. It's because if God left us alone to continue to suffer from the mortal disease of sin, all our flesh would have rotted away, we would have been reduced to just bones, and ultimately we would have all perished. It's because the Lord had compassion for such people like us that He came to this earth, looking for us to save us from all our sins. He had come to this earth to save everyone from all sins.

It is for people like the tax collectors and the prostitutes in this world that the Lord came to this earth. Although these people did not want to turn into what they eventually became, because of the sin committed by their forefathers, they were born into this world destined to die for all the sins they inherited. We are such people, and it is to save us from all our sins that the Lord came to this earth by looking for us. And thanks to the righteousness of our Lord, we were chosen and saved by faith.

Whom Does Jesus Christ Choose?

Jesus chooses the sinners who are bound to hell for their sins. On account of the righteousness of Jesus, God the Father chooses those who truly know that they themselves are sinners before God, who acknowledge His Word and recognize His righteousness, and who know and admit that they are bound to be put to death and cast into hell by God for their sins. To such people who believe in His righteousness, God says, "You belong to Me now. Do not worry anymore, for I have remitted away your sins. Son, your sins are forgiven you. You are now healed from your illness. Arise, take up your bed, and go to your house. There is now no condemnation to those who are in Christ, for the law of the Spirit of life has set you free from the law of sin and death." God the Father Himself has personally saved us from all our sins once and for all in Jesus Christ. He has delivered you and me from all our sins at once.

My fellow believers, you and I had been spiritual lepers by our nature. We were all destined to die for our sins. However, our Lord has saved us through the gospel of the water and the Spirit. God the Father chose you and me in the righteousness of Jesus Christ. And He has saved us. Having chosen us in the righteousness of Jesus Christ, God the Father has made us righteous. He has turned us the believers in the righteousness of Jesus Christ into His own children. He has made us sinless. God has told us clearly that we are made into His children by believing in His righteousness. It is only by believing in the righteousness of God that we are made righteous. It is not by not sinning that we are chosen by God. On the contrary, it is precisely because we commit countless sins as human beings that we were chosen and saved from all our sins, all thanks to the righteousness of Jesus.

Do you then believe that Jesus Christ has saved us from all the sins of the world through the righteousness of God? Do you believe that you were chosen in Jesus Christ on account of your faith in the righteousness of God? Who, then, is yet to be chosen by God? Who has been called but not chosen? Who has still not put on the garment of salvation by faith? It is those who do not believe in the righteousness of God, and therefore have not been chosen. Just as Jesus said, "Many are called, but few are chosen," the chosen are indeed few, while countless people on this earth today believe in Jesus as their Savior without knowing the gospel of the water and the Spirit. That is why there are so many people who have not been chosen yet.

Those who have not been chosen by God are none other than those who do not acknowledge the righteousness of God and do not admit that they themselves are sinners bound to hell. Such people have not come out to the priests to be diagnosed with the Word of God. Such people must come out from the shadows to God, admit their sins, ask His priests to examine them spiritually, and be healed from their spiritual leprosy.

The problem, however, is that many people do not recognize the diagnosis of these spiritual priests. Earlier today, I spoke about Lazarus and the rich man, and like this rich man, many people do not take the spiritual diagnosis of the priests of God seriously. They do not accept the admonishment of the servants of God, nor do they acknowledge His righteousness. As a result, they are clinging to their sins even as their spiritual leprosy is ravaging them. In the end, they will all perish and face death alone.

Anyone who still does not believe in the righteousness of God, and has therefore not been chosen by Him, is someone who is still deceiving himself. Whoever does not recognize the Word of God is fooling himself. It's your faith in the righteousness of God that should be shown to Him, not your own self-righteousness. You must realize from the Word of God what kind of a person you really are and admit it. If you don't know yourself, then you need to turn to the Word of God, acknowledge it, and thereby be washed from all your sins. From listening to the Word of God, you must realize and admit who you really are.

Whoever comes to God and admit his sins will be saved without exception. God has chosen in His righteousness whoever needs Jesus Christ's grace of salvation. He has saved all such people once and for all through His righteousness. He has washed away all their sins once and for all with His righteousness. He has enabled them to be born again of the gospel of the water and the Spirit once and for all. And He has blessed them to become His own children once and for all.

The Scripture says that when General Naaman dipped himself seven times in the Jordan River as instructed by Elisha, his flesh was cleansed and became like that of a little child. Likewise, the Lord has transformed us the believers in the gospel of the water and the Spirit from our old selves into completely new people. God the Father has saved you and me through the gospel of the water and the Sprit. He has blessed us to be born again. This means that God the Father chose us the believers in the gospel of the water and the Spirit in Jesus Christ. And having chosen us in Christ, He has made us His own children.

Dear saints, I admonish you all to know clearly that we have been saved from all ours sins by believing in the gospel of the water and the Spirit, and that it is on account of this faith that we were chosen. Moreover, it is not because we were perfect and clean that we were chosen. On the contrary, it is because we were full of shortcomings that we were chosen to be washed from all our sins with the gospel of the water and the Spirit. Be grateful for this. And be grateful for God's grace of redemption.

In the Scripture, those who were not chosen by God were the Pharisees, the scribes, and other such people who rejected the righteousness of God outright in their arrogance. Those who deceived themselves before God, those who did not recognize His righteousness, those who did not acknowledge His Word, those who boasted of their own religious piety, and those who practiced hypocrisy—all these people were not chosen by God.

Why did God choose some people while not choosing others then? God's elect are chosen in the righteousness of Jesus Christ. We are chosen only if we realize the righteousness of God in the gospel of the water and the Spirit, understand it fully, and then believe in it. God does not just choose some people while rejecting others arbitrarily. Speaking of Jacob and Esau in the Old Testament, God said that He rejected Esau and chose Jacob.

Why did God do this? From a human perspective, Esau was nearly a perfect man while Jacob was a weak conniving thief. But whom did God choose? God chose Jacob, a devious man with many shortcomings. Why was Jacob chosen over Esau? Jacob was chosen precisely because he was a conniving, devious liar who desperately needed God's grace. God had compassion on such a wretched man like Jacob and saved him perfectly through His righteousness. Jacob had stolen his brother's birthright as the firstborn with a bowl of lentil soup, deceived his own father by imitating Esau's voice by pretending to be him, and usurped the blessings that Esau should have received. God the Father knew very well that if He left Jacob to his own devices, he would have no choice but go to hell. Jacob was such as completely worthless man. That is why God couldn't resist but to save people like Jacob, and this is what God's mercy and grace is all about. Put differently, our Lord could not help but save such a sinner like Jacob from all his sins, and for that reason, He bore all his sins once and for all by being baptized by John the Baptist.

342   The Lord Has Saved Those Who Are Inadequate

The Lord also bore Esau's sins, not just Jacob's sins, but Esau was not chosen because unlike Jacob, he was too self-righteous. In fact, there are two types of people on this earth, those who are like Jacob, and those who are like Esau. Those who, like Jacob, know that they themselves are completely worthless can put on the grace of salvation by believing in the gospel of the water and the Spirit that constitutes the righteousness of Jesus. If such people walk in the way of righteousness that John the Baptist came in, and believe in the gospel of the water and the Spirit that constitutes the righteousness of God, then they can all be saved by faith, be chosen by the just God, and become righteous. In contrast, those who are like Esau boast of their own strength, their own righteousness, and their own goodness; and that is why they cannot be chosen by God.

In other words, we cannot be chosen by God if we do not recognize His righteousness and instead advocate our own righteousness. If we don't recognize God's servants who believe in His righteousness, and do not acknowledge those who have become God's own people, then we cannot be elected either. The righteousness of God has saved us from all the sins of the world. I hope and pray that no one here would be left out of God's elect only to be cast into hell by refusing to believe that God has saved us from all our sins.

Let's consider ourselves here for a moment. How have we become righteous? Have we become righteousness because our acts are upright or we have something that's truly meritorious in God's sight? No, of course not! The problem, unfortunately, is that there are far too many people on this earth who are exceedingly arrogant. But, those who are arrogant before God are left out of becoming His elect.

My fellow believers, I myself had lived without knowing

Free book request www.nlmission.com

the righteousness of God for ten years since I first believed in Jesus, and I tried so hard to be loved by God over all those years. Once I realized the righteousness of Jesus Christ, however, I also realized that all my effort had been completely in vain and empty-handed. It dawned on me that the Lord saves those who are inadequate. It is such people to whom God has given the gospel of the water and the Spirit, thereby bestowing His grace of salvation on them and clothing them in His everlasting righteousness.

We were chosen in Christ before the foundation of the world because we were full of shortcomings. That is why God chose us through the gospel of the water and the Spirit. Because we were all born as the descendants of Adam, the first man and a sinner, we cannot help but commit sins; but because we believe in the God-given gospel of the water and the Spirit, we have been saved from all our sins. God the Father chose such people like us in Jesus Christ, and He has made us His own people. None other than this is the grace that God has bestowed on us, and it is also what God's love is all about. The gospel of the water and the Spirit is God's amazing grace of salvation. It is by the grace of God and His love that He has given us the gospel of the water and the Spirit, so that He may heal us and deliver us from the leprosy of our sins.

As those who know and believe in the gospel of the water and the Spirit, you and I have been saved from all our sins. Everyone else on this planet earth, however, is still from spiritual leprosy. The entire human race is infected with the disease of sin that is leading countless people to perish in both body and soul. We must preach the gospel of the water and the Spirit to all such people. Think about just how much these people must be struggling with their lives, tormented by the fact that they cannot help but sin all the time? They must loath themselves for their wretched uncleanness. Knowing that they are approved neither by God nor by man, sinners arc living under the constant shadow cast by the sins they commit even in broad daylight. The gospel of the water and the Spirit, however, will be a great comfort to them.

Those who know their sins, and who know the suffering caused by their sins, will be blessed to be chosen by God if only they realize the gospel of the water and the Sprit, the power of the love of God. For admitting their sins, they will be blessed to be chosen and perfectly saved. In contrast, those who do not realize that they themselves are sinners even as they were born with sin and cannot help but sin repeatedly throughout their lifetime, will be forsaken by God as long as they continue to live without believing in the gospel of the water and the Spirit, thinking that they have no sin. Even to such people, we must spread and teach the gospel of the water and the Spirit.

I urge you to realize that all of us are sinners, but God has still saved every sinner through His righteousness and His love; and with this knowledge, I urge you to entrust yourself to the mercy of God to receive His true blessings. You must know and believe that it is sinners whom God saves, and that this salvation is fulfilled in the righteousness of our Lord Jesus Christ. Know that all of us the human beings were spiritual lepers doomed to perish, and acknowledge the righteousness of God in His sight, and accept the true salvation He is offering you. I hope and pray that you would believe with thanksgiving that God the Father chose us in the righteousness of Jesus Christ for true salvation, and I also hope and pray that God's grace and blessings would be with you all. Let us then all thank God always by faith, for it is by His righteousness that we were chosen by God to become His own children. ✉

SERMON

14

You can download Rev. Paul C. Jong's Christian Books on iPhone, iPad, or Blackberry by going to Amazon's Kindle e-bookstore (www.amazon.com).

The Sacrifice of
The Day of Atonement
In the Old Testament

< Leviticus 16:6-22 >

"Aaron shall offer the bull as a sin offering, which is for himself, and make atonement for himself and for his house. He shall take the two goats and present them before the Lord at the door of the tabernacle of meeting. Then Aaron shall cast lots for the two goats: one lot for the Lord and the other lot for the scapegoat. And Aaron shall bring the goat on which the Lord's lot fell, and offer it as a sin offering. But the goat on which the lot fell to be the scapegoat shall be presented alive before the Lord, to make atonement upon it, and to let it go as the scapegoat into the wilderness. And Aaron shall bring the bull of the sin offering, which is for himself, and make atonement for himself and for his house, and shall kill the bull as the sin offering which is for himself. Then he shall take a censer full of burning coals of fire from the altar before the Lord, with his hands full of sweet incense beaten fine, and bring it inside the veil. And he shall put the incense on the fire before the Lord, that the cloud of incense may cover the mercy seat that is on the Testimony, lest he die. He shall take some of the blood of the bull and sprinkle it with his finger on the mercy seat on the east side; and before the mercy seat he shall sprinkle some of the blood with his finger seven times. Then he shall kill the goat of the sin offering, which is for the people, bring its blood inside the veil, do with that blood as he did with the blood of the bull, and sprinkle it on the mercy seat and before the mercy seat. So he shall make atonement for the Holy Place, because of the uncleanness of the children of Israel, and because of their transgressions, for all their sins; and so he shall do for the tabernacle of meeting which remains among them in the midst of their uncleanness. There shall be no man in the tabernacle of meeting when he goes in to make atonement in the Holy Place, until he comes out, that he may make atonement for himself, for his household, and for all the assembly of Israel. And he shall go out to the altar that is before the Lord, and make atonement for it, and shall take some of the blood of the bull and some of the blood of the goat, and put it on the horns of the altar all around. Then he shall sprinkle some of the blood on it with his finger seven times, cleanse it, and consecrate it from the uncleanness of the children of Israel. And when he has made an end of atoning for the Holy Place, the tabernacle of meeting, and the altar, he shall bring the live goat. Aaron shall lay both his hands on the head of the live goat, confess over it all the iniquities of the children of Israel, and all their transgressions, concerning all their sins, putting them on the head of the goat, and shall send it away into the wilderness by the hand of a suitable man. The goat shall bear on itself all their iniquities to an uninhabited land; and he shall release the goat in the wilderness."

Today I would like to share with you the Truth of the remission of sins shown in the Day of Atonement as described in the Book of Leviticus. The Day of Atonement fell on the tenth day of the seventh month in the Jewish calendar. It's written in Leviticus 16:29-34: *"This shall be a statute forever for you: In the seventh month, on the tenth day of the month, you shall afflict your souls, and do no work at all, whether a native of your own country or a stranger who dwells among you. For on that day the priest shall make atonement for you, to cleanse you, that you may be clean from all your sins before the LORD. It is a sabbath of solemn rest for you, and you shall afflict your souls. It is a statute forever. And the priest, who is anointed and consecrated to minister as priest in his father's place, shall make atonement, and put on the linen clothes, the holy garments; then he shall make atonement for the Holy Sanctuary, and he shall make atonement for the tabernacle of meeting and for the altar, and he shall make atonement for the priests and for all the people of the assembly. This shall be an everlasting statute for you, to make atonement for the children of Israel, for all their sins, once a year.' And he did as the LORD commanded Moses."*

This was the day when the people of Israel were washed from their sins. On this day, in order to wash away the sins of the people of Israel, the high priest had to first offer a sacrifice for himself and his household. This was necessary because the high priest could only fulfill his priestly duty and blot out the sins of the people of Israel if he himself was washed clean from his sins. Through the Day of Atonement, God not only blotted out the sins of the Israelites, but He also promised the special gift of salvation to the entire human race.

Among the twelve tribes of Israel, Aaron and Moses belonged to the tribe of Levi. Aaron and the Levites were responsible for ministering sacrifices in the Tabernacle of Meeting, doing such things as collecting, chopping up and preparing the firewood, drawing water, cutting up the sacrificial animals into pieces, and burning them by fire. Their only task was ministering sacrifices to God like this in order to blot out the people's sins. On the Day of Atonement established by God, it fell on the high priest to pass the sins of the people of God to the live sacrificial animals and blotting them out by laying his hands on their heads.

On this Day of Atonement, Aaron first laid his hands on the head of a bull to pass all his sins and his household's sins. After this, Aaron took two goats for the people of Israel, as it's written: *"He shall take the two goats and present them before the LORD at the door of the tabernacle of meeting. Then Aaron shall cast lots for the two goats: one lot for the LORD and the other lot for the scapegoat" (Leviticus 16:7-8).* As indicated in this passage, there were two sacrificial animals given as the offering of the Day of Atonement. One of the two animals was offered to the Lord God, while the other was offered for the people.

To recap, for the entire nation of Israel, for them to receive the remission of sins on the Day of Atonement, Aaron had to first of all receive the remission of his sins and the sins of the Levites by passing them to a bull. After this he had to bring two sacrificial goats for the people of Israel: one of these goats was for God, while the other goat was offered for the people. This sacrifice of the Day of Atonement was offered to cleanse the hearts of the people of Israel from their sins. Why did God specify two sacrificial offerings for the Day of Atonement? He did this to show the people of Israel that all their sins were passed on to the sacrificial goats. This was demonstrated by the use of the live scapegoat, the second sacrifice offered on the Day of Atonement.

The Sacrifice of the Day of Atonement

On the Day of Atonement, the high priest had to offer two sacrifices for the people of Israel: one goat, whose blood was offered inside the Holy Place, was killed, while the other goat was released into the wilderness. In both cases, the high priest passed all the sins of the people of Israel to the goats by laying his hands on their heads without exception.

Let's turn to Leviticus 16:15-20 here: *"Then he shall kill the goat of the sin offering, which is for the people, bring its blood inside the veil, do with that blood as he did with the blood of the bull, and sprinkle it on the mercy seat and before the mercy seat. So he shall make atonement for the Holy Place, because of the uncleanness of the children of Israel, and because of their transgressions, for all their sins; and so he shall do for the tabernacle of meeting which remains among them in the midst of their uncleanness. There shall be no man in the tabernacle of meeting when he goes in to make atonement in the Holy Place, until he comes out, that he may make atonement for himself, for his household, and for all the assembly of Israel. And he shall go out to the altar that is before the LORD, and make atonement for it, and shall take some of the blood of the bull and some of the blood of the goat, and put it on the horns of the altar all around. Then he shall sprinkle some of the blood on it with his finger seven times, cleanse it, and consecrate it from the uncleanness of the children of Israel. And when he has made an end of atoning for the Holy Place, the tabernacle of meeting, and the altar, he shall bring the live goat."*

On this day, after passing the sins of the people of Israel to the sacrificial goat by laying his hands on its head, the high priest had to draw its blood and take this blood into the Most

Holy Place, where the mercy was found. This was God's dwelling place of the Tabernacle, and this place was above the cover of the Ark of the Testimony inside the Most Holy Place. This cover of the Ark is also known as the mercy seat. The house indwelt by God was divided into the Holy Place and the Most Holy Place. In the Holy Place, there were the table of bread, the altar of incense with four horns, seven lamps. Before taking the blood of the sacrifice into the Most Holy Place, the high priest had to first light the altar of incense.

All of these things teach us that the remission of all sins is fulfilled only if there is death as their condemnation. Spiritually speaking, the altar of incense refers to the condemnation of sins and prayer. The Most Holy Place could be entered only by the high priest. And when the high priest did so, He had had to first pass all the people's sins to the sacrificial offering by laying his hands on its head, cut its throat and draw its blood, and take this blood with Him. This teaches us that we are qualified to pray to God only after all our sins are condemned.

The Bells on the Hems of the Robe of the High Priest

There were small golden bells attached to the hems of the robe of high priest. These bells rang when the high priest sprinkled the blood of the sacrifice on the mercy seat. And this sound was heard by the people standing outside the Sanctuary. Hearing the sound of the bells ringing, the people outside the Sanctuary were able to realize that the sacrifice of the Day of Atonement was over, even though their eyes could not see what the high priest was doing inside the Most Holy Place. In this way, the high priest ministered the sin offering inside the

Most Holy Place for himself, his household, and the whole assembly of Israel.

What's important for us to realize here is the fact that on the Day of Atonement, the high priest passed the sins of the people of Israel to the sacrificial animal by laying his hands on its head. It was through the laying on of his hands that the sins of the Israelites were passed on to the sacrificial animal. When we turn to Leviticus chapter one, we see the Scripture saying, *"Then he shall put his hand on the head of the burnt offering, and it will be accepted on his behalf to make atonement for him" (Leviticus 1:4).* And the Scripture also says that the high priest sprinkled the blood on all the instruments in the Holy Place and the Most Holy Place and so cleansed them.

The Shedding of Blood for the Remission of Sins

Hebrews 9:22 says, *"Without shedding of blood there is no remission."* That is why the high priest sprinkled the blood of the sacrifice seven times on the mercy seat before God, where His grace was bestowed. The blood of the sacrifice sprinkled over the whole of the Ark of the Testimony which was located in the Most Holy Place. The Scripture says that below the Altar of Burnt Offering located in the outer yard of the Sanctuary, blood was flowing like a river. Blood flowed like a river there because the people of Israel committed so many sins and sacrificed so many animals for their sins. Can you imagine just how many animals had died there?

For the people of Israel to receive the remission of sins from God, all the instruments in the Sanctuary had to be cleansed first, the high priest himself also had to be clean, and this required a sacrificial animal. This animal had to accept all the sins of the people of Israel so that they may receive the remission of sins, and Aaron and his household had to be clean. How was this cleanness obtained? It was obtained through the laying of hands on live sacrificial animals such as goats, bulls, or lambs, and then the shedding of their blood.

The people of Israel were prohibited from looking into the Most Holy Place, nor could they do this as the Sanctuary was walled up covered in the skins of animals. However, because golden bells were attached to the hems of the robe of the high priest, from hearing the sound of these bells ringing out, they could know what was happening inside the Most Holy Place. Through the sacrifice of the Day of Atonement ministered by Aaron the high priest, his household, his children, and the people of Israel all made atonement for their sins, and whoever believed in this sacrifice received the remission of sins. However, there still remained a question: how could the people of Israel, who were all standing outside the Sanctuary as they were not allowed to come in, confirm that they were indeed remitted from all the sins they committed out of their shortcomings and weaknesses, which were also written in the tablets of their hearts?

On the tenth day of the seventh month, the Day of Atonement set by God, all the people of Israel received the remission of sins without exception. The sacrificial offerings of the Old Testament teach us that in the age of the New Testament, our Lord Jesus bore all the sins of this world once and for all by being baptized by John the Baptist and remitted them all away by shedding His blood, leaving absolutely no one's sins behind. God did not remit away just some people's sins while not remitting away others' sins. Rather, on the tenth day of the seventh month, God remitted away all the sins of the people of Israel 100%, no one was exempt. This meant sin had disappeared from the assembly of Israel as a nation. On this day, God blotted out all the sins of the Israelites through the sacrificial animal, regardless of whether they wanted it or not. The fact that God remitted away all the sins of the people of Israel when the sacrifice of the Day of Atonement was offered on the tenth day of the seventh month is evidence of the fact that Jesus has remitted away all the sins of everyone in this world once and for all by being baptized by John the Baptist and shedding His own blood.

It's absolutely important for all of us to realize that Jesus bore all the sins of all the people in this world when He was baptized by John the Baptist, and that He has blotted all these sins out by shedding His blood. But, were we there when Jesus was baptized by John the Baptist? No, of course not. Has anyone here been inside the Tabernacle of the Old Testament? No, none of us has ever set a foot inside the Sanctuary. After all, how could we, as the Gentiles ever be allowed to enter into the Sanctuary when even the people of Israel could not do so? How, then, can we know and believe that Jesus Christ has become our Savior? We know and believe so because of the baptism through which the Lord bore all our sins once and for all, and including the blood He shed on the Cross. The evidence of this salvation comes from the baptism of Jesus and the blood of sacrifice He shed as our own live scapegoat.

The word "scapegoat" means to become and to give up. What was given up on the Day of Atonement? An unblemished live goat was given up, as it's written, *"And when he has made an end of atoning for the Holy Place, the tabernacle of meeting, and the altar, he shall bring the live goat."* This was the shadow of Jesus Christ who would come by water and blood in the age of the New Testament. It prophesies, in other words, that Jesus would blot out all our sins once and for all by being

356 The Sacrifice of the Day of Atonement in the Old Testament

baptized by John the Baptist and shedding His blood on the Cross.

It's written in Leviticus 16:21-22: *"Aaron shall lay both his hands on the head of the live goat, confess over it all the iniquities of the children of Israel, and all their transgressions, concerning all their sins, putting them on the head of the goat, and shall send it away into the wilderness by the hand of a suitable man. The goat shall bear on itself all their iniquities to an uninhabited land; and he shall release the goat in the wilderness."*

The Spiritual Significance of the Live Sacrificial Goat

Spiritually speaking, the live sacrificial goat here refers to Jesus. Where the Scripture says, *"Aaron shall lay both his hands on the head of the live goat,"* the live goat here refers to Jesus Christ in the New Testament, teaching us that the Savior would be baptized by John the Baptist and shed His blood on the Cross .

Let's turn to Hebrews 9:9-12, *"It was symbolic for the present time in which both gifts and sacrifices are offered which cannot make him who performed the service perfect in regard to the conscience—concerned only with foods and drinks, various washings, and fleshly ordinances imposed until the time of reformation. But Christ came as High Priest of the good things to come, with the greater and more perfect tabernacle not made with hands, that is, not of this creation. Not with the blood of goats and calves, but with His own blood He entered the Most Holy Place once for all, having obtained eternal redemption."*

In the Old Testament Aaron the high priest was the head of all the priests. When his sons turned 30, they could succeed his ministry as the high priest. The Scripture says that in the age of the Old Testament, Aaron laid his hands on the head of the goat. Why did Aaron lay his hands on the head of this sacrificial animal? He did so to pass the sins of his people. It's written that Aaron confessed all the iniquities of the people of Israel and all their transgressions, and put all these sins on the head of the goat in this way. It was at that time that the Israelites' sins were passed on to the sacrificial animal through the laying on Aaron's hands.

The sacrificial goat, bearing the lawlessness of all the people of Israel, was then led far into the wilderness to die. Spiritually speaking, who does this sacrificial animal refer to? It refers to none other than Jesus Christ our Lord. When Jesus came to this world, He shouldered all the sins of this world once and for all by being baptized by John the Baptist, was dragged out of Jerusalem to Golgotha, and shed His blood on the Cross to death. Just as the sacrificial goat of the Day of Atonement had accepted all the sins of the people of Israel in the age of the Old Testament becoming sin for them, so did Jesus accept all the sins of His people once and for all by being baptized. That's why the Scripture says that Jesus Christ has become the Savior by giving up His own body, by being baptized by John the Baptist and shedding His blood, rather than using the blood of goats and calves which was done in the age of the Old Testament.

This was done to fulfill the Word promised in the Old Testament. Through the baptism Jesus received from John the Baptist, a direct descendant of Aaron, He could bear all the sins of the world. John the Baptist was born into this world six months before Jesus was born. He was born from Zacharias and Elizabeth, both of whom were Aaron's descendants. Born in the household of the high priest six month earlier than Jesus, John the Baptist was raised by God to be the greatest of all those born of women, and God made him pass the sins of the world to Jesus by baptizing Him. Like the sacrificial animal of the Old Testament, Jesus accepted all the sins of everyone in this world on His own body completely and offered Himself to God the Father; and by doing so, He has blotted out all the sins of all the people in this world, and He has perfectly saved all those in this age and time from all their sins who believe in the gospel of the water and the Spirit.

As the Lamb of God, Jesus shouldered all our sins once and for all by being baptized by John the Baptist, and He was condemned for these sins by dying on the Cross in our place, even though none of us actually saw this with our physical eyes. That is how Jesus has made it possible for all of us be freed from all our sins by faith. Put differently, the spiritual significance of the Day of Atonement is found in none other than the baptism Jesus received from John the Baptist and the blood He shed on the Cross.

Now in this age of the New Testament, the sacrifice of the Day of Atonement is offered spiritually by faith, through the gospel of the water and the Spirit. Jesus Christ our Savior accepted all the sins of mankind once and for all through the baptism He received from John the Baptist, and by offering His own body to God the Father, He has saved His people. It is by being baptized by John the Baptist that Jesus took upon all the sins of this world once and for all. To offer His fundamentally sinless and unblemished body to God the Father as our own sacrificial offering, Jesus Christ received His baptism from John the Baptist and shed His own blood; and by doing this, He has made it possible for everyone who believes in the righteousness of God to receive the remission of sins. Like this, the baptism of Jesus Christ and the shedding of His blood has enabled us the believers in the righteousness of God to receive the perfect remission of sins.

Jesus is fundamentally sinless. He never committed any sin at all. Yet, He still accepted all the sins of mankind by being baptized by John the Baptist in order to save us from all our sins, and to obey the will of God the Father. It was God the Father's will to sacrifice His own Son to save everyone in this world from all sins. It was in obedience to this will of God the Father that Jesus accepted all our sins on His body by being baptized and shed His blood on the Cross in our place. In short, the Lord has made it possible for us to receive the remission of sins from God if only we will believe in His righteousness.

By believing in the righteousness of Jesus Christ, the unblemished and spotless High Priest of the Kingdom of Heaven, we can be saved and remitted from all our sins. It was to save us from all our iniquities that Jesus Christ came to this earth, accepted all our sins once and for all by being baptized in the Jordan River, died on the Cross in our place to bear the condemnation of our sins, and rose from the dead again. The sacrificial offering that has blotted out the sins of mankind is none other than Jesus Christ, and this offering is an unblemished offering. Jesus Christ neither knew nor committed any sin at all. It was only to save us from all our sins that He became our own sacrificial offering to bear all the sins of every sinner and bore the condemnation of our sins in our place.

From the baptism of Jesus Christ and the shedding of His blood, we can believe that He is indeed our Savior, and we can also confirm it. God has made it possible for whoever believes in His righteousness, that is, all those who believe that Jesus Christ accepted all their sins by being baptized in the Jordan

River and sacrificed Himself on the Cross—to receive the complete remission of sins 100%.

Viewed from the perspective of our faith in the gospel of the water and the Spirit, we can see clearly that all the sins of all the people in this world have been blotted out, just as the sinful people of Israel were made completely sinless on the Day of Atonement. It's absolutely important for all of us to realize this glorious Truth and to believe in it. In the age of the New Testament also, all the sins of this world have disappeared completely without a trace, thanks to Jesus Christ, His baptism in the Jordan River, His Cross, His resurrection, His ascension, and His return. All the sins of everyone in this world have been blotted out. Each and every sin has disappeared in God's sight. God no longer accuses us of our sins. On the contrary, He is saying to us, "Receive the remission of sins by believing in Jesus Christ, in the sacrifice of atonement My Son made to blot out all your sins. I have blotted out all your sins. I am the God of love. It is not you who loved Me first, it is I who loved you first."

All those in this world who believe in the righteousness of God are sinless. It's just that the Devil is trying to hide the Truth so that people wouldn't know that our Lord Jesus has blotted out all the sins of the world. So, no matter who, anyone in this world can be made sinless if only they would come to know and believe in the gospel of the water and the Spirit. The problem, however, is that too many people still do not know this Truth.

We are the priests in God's sight, and as such, we must pass all our sins over through our faith in the righteousness of God and believe that Jesus Christ bore each and every sin of ours through the baptism He received from John the Baptist, no matter what kind of sins we might have committed. And we must also believe and preach that Jesus Christ took up all the sins of all the people in this world. Thanks to the righteousness of God, everyone in this world is sinless. How about you then? Do you still have your sins remaining intact? No, you have no more sin. All your sins and mine were passed on to Jesus Christ through His baptism.

It's also very important for the believers in the righteousness of God to realize that no one in this world has any sin in their hearts, even the nonbelievers. It's just that these people do not know it. It's when we know this clearly that we can bear witness of the gospel effectively. Not only are we ourselves sinless as the righteous, but everyone else is also sinless, including our households and even those who still have not come into our gathering. In Christ, no one can have any sin. Like this, when we have the full conviction that there is no sin in the believer, we can preach the gospel boldly. And we can establish God's Church by faith. Unless we have this faith, we cannot preach the gospel.

This is a fact. It is the truth. The Lord said that the truth shall set us free. I give all my thanks to our Lord for blotting out all our sins with the gospel of the water and the Spirit first of all, and for eradicating all the sins of each and every person, all the sins of all the people all over the world, and all the sins of our brothers and sisters. ✉

SERMON

15

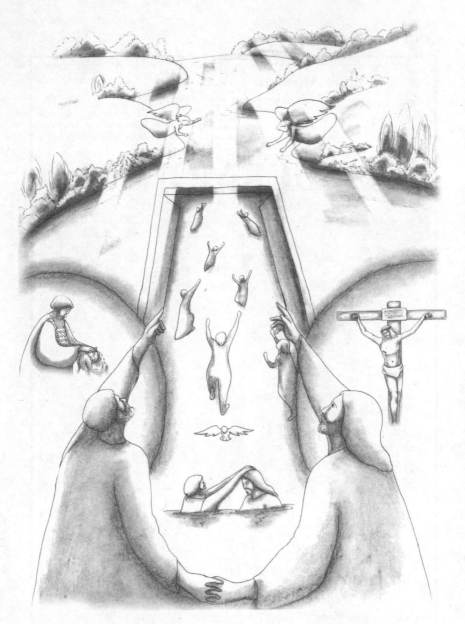

You can download Rev. Paul C. Jong's Christian Books on iPhone, iPad, or Blackberry by going to Amazon's Kindle e-bookstore (www.amazon.com).

Devote Your Life to Saving Lives

< Leviticus 17:10-16 >

"'And whatever man of the house of Israel, or of the strangers who dwell among you, who eats any blood, I will set My face against that person who eats blood, and will cut him off from among his people. For the life of the flesh is in the blood, and I have given it to you upon the altar to make atonement for your souls; for it is the blood that makes atonement for the soul.' Therefore I said to the children of Israel, 'No one among you shall eat blood, nor shall any stranger who dwells among you eat blood.' Whatever man of the children of Israel, or of the strangers who dwell among you, who hunts and catches any animal or bird that may be eaten, he shall pour out its blood and cover it with dust; for it is the life of all flesh. Its blood sustains its life. Therefore I said to the children of Israel, 'You shall not eat the blood of any flesh, for the life of all flesh is its blood. Whoever eats it shall be cut off.' And every person who eats what died naturally or what was torn by beasts, whether he is a native of your own country or a stranger, he shall both wash his clothes and bathe in water, and be unclean until evening. Then he shall be clean. But if he does not wash them or bathe his body, then he shall bear his guilt."

Jesus Is Sovereign over Life

During the age of the Old Testament, the people of Israel were forbidden from eating any kind of blood. This was one of the first commandments that God gave to the people of Israel. By prohibiting them from eating blood, God was commanding them not to eat any life of the flesh. This is what God meant when He told the Israelites that while they could eat the flesh of animals, they could not eat their blood. That's because God is sovereign over life.

On this issue, it's very important for us the believers in the gospel of the water and the Spirit to realize that God is telling us here to save lives. In other words, it is incumbent upon us to share life rather than letting it perish. We ought to save souls and bring the remission of sins to them through the gospel of the water and the Spirit. What, then, should we do to bring the remission of sins to people and save their lives?

The Works of the Flesh Are Evident

For us to save souls from their sins, we must be guided by the Holy Spirit. To ensure this, we must first of all believe in the gospel of the water and the Spirit. We must not become conceited, provoking one another, envying, or being in competition with one another (Galatians 5:26).

What, then, is the work that saves lives? We know very well that the fruit of the Spirit is different from the fruit of the flesh. The works of the flesh are evident, and these include such things as adultery, fornication, and rejecting the righteousness of God. They also entail idolatry, sorcery, and enmity with the righteousness of God. Other attributes characteristic of the works of the flesh are contentions, jealousy, outbursts of wrath, and selfish ambitions. They also include, swearing, dissensions, heresies, envy, drunkenness, and revelries. Like this, the works of the flesh are revealed evidently. When we turn to Galatians 5:19-26, we can see the Scripture describing what such a fleshly life is like. We can see that it's completely opposite to following the Holy Spirit and saving lives. The Bible says in Galatians 5:19-21, *"Now the works of the flesh are evident, which are: adultery, fornication, uncleanness, lewdness, idolatry, sorcery, hatred, contentions, jealousies, outbursts of wrath, selfish ambitions, dissensions, heresies, envy, murders, drunkenness, revelries, and the like."* Those who lead such a life cannot do the work of saving lives.

It's written in Leviticus 17:12, *"You shall not eat the blood of any flesh, for the life of all flesh is its blood. Whoever eats it shall be cut off."* This prohibition against eating any blood is also found in Genesis chapter 9. When God said that we should not eat any blood, He was commanding us not to kill any soul that can be saved.

What Is the Work That Saves People's Lives?

There was a special commandment that God gave to all the people born after Noah's flood. This commandment was the prohibition against blood, as it's written, *"Every moving thing that lives shall be food for you. I have given you all things, even as the green herbs. But you shall not eat flesh with its life, that is, its blood"* (Genesis 9:3-4). By this, God was telling us to never do anything that would kill and devour another person's soul, even though we all do the things of the flesh from time to time. Accordingly, we should never do anything that can lead another person's soul to perish. God commanded us not to eat the flesh of any animal with its blood, because the life of the flesh is the blood, and the blood is the same as life itself. Therefore, we must never allow ourselves to preach a false gospel and consequently kill the souls that would have otherwise been saved. We ought to do the things that save lives rather than killing them.

Everyone has a life. We must therefore work to save this life. To do so, we must refrain from following the flesh and devote ourselves fully to saving the souls of those who are perishing. If we commit any sin with our flesh, then it's only a matter of course that we ought to wash it away again by believing in the gospel of the water and the Spirit.

When we turn to Leviticus 17:15-16, we see the Bible saying, *"And every person who eats what died naturally or what was torn by beasts, whether he is a native of your own country or a stranger, he shall both wash his clothes and bathe in water, and be unclean until evening. Then he shall be clean. But if he does not wash them or bathe his body, then he shall bear his guilt."* Spiritually speaking, those who eat what died naturally or what was born by beasts here refer to those who believe in something else other than the true gospel. Because they committed sin with our flesh, we had to wash their clothes and bathe in water, and be unclean until evening. Then they became clean.

How should we wash away our iniquities? We should wash them away with our faith in the gospel of the water and the Spirit. We should go to the Jordan River where the Lord bore all our sins, and wash them away with our faith in the righteousness of God. Spiritually speaking, if we ate what was torn to death by beasts, we must wash ourselves by believing in the righteousness of Jesus. That's when our sins are passed on to Jesus. The remission of sins is then received by faith. We must wash our hearts with our faith in the baptism of Jesus and His blood. Our hearts will then become clean again.

But what would happen if we sin again after receiving the remission of sins, but neglect to pass these sins by ruminating on the gospel of the water and the Spirit nor wash it away with faith? We will not recover. Indeed, we will suffer from the sins that remain with us. Therefore, if we commit a sin again by chance, we must wash it away immediately by believing in the gospel of the water and the Spirit. This does not mean that we are to wash away our sins by offering our prayers of repentance, but rather, by trusting in the gospel of the water and the Sprit that constitutes the righteousness of God. We ought to go to the Jordan River, confess that these sins of ours were indeed passed on to the Lord through the ministry of John the Baptist, and confirm this again with our faith. All our sins must be washed away like this with our faith in the gospel of the water and the Spirit.

Therefore, if we ever find ourselves sinning with our flesh, we must wash this sin away as soon as possible with our faith in the righteousness of God. Without this faith in the gospel of the water and the Spirit, we cannot wash away our sins, just as the Scripture says, *"But if he does not wash them or bathe his body, then he shall bear his guilt."* Therefore, we must go to the Jordan River and wash away our sins as soon as possible with our faith in the righteousness of God. We must cleanse away our sins, believing that the Lord took away these sins also.

We must do the work that saves the lives and souls that died. To do this, we must refrain from following the flesh. We ought to be joyful and pleased with this work that saves souls by faith. It is by faith that we do the work of the Spirit, that is, the work that saves souls from their sins. We must fulfill our roles, which is washing away people's sins with the clear water of the Jordan River. To this end, we must live only by our faith in the righteousness of God.

How then can we save lives? You and I can firstly pray for the souls that we have in mind. These souls could be from your workplace, friends, or our own family. Whoever they might be, we ought to guide their souls to receive the remission of sins. It's through us that God brings the remission of sins to them. We must do this work throughout our entire lifetime. Preaching the gospel of the water and the Spirit is what you and I can do as the redeemed to save lives. We should no longer live only for our flesh, worried about how to make a living or what to eat or drink. The works of the flesh are very evident, including that of adultery, greed, and the likes, and such things are not what we should be living for. From now on, we must make up our minds and devote the rest of our remaining lives to saving the lives of others. It's absolutely crucial for us to realize just how precious thing it is save the lives that were dead in sin.

One soul is more precious than everything under the heavens. The gospel of the water and the Spirit, the gospel of the remission of sins, is the precious Word of God that can save every single soul. We must preach the gospel of the water and the Spirit to all the souls so that they may believe in this gospel wholeheartedly, and thereby, receive the complete remission of their sins. It is incumbent upon us to help them realize just how precious and valuable this remission of sins really is. We must do this work without fail. How precious is each and every life? This preciousness of life is appreciated when one is facing certain death. When death is imminent, one realizes just how precious and valuable life really is.

Saving the lives that are dead in their sins by sharing with them the work of the baptism of Jesus and of His blood on the Cross is what preaching the gospel is all about. Spreading this gospel of the water and the Spirit is what save lives. We are laboring to save people's lives one by one. We are working to wash away their sins, and this work that brings the dead back to life is what spreading the gospel is all about.

What a precious work this is? Can there be any work on this earth more precious than this? No, saving lives is the most precious work. It's written, *"For the life of the flesh is in the blood, and I have given it to you upon the altar to make atonement for your souls; for it is the blood that makes atonement for the soul" (Leviticus 17:11).*

The Most Precious Work

The most precious work is sharing God's love, and this is sharing the work of the water and blood of Jesus Christ. With the water, Jesus Christ washed away people's sins, and with His life, He was judged for their sins, and, gave them new life. He also delivered them from the Judgment and enabled them to be born again. This work is more precious than any other work in the world. The gospel of the water and the Spirit we are preaching is what saves people's lives. So by remembering just how precious it is to save lives, let us all devote ourselves even more to preaching the gospel of the water and the Spirit and saving lives.

We must dedicate ourselves to this work, inviting and guiding souls. For us to do the work that saves souls, spiritually speaking, there must be dry firewood for the Altar of Burnt Offering, as there must be water and fire also. There must also be the servants ministering, and there must be the Word of God and His faithful working servants as well. Our God must be with us also, and we must, of course, have the necessary financial resources also. Feel free to invite to this revival meeting as many souls as you want. If you don't have anyone to invite, then participate in this work with material and financial contributions. Everyone who wants to take part in this revival meeting is welcome. We are doing so voluntarily by our faith in the righteousness of God.

Saving lives is a truly precious, beautiful, and blessed work. Those who have the gospel of the water and the Spirit—that is, those who have received the remission of sins—preach this gospel of the water and the Spirit to those who still have not received the remission of sins. Those who already believe in the gospel of the water and the Spirit enable the sinful to receive the remission of sins by preaching this gospel to them. Sinners will then be washed clean from their sins and become sinless. This is the most beautiful picture in the world. This picture is the most beautiful picture of all, more stunning than any other picture in the world.

Those who are serving God to save lives are also very beautiful. How wonderful is it to see a physician saving a person's life? Physicians heal the sick. It's with a sense of calling that they deal with their patients, treat them, perform surgeries on them, and save their lives. They also encourage their patients' hearts. What an amazing work is it to save a life that's perishing? We are doing such a truly marvelous work. What a worthy and fulfilling work it is? We are serving the most beautiful and precious work that saves lives.

My fellow believers, you and I have received the remission of sins by believing in the gospel of the water and the Spirit. We are now preaching the gospel to the souls that are dead in their sins. These souls are then washed from their sins, and they come to live again by believing in the gospel and in Jesus. What a beautiful and precious work this truly is? We must remember that saving lives a truly marvelous and beautiful work.

In the Scripture, God told the people of Israel that no one, whether an Israelite or a Gentile, should eat the flesh of any animal with its blood, and that whoever does so will be cut off from them. Any Israelite who killed another person's soul was cut off from the people of Israel. Even to the people of Israel, God warned that if any of them killed another person's soul, He will cut him off. He said so because it's such an important and precious work.

My fellow believers, you and I have the kind of life that can wash away people's sins and save their dead souls. We have the one thing that can save lives—that is, we have the gospel of the water and the Spirit. We are indeed capable of great things. If only we decide to save the souls that are dead in sin, we will indeed save them. However, if we decide to serve just our flesh, then we will not gain anything from God. We all have a soul and a body. In our hearts, we have the gospel of power that can save souls. We have the gospel of God and His righteousness. That's why we can save souls. We know that this work is precious. It is all about saving lives by faith. If we just set our minds to it and then actually do it, then we can all carry out the precious work that brings countless dead souls back to life and enables them to receive new life.

We are the ones who have the righteousness of God that can save countless people. We have the righteousness of God that can deliver everyone and bring the dead back to life. We have the faith that can save souls, and we know the mystery of faith. We are the ones who possess the Kingdom of God and His life. We are the pathway to God's blessings. We are the pathway to God's life also. You and I are the pathway to sharing life. We must never eat any blood. We must do the work that saves people's souls and lives, leading them to have God's life. Throughout our entire lifetime, you and I must cherish the work that saves lives. We must do the work that saves lives.

What is the purpose for living in this world? Our purpose is to save people's lives. We must not boast of anything else. We must not boast of our flesh. Instead, we ought to take pride in the work we have done to save souls. I give all my thanks to God for using us as His set apart and holy workers. All that I have done is just preach the gospel, but God has saved many souls and made them receive the remission of sins. These are the things that we should be grateful for and proud of.

There is only one thing that you and I can boast of throughout our entire lifetime, and that is that God has saved people's lives. He has given us His righteousness. God has shared the flesh and blood of Jesus Christ with us and with everyone else. We ought to be proud of the fact that God has used us as His workers sharing His flesh and blood. Boasting of the flesh is not something the righteous should be doing. Instead, they ought to be proud of the work they are doing to save souls. We ought to boast of Jesus our Lord, who has given us new life.

God said to pour all the blood out on the ground. The ground refers to the human heart. It means that God has given us new life. He has given new life to the souls that had once been dead in sin. He has brought our souls back to life and saved us. Not only this, God has also entrusted us with His precious work. I am so grateful for this wonderful blessing. I pray with all my heart that we will never allow ourselves to eat any blood spiritually. I hope and pray that we would instead save lives by sprinkling the baptism and blood of Jesus on the Altar of Burnt Offering. Hallelujah! ✉

SERMON

16

Keep My Statutes and Perform Them

< Leviticus 20:8 >
    "And you shall keep My statutes, and perform them: I am the Lord who sanctifies you."

I am very grateful to be here today and share the Word of God with you. I know it's not easy on your back to be sitting on the hard floor and listening to my sermon like this, parts of which you may already have heard. So I am very thankful for your patience. After today's worship service, there will only be one more service left for tomorrow, which will bring this revival meeting to a close. There is a wedding the day after tomorrow. The day after this, we will gather together in the Church again to share fellowship with God's people, praise God, and worship Him. On Monday, we will pray for the lost souls, go out looking for them, and do various other things for them. And we must spread the gospel to North Korea also.

    Rev. Kim and I are not that knowledgeable when it comes to current world events, but given what we have been hearing lately, we think that the time is nearing for us to spread the gospel to North Korea. It's believed by many in North Korea are on the verge of total collapse. This week, as I share the Word with you regarding God's statutes, which are the laws established by God, I'm thinking increasingly that the time is nearing for us to preach the gospel to North Korea, as its cruel dictatorship regime is about to collapse and profound social changes are about to be unleashed.

Rev. Kim, let's go to North Korea when it opens up. We will each carry a backpack, with a tent and 50 Bibles. We will pool our strengths together. When that time comes, it's not just our pastors, evangelists, and their wives who will go, but all the brothers and sisters who have received the remission of sins must also go. We must go boldly, preaching to the people of North Korean that Jesus Christ has blotted out all their sins, and that it is God, not Kim Jong-un, who provides for all their needs. North Koreans are even more likely to receive the remission of sins once the gospel is preached to them, as their hearts have been untouched by the false doctrines of modern Christianity.

When painting, what you draw with the first stroke of the brush on the blank canvas is very important. I have no doubt that when we preach the gospel clearly to North Koreans, they will receive the remission of sins for sure. There are so many fake religious teachings nowadays, just as there are many fake designer bags and clothes. It's inevitable for fake products to outnumber genuine products, and they even look better than the original products. This morning, I had some rice mixed with sesame oil for breakfast, and Rev. Kim's wife told me that the sesame oil was genuine. I was shocked to find out that some unscrupulous people were faking even sesame oil. In the old days, venders couldn't deceive their customers as it would have ruined their reputation. News spread quickly as everyone knew everyone else. However, once urbanization began, some businesses began to tamper with the production process. For instance, sesame oil used to be made in a Mom-and-Pop store relying on a manual production process. Modern machinery changed all this, as it made mass production of sesame oil possible. Apparently, nowadays fake sesame oil is made easily by mixing in some other type of inferior oil and chemical additives. It's hard to believe how far some people would go just to make some money, cooking up all kinds of schemes for such an unscrupulous end. What's the point of making money so dishonestly like this?

I meant to speak about false gospels, but I digressed here a little. At any rate, the day will come soon when we will go to North Korea and preach the true gospel. So let us renew our strength, tighten our belt, and strap our boots. We must prepare ourselves diligently now, so that when the time comes, we can pounce upon the first opportunity to head to North Korea and spread the gospel there. If only we go there and preach the Word, many, many people will receive the remission of sins. Just as the people of Israel entered into the land of Canaan and settled down there even though the land was already inhabited by other tribes, if we just raise a flag and draw a line on the ground, it will all be ours. Of course, I am not speaking of grabbing some North Korean land, but rather, I am speaking about preaching the gospel to North Koreans. God will deliver them to us so that we can preach the gospel to them.

We Must Live with a Clear Vision of Faith

We need to have a plan for the future, thinking ahead what we will do in the years to come, such as where to plant a church next spring, and when to preach the gospel to North Korea. It's really not an easy thing to do. In fact, it's extremely difficult. We need even more workers of God in times like these. So let's plan ahead for the future. Let's plan on going to North Korea and preach the gospel there, just as we have a plan for South Korea. There are many, many places here in South

Korea where our Church is not present. Our gospel workers have been looking long and hard at some of the possible locations for church planting. We must dig a well everywhere we go, so that the Word can spring forth everywhere.

When we turn to the Bible, we see that Isaac and Jacob dug a well everywhere they went. They did this in the desert. Some of Jacob's wells still remain even to this day. Digging a spiritual well like this is what life is all about for us holy Christians. It is not easy to dig a spiritual well. It's even more difficult that we have to dig it deep. However, once it's dug, many thirsty people will be able to quench their thirst from this well for thousands of years to come. They will drink the living of water of Truth from the wells dug by us and receive new life. The work of life will unfold. We must therefore plant churches diligently, and spread to even more people this blessed Word that we have in our hearts.

Let us plant churches everywhere. I am not saying that we should seek to gratify our own ambition. Rather, by planting churches, we must bring the living water to the many people who are thirsting for it. Countless people are perishing from drinking dirty contaminated water mixed with all kinds of filthy and toxic waste material. They are all crying out in pain. Can you not see such souls? They are so many that they are everywhere. We are the only people who can bring the water of life to them. Even though we still have many shortcomings on our own, we can still deliver them, for the Lord is with us.

All that we have to do is preach the gospel wherever we find ourselves. The elderly can teach their fellow seniors the way to Heaven; our working brothers and sisters can preach the gospel of life at their workplaces; and our young adults can preach the gospel to college students and to other young people. Like this, from each of our positions, we must lead as many people as possible to the way of receiving the remission of sins. What is it that we are supposed to do? The Scripture says that whatever we do, whether we eat or drink, we must do all things for the glory of God. We must therefore live for the gospel. Even though we are inadequate and may even be useless in this world, in the Kingdom of God, we can all be used for an urgent and noble purpose.

So, we have no time for idling around. Words cannot describe just how busy we all are. Don't you agree with me Rev. Kim? I've been so busy that I can't even find time for the restroom. Wherever I go and whatever I do, I find myself so busy with so many things to do that it all seems endless. Even at home I don't have much time to rest, to say nothing about how busy I am at the church with my ministry. However, despite such a hectic schedule, I'm still calm and at peace. Seoul is a very modern and busy city by its nature. It's all hustle and bustle here.

Soon, the Church of Seoul will have to relocate to another place, but we have been so busy that we are not sure when we can do this. For now, the congregation is sitting on the floor during the worship service. While this is good for our brothers and sisters to share fellowship with one another more closely, it does exact a toll on their backs. I heard that it costs $2,000 to rent a commercial wedding chapel. With that money, the wedding ceremony could be held here and even hire a professional for video shooting. You might as well get your electronic equipment with the money to rent a wedding place. You could just as well buy a smartphone or video camera and do it yourselves.

My fellow believers, faith is the substance of things hoped for and the evidence of things not seen. If we believe in God and His Word, everything will be fulfilled. However, someone who has no vision at all is an already a dead person. Such people are indeed no different from the dead. So, let us prepare ourselves to spread the gospel to North Korea, and to preach the gospel and plant God's Church here in South Korea as well. Let us do our best, believing that our hopes and desires will all be fulfilled. Let every church throughout Korea pray for this, and let us all pool our strengths together. Let us pool the power of prayer and supplication. This power of prayer is extremely important. It is more important to pool the power of prayer than financial resources.

I know that many of you are tired. Some of you are shaking your head, but I can tell it from your voice. During the praise service this morning, I noticed that many of you had hoarse voices. That's the evidence showing that you are tired. We had such a wonderful fellowship last night that many of us here stayed up until 2 in the morning. We even had instant noodles at that hour! And now you are back here this evening for another service, so I know that you must all be quite tired. I was very happy to get together like this and talk and laugh for hours late into the night. I didn't know that instant noodle tasted so good in the wee hours of the morning! I don't eat instant noodle that often, but I've had it quite a few times since coming here to Seoul for the revival meeting. With everyone saying that they will have instant noodles, I felt it would be awkward for me to ask for something else. More importantly, I believe that everything should be done together no matter what. I've been so happy to share the Word with you at this revival meeting that I am filled with joy in both body and soul, and my heart has the fullness of the Holy Spirit. It's true that I feel a bit tired when I wake up in the mornings, but I am still very happy as I am filled with the Holy Spirit.

Whatever we do, we must share everything and be one

like this. We must do all things together in unity. Try eating instant noodle by yourself. It will be tasteless. You will just fill stuffed without getting any nutrition. Likewise, if you are by yourself, only self-righteousness will arise out of your heart and you will come to just complain for no reason. In contrast, when we share good things with one another, everything tastes good, and everything is joyous and fun. Whatever we do, we must do all things together. We ought to pray together, and when we do God's work, we ought to do it together in unity. I urge you to open your heart. We can all walk together.

It looks like Brother Dochun has some trouble with his eyes, as he keeps rubbing his eyes. Perhaps it's because he didn't get enough sleep last night. Even so, please find the strength to bear this hour, as the Word of God is about to be preached. I said just a while ago that we must have a vision in everything we do. Today, we will examine the statutes of God, the topic for this week.

The Statutes Established by God

Leviticus 20:8 which we just read today says, *"You shall keep My statutes, and perform them: I am the LORD who sanctifies you."* Those who have the law of God are the happy ones. Indeed, those who have a leader to guide them are the happy ones. Those who have God at their side are the happy people. Those who have a shepherd are the happy. And those who have brothers and sisters are also the happy ones, as are those who dwell in the Kingdom of God. God told us here clearly, *"You shall keep My statutes, and perform them: I am the LORD who sanctifies you."* What does the Scripture say God is? He is the Lord who sanctifies us. What did the Lord command us? He commanded us to keep and perform His statutes. These statutes refer to the decrees and rules set by God. There is nothing bad in any of the rules God set for us. Although these statutes number no less than 613 different laws, far from being bad, they are what we must remember, and they are indispensable to us. God has given us His statutes and everything else as well. Within the confines of these statutes of the Law, God has also given us the sacrificial system, thereby sanctifying us. Just as our God said here, *"I am the LORD who sanctifies you,"* He has indeed sanctified us through the sacrificial system as set by Him, and by sending His Son to us. Words cannot describe just how thankful we are for this.

We were able to be sanctified by believing in the gospel of the water and the Spirit and making our spiritual offering according go these statutes of God and the requirements of His sacrificial system. Let us then reflect upon these God-given statutes thoughtfully. Let's turn to Exodus 30:11-16, *"Then the LORD spoke to Moses, saying: 'When you take the census of the children of Israel for their number, then every man shall give a ransom for himself to the LORD, when you number them, that there may be no plague among them when you number them. This is what everyone among those who are numbered shall give: half a shekel according to the shekel of the sanctuary (a shekel is twenty gerahs). The half-shekel shall be an offering to the LORD. Everyone included among those who are numbered, from twenty years old and above, shall give an offering to the LORD. The rich shall not give more and the poor shall not give less than half a shekel, when you give an offering to the LORD, to make atonement for yourselves. And you shall take the atonement money of the children of Israel, and shall appoint it for the service of the tabernacle of meeting, that it may be a memorial for the children of Israel before the LORD, to make atonement for yourselves.'"*

God told the people of Israel to offer a ransom for themselves when their number is counted, so that there may be no plague among them. This means that each and every Israelite was assigned a certain amount of money as his atonement money to offer to God for the service of the Tabernacle. By this, God is telling us that instead of us dying for our own sins, we should offer Him something else equivalent to make atonement for ourselves. What are the statutes established by God? What has God determined for mankind? It is that every human being is under the judgment of God. In God's sight, no human being can avoid but be under His judgment. It's very important for us to realize this, and appreciate why it is that God must judge everyone. This is a God-established statute. It is not something that we can change to our liking, for in God's sight, whoever has not received the remission of sins and not been born again must be judged by Him. This is a statute established by God Himself.

In God's Sight, We Should Be Put to Death for Our Sins

This is why God told us to give a ransom for ourselves—that is, to pay the wages of sin. God demands us to pay the wages of our sins. No sinner can escape from this, and every sinner must pay for his sins. The ransom demanded by God is life itself, and we can avoid death only if we find something else that can make atonement for our sins. Only then can we avoid being condemned by God for our sins. It's absolutely indispensable for us to realize that we must pay a ransom to make atonement for our sins. We must realize that we cannot avoid but be put to death for our sins. Every sinner must realize that he is destined to hell inevitably for the wages of his sins. Because our forefather sinned against God we were born as sinners. As a result, unless this ransom of life is paid, all of us must bear the condemnation of sin without fail. This is why everyone must come to the full understanding of the gospel of the water and the Spirit. For us to be saved from our sins, we must pay the wages to God.

Those who know this truth are truly blessed people. Unless you pay the wages of your sins to God, you will all be put to death. Therefore, if we want to save ourselves, then you must pay the ransom of life to God. Realizing this, that we ourselves are destined to face death by God for our sins, we must pay the wages of life and receive redemption in our lives.

Today, we must examine ourselves to see if God is with us or not, and if we have not thought and or done everything on our own. Rather than thinking and doing things without God, we must reflect upon ourselves before Him. We must realize that unless we pay the wages of our sins to God, we cannot avoid but face death. There are many things that are visible to our eyes in this world that all too often we cannot see God by faith and our hearts become devoid of Him. This is all the more reason why we must remind ourselves of God's statutes. We must accept by faith what God has set. What God has set has come about because our ancestors Adam and Eve sinned against Him, and we were all born as sinners destined to be put to death. For us to be delivered from this destruction because of our sins, we must pay their wages. This means we must first of all know ourselves, realizing what kind of beings we really are. In other words, we must grasp here who we really are by nature before even considering our thoughts and our actions.

Anyone who lives without God faces ruins in both body

and spirit. It's written in Psalm 49:20, *"A man who is in honor, yet does not understand, is like the beasts that perish."* As the Scripture says here, anyone who does not realize God is like the beasts that perish. I don't know about you, but I hold God's statutes close to my heart. If God had set the way of salvation unfairly, then there would be no need for us to follow it. We would never have any assurance, not knowing when God might get offended and be cast us to hell. But that is not what God has done. Having established His statutes, God fulfills everything and saves us exactly according to His Word of promise. This law of salvation is never changing. And this law is the Truth of the water and the Spirit. It is the law of salvation God that has been established justly.

How wonderful it is that we have such a clear and exact statute. We belong to this just and fair salvation of God. We belong to the just Word of God. God told us to pay a ransom for our sins. He told us to give half a shekel to make atonement for ourselves. While we don't know exactly what the shekel of the Sanctuary was, we do know that there were half a shekel and full shekel as its units of account. Of these two units, God said to pay half a shekel. He also said that the rich should not pay more than this, nor should the poor pay any less. That's because regardless of whether one is rich or poor, each life is worth the same in God's sight. In other words, our lives are all equally precious, and for us to receive redemption equally, we must pay the same ransom of life. It is not the case that some people's lives are more important or less precious than anyone else's life. Far from it, each and every one of our lives is equally precious.

Whenever I read this passage, I can't help but thank our Lord Jesus Christ. We all had to pay half a shekel for our sins, but to completely blot out our sins, Jesus laid down His own life for us. My fellow believers, this is the statute established by God. In our human thoughts, we might wonder how the rich and the poor are expected to pay the same ransom money to God. It would make more sense to us for the poor to pay less and the rich more, wouldn't it? But God set the same price for both the rich and the poor alike, demanding them all to pay the same random. This is a God-established statute, so we should not think or believe according to our own wishes. In other words, when it comes to receiving the remission of sins, we shouldn't expect that God will somehow just gloss over us, thinking to ourselves, "I believe in Jesus as my Savior, and I'm leading a godly life like this. I've also given a lot of offerings and donations to my church, I've kept the Lord's Day holy, and I've been very diligent and pious for the Lord. So I'm sure God will give me a break and gloss over some of my mistakes. Since I've done all these things, I'm pretty sure that I don't really have to know the Word of God and believe in it exactly as it is. Even if I believe blindly just as long as I believe, God will surely gloss over it, if not for anything else than my devotion."

This however, is absolutely not the case. Apart from the fact that Jesus has saved us, no one can be saved by adding anything of his own works or efforts or whether it's his own piety or riches. Salvation is reached only if we believe that God has saved us through the gospel of the water and the Spirit. That's why I am so glad that God has set His statutes in the way He has, for He is not demanding much from us in return for our salvation. Our God is faithful and righteous. Once God makes a promise, He fulfills it without fail. Even though we are fickle, God is not. How wonderful our God is. I am so glad that our salvation is the same today and tomorrow, day after day, no matter how we think about it. Once we receive the remission of sins by believing in the God-given gospel of the water and the Spirit, all that we have to do is just ruminate on this gospel.

Words cannot describe just how grateful we all are to God for bestowing such a wonderful blessing upon such undeserving people like us. How marvelous is it that our God is never changing? Would you like God to be fickle? Of course not! What would happen to this world if God were fickle? What would happen if the law of salvation were to change every single day? It would be impossible for anyone to reach salvation. Like this, God has set the gospel of the water and the Spirit as the law of salvation. Yet, many Christians think that they have received the remission of sins by just asking God for forgiveness with their mouths. In reality, none of them have actually received the remission of sins. These people do everything by themselves, so much so that they even think all on their own that they have received the remission of sins. This is nothing more than a belief all of their own making without taking into regard to what God has set for them. That is why God has established His statutes clearly, knowing fully well that human beings, His creatures, would follow their own wishes even when it comes to their salvation.

As a witness of God, I can tell you and testify that God has indeed saved us all, for the Scripture is the Word of God that everyone can read and believe. The only thing that never changes and that we can believe in is the Word of God. All that we have to do is believe in and live according to the statutes as established by God. And for this opportunity I give all thanks to our Lord! The Lord said here to take the ransom money and use it for the service of the Tabernacle of the Meeting. This means that when the Israelites paid the ransom money—that is, when they gave half a shekel to God—this money had to be used for the Tabernacle of Meeting. This statute applies to us also. Put differently, God is telling us also to take the ransom money and use it for His work.

Our Lord has already paid all the ransom money for our lives, even the half a shekel that we were supposed to pay. It's all thanks to this price that our lives have been spared. You and I are indebted to the Lord for our lives. That is why the Lord told us to devote our lives to help others receive the remission of sins. Therefore, all of us who have been saved must dedicate our lives to God's good work. It is only a matter of course that for whoever has received the remission of sins through the price of life paid by Jesus Christ to offer his life to God and devote it to His work and His Church in return. Where else could we dedicate ourselves, when God has saved us by paying the price of life in our place? We ought to offer ourselves only for the work of the Lord. That's because our lives are such precious things that God has saved by paying the price of life in our place. We cannot waste such a precious life on any worthless cause. That is why God told us to offer ourselves to the service of the Tabernacle. This means that God will use us as His precious instruments.

Our God Uses Us as His Precious Instruments

When the Lord sent His disciples to free a donkey and a colt which were tied up, He told His disciples to bring themt to Him, and also told them to say to its owner, "The Lord has need of them." This colt when fully grown would have done nothing else but carry heavy loads on its back for the rest of its life. But our Lord had this colt freed from its yoke and used it for noble purposes by riding on its back into Jerusalem. In the same manner, the Lord is also using us for noble causes. Our

Lord has saved us from all our sins by paying the wages of our sins with His own life. Having done so, He does not make us bear any heavy loads of the world, but instead, He uses us for the service of the Tabernacle of God, all to save lost souls. What a wonderful blessing this is. Are you also truly thankful to our Lord for this blessing? What are we that the Lord would treasure us so preciously? He could have just left us to our own devices once we were born again, but far from this, He has made it possible for us to live the most worthwhile life on this earth.

God also said, *"That it may be a memorial for the children of Israel before the LORD, to make atonement for yourselves" (Exodus 30:16).* God told us to make atonement for ourselves by paying a ransom price. This means that we must be saved from our sins by paying the specific ransom money—that is, the price of life. Without paying the price of life, there can be no salvation. You can never be saved from your sins unless you pay the price of life. You must give half a shekel. That's because God told us to pay this ransom money without fail to make atonement for ourselves. This reminds me of the testimony given by one of our brothers just a short while ago. As I recall, this brother said that he attended a seminary for a semester, and that it had something to do with sports ministry, right? But he couldn't find any satisfaction there. There is nothing surprising about this. It's all because there was no life in that seminary. Where all of us really ought to offer ourselves is found inside the Church. Wherever our brothers and sisters might be used by God, it is when they offer themselves inside God's Church that they devote themselves to the most precious cause. Don't you agree? Jesus Christ has saved us once and for all by laying down His life in our place and becoming our own propitiation.

God's Statutes Found in the New Testament

God's statutes are also found in the New Testament. What kinds of statutes has God set for us in the New Testament? To find the answer to this question, let's turn to the Gospel of Matthew to further examine these statutes of God. Let's all read Matthew 7:7-12 together, *"Ask, and it will be given to you; seek, and you will find; knock, and it will be opened to you. For everyone who asks receives, and he who seeks finds, and to him who knocks it will be opened. Or what man is there among you who, if his son asks for bread, will give him a stone? Or if he asks for a fish, will he give him a serpent? If you then, being evil, know how to give good gifts to your children, how much more will your Father who is in heaven give good things to those who ask Him! Therefore, whatever you want men to do to you, do also to them, for this is the Law and the Prophets."* Amen!

What statutes of God are found in the New Testament? What has God set for us in this age of the New Testament? It's absolutely important for us to first of all know what it is that God has set for us. We shouldn't just lead our lives of faith blindly without even knowing what God has in store for us. Before we do anything else, we ought to know what God has set for us. And here in the New Testament God said that He would give us whatever we ask. To those who ask, God gives; to those who seek, God enables them to find; and to those who knock, God opens the door. Jesus also said, *"Therefore, whatever you want men to do to you, do also to them, for this is the Law and the Prophets."* This is the statute that God has established for us in this age of the New Testament.

Referring to Himself, Jesus said that He is the Prophet. This means Jesus is the Prophet for all mankind. With His statutes God shows us the model of how to believe. If we really want to receive the remission of sins, then God gives us the gospel of the water and the Spirit. With the gospel of the water and the Spirit, God makes righteous whoever truly wants to it. That is how God has set the law of salvation. God does not bestow the blessings of receiving the remission of sins or becoming righteous on anyone who says, "I don't want anything to do with it. I don't really care. I don't need God's righteousness." Although God helps those who have the desire but no ability, He does not help anyone who does not even have such a desire. Do we want to be made righteous and sinless before God? Do we want to go to Heaven? This is what we wanted, right? So what happened to us then? Because we yearned to receive the remission of sins and go to Heaven, God remitted away our sins and made us righteous so that we would indeed be able to go to Heaven. It's because we longed to become righteous that God made us righteous through the gospel of the water and the Spirit. And this is all according to God's statutes.

Like this, salvation can be reached only if people know the God-established rules, realize and believe in the Truth of salvation, yearn to receive new life, look for God, ask, seek, and knock. If anyone truly wants to receive the remission of sins, become righteous, and go to Heaven, then God will save all such people without fail. So why would anyone not ask God, seek and knock? This is all according to the statutes established by God. You must realize here that you cannot neglect your salvation, thinking, "I'm sure God will take care of it somehow even if I don't ask for it." That is not what God's statutes say. According to the statutes of God, God gives to those who ask, reveals Himself to those who seek Him, and opens the door to those who knock. This is how God has decided to deal with us.

It is absolutely not the case that you can just say, "Salvation will come to me somehow. God will take care of it." God reveals Himself without faith to those who seek Him. The door is opened without faith to those who knock. God gives without fail to those who ask. The Lord also said, *"Therefore, whatever you want men to do to you, do also to them."*

If you sincerely yearn to receive the remission of sins from God, if you really want all your sins to be remitted away like this, then you must pray. You must look for God. Why do we pray? We pray because God give us whatever we ask. It's because He lets us find whatever we seek. And it's because He opens the door whenever we knock. If one neither seeks nor asks for the remission of sins, then such a person is little more than a fat pig, saying, "I don't really want to receive the remission of sins, nor do I see much need for it. I'm ok. I don't really care either way." It's with such people in mind that Jesus told us not to cast our pearls before swine (Matthew 7:6).

If one does not have the heartfelt desire to receive the remission of sins despite the fact that his heart is sinful, then even if God gives him His precious Word, he cannot realize its value. It's such people who are like swine. Can such people realize the value of a pearl? No, of course not; they will just tramp on it. The Word of God tells us to deliver all those who are drowning in their sins. As we carry on with our lives of faith before God, we ought to ask Him for help always. God gives as we ask, opens the door as we knock, and lets us find as we seek. It is not the case that God answers us even if we don't pray. We must therefore realize the rules God has set for us. God does everything according to His rules. He does not act according to how we think about Him. God is never-changing. He is immovable. That is God's statute, and it's His justice. But if we pray, then God will answer us without fail.

You wanted to receive the remission of sins, right? So what did you do then? Since your heart yearned for this, you prayed for it. And hearing this prayer, God blotted out all your sins through sacrificial system of atonement, through Jesus Christ. When we had the heartfelt desire to become righteous and asked God for it, our God indeed made us righteous. We ought to remember here that God made us righteous only when we sincerely yearn for it. Worshiping God and living out our faith with the knowledge of the statutes of God is fundamentally different from trying to lead a life of faith without this knowledge. God is saying to us, "Ask Me for anything. I have so much in store for you. I have so much to give. I will give you everything you ask. But you must ask first. Only then will I give." We must therefore ask.

The Rule of Prayer Is Simple

All that you have to do is just ask, seek, and knock, just as Jesus said, *"Ask, and it will be given to you; seek, and you will find; knock, and it will be opened to you" (Matthew 7:7)*. It's all very simple, isn't it? God will give us if ask, but not give us if we don't ask. He will give us anything as long as we ask. That's why we must pray to God. Herein lies the very reason why we pray. We must pray to God because that is how He has set it for us. If you have any desire in your heart, you should just ask God for it. We are so blessed to have such a wonderful statute. A nation without any law is truly wretched. The rule of law must be there. Since we are God's people, we must know and follow God's law.

It is absolutely indispensable for us have the rule of law. Those who have the law are bold, orderly, and wise in God's sight. In contrast, those who have no law do not even know what to do and how they ought to conduct themselves. We must have the law of God—that is, His statutes—to guide us. No one can lead a proper life of faith just blindly without such statutes. It's when we sinners ask God to make them righteous and God listens to the prayers of such sinners and makes them righteous. We can confirm from the Word that the Lord made us righteous when we were still sinners—by asking Him for it.

For this reason, it is very important to know the Law first of all. Because we are God's people, we must be under His law. If God's people are not under His law, then they will be no different from anyone else. We must have the rule of law. We must have the statutes to guide us. We must live under the God-given statutes. Only then are we secure, and only then can we live a blessed life. We should never try to lead our lives of faith without the law. The rule of law is found in God's Church also. For instance, we must be one with the Church leaders, being God's servants. It is God's law for us to unite our hearts with those of the servants of His righteousness. This is a statute set by God. Even God's servants are not perfect. But just because they have some minor flaws, we shouldn't be talking behind their backs or criticizing them, for God has said that we would never be blessed if we do so.

It's so wonderful that we are sharing fellowship with one another, just as it's written in Psalm 133:1, *"Behold, how good and how pleasant it is for brethren to dwell together in unity!"* Although all of us have our own shortcomings, if we march forth in unity with our brothers and sisters, God will guide us to the path of righteousness through His redeemed servants. God will lead us to the way of righteous for His name sake. It's because His name is riding with us that He guides us to the path of righteousness. We must have faith. We must unite our hearts. No matter what, whether we live or die, we must be one in unity. We should never be arrogant, trying to raise ourselves and putting down everyone else. Worldly churches are full of people who are boastful. We should never let this happen in God's Church. No work of the Church is achieved by one person. Everything we do, we do it together.

God's Church throughout the country must march forth together. The same goes for preaching the gospel to North Korea. It's not something that Pastor Kim can do just by himself, but rather, all of us are God's workers responsible for this ministry. We are the true warriors of faith. When Pastor Kim lays the foundation, we will all go there and work. Everything under the heavens and on the earth is made God's and ours only if we ourselves work.

I cannot emphasize enough just how important it is for us to be one with God. No matter what, we must seek the will of God in unity, pray to Him, and seek and knock as we go forth. Only then are we blessed. This is a statute God has set for us. Whatever God has set for us, we ought to follow it to the letter, or otherwise we will be cursed. Trying to do good by relying on your own strength is completely useless. When you run an errand for someone else, you ought to do what you were asked to do. You can't just do something else entirely different. Let me illustrate this with an example. Let's say that there is a kid named "Obedience," named after his faithful obedience to his parents. Obedience is so eager to obey his parents that at the first suggestion of an errand, he dashes off to run that errand. But, he does not always listen carefully to what his parents are asking him to do. One day, his parents asked him to go to another town to buy some cheese. Eager to obey his parents, Obedience took off the moment he heard this. But half way to the town, he realized that he didn't know what kind of cheese he was supposed to buy, so he had to return empty-handed. Would his parents be pleased by this? No, of course not! In the same vein, we cannot please God just by obeying Him blindly on our own. We must first of all know what it is that God wants from us, and then obey Him.

Indeed, you can unite with God's Church properly only if you listen carefully to your Church leaders, unite your hearts with theirs, and know their intention. You can't become one with the Church blindly without even knowing its will. There are quite a few people in God's Church who are beaten down spiritually. Who are they? They are the ones who walk on their own rather than according to the statutes. God has given us His statutes for our everyday lives. He told us clearly that whatever we do, whether we eat or drink, we must do all things for His glory. We must therefore walk in unity in all aspects for the glory of God.

We ought to give up our own thoughts if it's for the glory of God. Yet, there are too many people who are still beholden by their own thoughts and are ignorant of God's statutes. We shouldn't insist on our own way so stubbornly without even knowing what God has set for us. We must cast aside such attitudes. We must walk according to the statutes. Our lives of faith must also be led according to the statutes, just as we must obey God according to the statutes. We ought to ask God for our everything, knowing fully that God gives us only when we ask. And as we rise up to the many challenges facing us, we ought to seek and knock. Like this, we must do everything according to the statutes. We shouldn't be swayed by the ups and downs of our own emotional feelings, laughing one day when we feel good and sulking the next day when we feel bad. What is there to like and dislike before God? We must do everything according to God's statutes.

As God's servants, we ought to run His errands knowing His will. We ought to believe according to how God has set His statutes. Believing according to these rules is the best thing we can do. Living our lives according to God's rules is also the right thing to do. If God has set a certain path for our lives, then this path is the path of truth. Too many Christians claiming to live a life of faith do not know these statutes. That's why these people have no idea what to do. They believe according to their own wishes precisely because they do not have the God-established law in their hearts.

Everyone must always follow the will of God, including our ministers. Whatever they do, whether they hold a revival meeting like this, open a prayer meeting, or make any other decision, they must obey the will of God. They should first ask what would please God, and then take the course that is most pleasing to Him. Once they make a decision together according to the statutes, they should pray for it and act upon it. They will then be blessed by God. Many of our ministers are here today, and I ask them in particular to take this lesson to heart. This is not some man-made up thought. Our ministry is not something that can be done according to our own wishes. Rather, we must pray for it, decide together, and carry it out in unity. It is not something that we can do according to our own man-made thoughts.

In many aspects, we are still living according to our own wishes. That's why it's all the more important for us to learn about our God's statutes over this week. These statutes of God bring so much comfort, strength, and courage to us. They illuminate clearly for us the path that we should follow. Only when we have God's statutes in our hearts do we become bold and clear-sighted. Without knowing such good statutes, we cannot even know how to walk. Once God's statutes are set for us like this, then from this moment on, obedience is better than any offering. So I ask you to obey God. And I ask you to obey God knowing what His will is.

The Truth of Atonement

Let's now turn to what our Lord said in Exodus 34:18-20: *"The Feast of Unleavened Bread you shall keep. Seven days you shall eat unleavened bread, as I commanded you, in the appointed time of the month of Abib; for in the month of Abib you came out from Egypt. All that open the womb are Mine, and every male firstborn among your livestock, whether ox or sheep. But the firstborn of a donkey you shall redeem with a lamb. And if you will not redeem him, then you shall break his neck. All the firstborn of your sons you shall redeem. And none shall appear before Me empty-handed" (Exodus 34:18-20).* This is God's statute.

God said here that the firstborn of the sons of the Israelites and of a donkey must be redeemed with a lamb without fail. What statute did God set here? It is that if the people of Israel wanted to save the firstborn of a donkey and the firstborn of their sons, they had to take a lamb as their sacrifice of atonement and offer it to God as the price of life. This is the way of salvation set by God. We shouldn't believe according to just our own wishes. What, then, is the spiritual meaning of the firstborn of a donkey and the firstborn of the sons of the Israelites? It means none other than the following, if human beings really want to save and preserve their lives before God, they must pay the full price of life. In other words, because we were all born as sinners in God's sight, for us to be saved from all our sins, we must make atonement to God by paying the price of life without fail. Only then can we save our lives.

None of us can be born again to live unless the remission of sins is received and atonement is made with a lamb. No matter how meritorious and virtuous one might be, everyone must make atonement and receive the remission of sins. It's absolutely indispensable for all of us to receive the remission of sins. What will happen if the remission of sins is not received? God said here that He will kill the firstborn of a donkey. This is the very statute by which the firstborn is redeemed with a sacrificial lamb. By tradition, if the firstborn son dies, the genealogy of that family is considered to have ended. If we want to spare our lives before God, we must give up our stubbornness and offer a lamb as our sacrifice of atonement to Him according to His statutes. Put differently, we can be saved only through our faith in Jesus Christ, by acknowledging and believing wholeheartedly in the remission of sins that Jesus Christ has fulfilled for us.

God said here to break the firstborn of a donkey if it was not redeemed. Why did God say this? Why did He specifically mention the firstborn of a donkey? The donkey is the strongest of domesticated animals. When God spoke of the donkey along with the people of Israel, He was speaking of none other than us the strong-willed stubborn human beings. In God's sight, we human beings are like an unclean animal. Indeed, we are filthy even to ourselves. Human beings are so wicked that when Adam and Eve sinned against God and brought His curse upon themselves, they hid themselves from God and made all kinds of excuses to avoid the consequences of their sin. That's how shameless human beings are before God. They are so dishonorable and stubborn that they are no different from a donkey. This is probably man's most shameful aspect before God.

Let's think about God's statutes here. God has set the law of atonement in such a way that for us to receive the remission of sins, we must break down our own thoughts and wills, keep God's statutes, and believe in His Word. It is according to this way of salvation the remission of sins is received. We ought to obey God with all our hearts according to His statutes. We ought to confess to God, "Lord, Your way is right!"

The Lord chose such a way to save us from all our sins, and we can be saved only if we believe in these statutes. It is those who break down their own thoughts that receive the remission of God from Him. God said clearly here to break the neck of the firstborn of a donkey, right? Have you broken your neck? Many of you are nodding, but there still are some people who have not broken their necks. And there also are those who have not broken their necks completely yet. These are the people who have too much righteousness of their own. Such people are so stiff-necked that they find it nearly impossible to break their necks.

This means that even though they have been born again, they are not grateful enough and they still are way too self-righteous. They do whatever they want to do. They might have an excuse if this were out of their ignorance, but if they are walking according to their own wishes even as they know God's statutes, then God will break their necks without fail. This is what God meant by breaking the neck of a donkey. Do you know what causes us the most anxiety as we carry on with our lives of faith before God? It is the self-loathing that comes from thinking that we are not right, and that we have all gone astray. We think to ourselves, "God is right, and everything He has set for me is right. But what about "me"?" It's because of such thoughts that we find it so hard to admit that we are wrong, and that we are indeed sinners. However, God will surely break all those who are trying to establish their own righteous, as the neck of a donkey is broken. It's absolutely important for all of us to realize this.

The clear truth is that we have been saved because the only begotten Son of God offered Himself as our Lamb, and we must all believe in this truth exactly as it is. We must throw out our everything. We should have nothing of our own. We should have neither our own thoughts, nor our own wills, nor our own stubbornness, nor our own judgments. What is then left? There is only the blood of the Lamb who offered Himself in our place, the life of this Lamb. And the only thing left for us to do is follow and obey this Lamb wherever He leads us. We have nothing of our own left anymore. Yet, there still are far too many people hanging onto their own thoughts.

The fog comes up from the ground, and wetlands are much more prone to get foggy in the morning due to greater differences in the temperature. It's not good for people to be exposed to such a fog too much, as it can damage their respiratory system. It's also unhealthy for many plants. Most plants can't grow and bear fruit in a densely foggy area, as they cannot get enough sunlight. Like this, when we are all fogged up by our own thoughts, we must remember that they are all our own flawed thoughts that run counter to the statutes of God. Just as the fog is lifted when the wind blows, we must blow away all such thoughts of our own making with God's clear and unambiguous statutes. We must admit that we were already destined to be put to death, that we have to break ourselves completely like the neck of a donkey, that Jesus Christ died for such people like us in our place, and that we died with Jesus Christ when He died. And with this faith, we must live in unity according to the guidance of the Holy Spirit and the Church. This is what God's statutes demand from us. That is how each and every one of us ought to live.

Although it may seem that we have been trained sufficiently to live this kind of life, we still have many shortcomings. Sometimes, we feel like our self-respect is hurt, and we even get angry with God. For those grappling with such a struggle in their lives of faith, their hearts are hurting because they are being broken by God just as the firstborn of a donkey was broken. God Himself is breaking them. All of this is so unnecessary and sad, for if they just acknowledge God and obey Him, nothing but sunny days would await them and they can all follow the Lord with a bright smile. Despite this, some of you still think, "I know God is divine, but even so, how can He ignore me so much? I believe in God with all my heart, so how can He dismiss me, one of His own people? I also have my pride, and I have my ego as well."

What ego are you speaking of? How can we have any ego left when we had already died on the Cross? Is there any ego left? Is there such a thing as "I"? If there is such a thing as "I," then it can only mean that you have still not died with Christ. Despite the fact that our ego had already died, we still cling to our ego out of self-delusion. That's why we get angry. To put it bluntly, we get all sullen and lash out like a rabid dog. Some of us stew in our miserable and depressive sulk for months. We think it's so unfair and so insulting, and we feel we are being totally ignored. This happens because we are still wrapped in our own self-respect and ego. It's all part of breaking this ego down.

Our ego must be broken, or otherwise we cannot be used by God. Anyone whose ego remains intact has not received redemption from God. Unless one truly seeks to receive new life from the Lord and save his life, he will be broken just as the neck of a donkey was broken. For those of us who have received this new life from the Lord, our necks have already been broken. Our ego has already disappeared. Where is our ego? Where is the ego of our old selves? Where are our own thoughts? We were such wretched beings that had Jesus Christ not died for us, we would all have been cast to hell inevitably. Yet, for such wretched people like us, Jesus Christ shouldered our sins and died for us, and when He died, we had also died with Him. Faith is all about believing in Jesus according to God's rules, and that is the true faith.

Faith is all about accepting what God has done for us exactly as it is, and acknowledging and obeying this work of salvation. It's actually a blessing to have God rule over you. You should therefore obey Him rather than deciding everything for yourself. That is how you can be one with God and the born-again Church. However, for the Church to be established properly, we must first of all break our necks. Our Lord has broken our necks. He has saved us. He has put to death our everything. Despite this, some of us still insist on our own pride, being deceived by Satan into thinking that you have not died yet. Do you think you are suffering alone? That's all an illusion. We are no longer our old selves that have all gone.

When you admit all these things, you can then obey the Lord in obedience and guide your brothers and sisters properly. When the brothers and sisters following in your footsteps struggle with their inability to break themselves and as a result suffer from it, you can say to them, "It's all in your own mind. Your ego is no longer there. It's just your own conscience and your own stubbornness." What does the Word of God say? It says that our old selves are gone. Even though we get angry and insist on our own way stubbornly when our old selves are ignored, in reality, our old selves no longer exist. Break yourself once first. Someone who broke himself once can do it again easily. Like everything else, you need training for this. It is no different from teaching your kids to greet the elderly politely. If your kids don't greet the elderly in your neighborhood, you would correct them and force them to greet properly. They would then eventually learn how to greet the elderly properly. Likewise, if you find it difficult to break yourself, you need to train yourself even if you have to force yourself.

The same principle applies to your life of faith also. The first step is always the most difficult, but once you take this step and get used to it, from then on you can follow the statutes of God easily. It's always this first step that is the most difficult to take. You need to train yourself for this. Of course, it would be easier if there were someone to train you at first, rather than training all by yourself. If you can learn from your righteous Church leaders, it would be easier for you to break yourself and follow God's statutes. If you can say 'Yes' just once to your Church leaders when they ask you to do the one thing that you dislike the most, then from then you will have no trouble living by God's statutes. I cannot emphasize enough just how important it is for you to be one with God. Would you then still insist on your own way stubbornly? You must walk according to God's statutes. You must realize just how important these statutes are. Someone who knows the statutes is bound to be spiritual enlightened. In contrast, someone who does not know the statutes is bound to fall into a great deal of confusion, and go astray without even realizing it. Such a person can even turn into an enemy of the Lord and the righteous.

We have been redeemed according to the statutes of God. We must therefore preach the gospel according to the statutes. If you don't know the statutes, and instead just insist on your own way stubbornly, then it's impossible for you to preach according to the statutes. You will end up preaching according to your own wishes, or not be able to preach at all. Nowadays, there are so many people claiming to be preaching the gospel. Setting aside the clueless, even among those who are renowned for serving God well, there are countless people who lack God's statutes. Whatever the Scripture says, everyone ought to follow it exactly as it is. Whatever God told us to keep and practice, we ought to keep and practice according to His statutes, just as God said in today's Scripture reading, *"You shall keep My statutes, and perform them. I am the LORD who sanctifies you" (Leviticus 20:8).*

We must walk according to how God has told us to walk, casting aside our own thoughts and our own desires. It doesn't matter even if you fail to reach your goal. If you have done exactly according to God's rules and walked according to His statutes, then that's all that matters. It's then that the work of God unfold, and it's then that your end can be greater even though your beginning may be small. In God's sight, it is better for you to follow His will in obedience even slightly than achieving something great according to your own stubbornness. You must never allow yourself to turn into someone who does everything all on his own, someone who loves and leaves at his own whim, someone who leads his life of faith in whatever way he wants. It's absolutely not the case that you can do whatever you want to do once you receive the remission of sins. If you do this, you will be ruined without fail. You will perish for sure.

Everyone knows about the parable of the prodigal son, right? In that parable, the younger son left his home only to face all kinds of troubles. This happened because he did not live according to God's statutes. All people can become God's people. Jesus has blotted out everyone's sins with the gospel of the water and the Spirit. However, unless we believe in the gospel of the water and the Spirit as God has determined, we can neither become His people nor be saved; and unless we obey God according to His statutes, we cannot live amid the blessings that God has prepared for us either. If all these blessings are out of your reach, then it is only because you have not lived in obedience to God according to the statutes He has set for you.

Let's turn to Exodus 15:22-26 here: *"So Moses brought Israel from the Red Sea; then they went out into the Wilderness of Shur. And they went three days in the wilderness and found no water. Now when they came to Marah, they could not drink the waters of Marah, for they were bitter. Therefore the name of it was called Marah. And the people complained against Moses, saying, 'What shall we drink?' So he cried out to the LORD, and the LORD showed him a tree. When he cast it into the waters, the waters were made sweet. There He made a statute and an ordinance for them, and there He tested them, and said, 'If you diligently heed the voice of the LORD your God and do what is right in His sight, give ear to His commandments and keep all His statutes, I will put none of the diseases on you which I have brought on the Egyptians. For I am the LORD who heals you."* Amen!

God is saying to us here, *"I am the LORD who heals you."* God is indeed our Healer. I don't usually quote this passage as it has been misinterpreted and abused by many unscrupulous liars claiming to have some sort of supernatural power to heal. That's not what this passage is about. Rather, it teaches us that the Lord has given us His statutes for our everyday lives as Christians. Our Lord said here, *"So Moses brought Israel from the Red Sea; then they went out into the Wilderness of Shur. And they went three days in the wilderness and found no water. Now when they came to Marah, they could not drink the waters of Marah, for they were bitter."* The people of Israel then blamed God for this predicament. God clearly told us to keep His statutes. The statutes are there to be observed. Even though these statutes may be bitter to our tongues, they must be kept without fail. As we carry on with our lives of faith, sometimes we hear a few words that sting our ears. However, the Lord told us clearly to observe the rituals of the Passover Day, and to eat bitter herbs along with the meat of a lamb.

I will hold back from discussing an issue that might be too complex for you right now. But there are certain things that all of us must know without fail in the sight of our Lord. Firstly, the very first statute for our everyday lives is serving God. Secondly, we must deny our own thoughts and judgments and instead follow God's statutes. Regardless of whether we think it's right or wrong, we must deny our own thoughts, know what God's statutes are, and obey them exactly as they are. Thirdly, we must live according to these statutes of God. The Lord is telling us clearly here to know the statutes He has given us and live our according to them.

What is our Lord saying to us? He is saying, *"If you diligently heed the voice of the LORD your God and do what is right in His sight, give ear to His commandments and keep all His statutes, I will put none of the diseases on you which I have brought on the Egyptians. For I am the LORD who heals you."* It's absolutely indispensable for us holy Christians to remember that diseases and all other curses stem from violating the statutes of God and His commandments. Let me remind you once again what our Lord said, *"If you diligently heed the voice of the LORD your God and do what is right in His sight, give ear to His commandments and keep all His statutes, I will put none of the diseases on you which I have brought on the Egyptians. For I am the* LORD *who heals you."* Just as God has allowed thorns and thistles in this world, He has also allowed suffering, diseases, and tribulations. That all such things are faced by everyone as the general rule set by God.

Put differently, God allows diseases and tribulations to come to everyone, regardless of whether one has been born again or not. However, our God promised that if we observe and practice His commandments and statutes in His sight, then He will remove from us all the diseases that He put on the Egyptians, reveal Himself to us as the God of healing, and heal us all. Do you believe in this amazing grace of God? Amen!

Herein lies the very reason why we must observe God's statutes and commandments. It is none other than to put on God's blessings. If we ignore the statutes of God and His commandments, boldness will disappear from our hearts. Just as 1 John 5:14 says, *"Now this is the confidence that we have in Him, that if we ask anything according to His will, He hears us,"* God will do everything as we believe. That is why it's so important for us to ask God properly according to His will and live according to His statutes. It's because God said that He will bless such people.

The question before us is this, now that we have received the remission of sins, will we live in suffering and curses, or will we live clothed in God's blessings by keeping His statutes and carry out the Lord's work? The answer will depend entirely on whether or not we observe God's statutes. If we keep God's statutes, we can all receive all the blessings of God in our lives and then go to His presence. This is what God's statutes and commandments are all about. The reason why I have spent so much time this week on the statues and commandments of God, and why I have emphasized them so much, that is, what God has set for us, is to illuminate the way of blessings for you. This is the Law. The Law is the Word of God, and God has given this Law to us His people because it is absolutely indispensable to us.

God has given us these statutes of the Law so that we would realize our sins and distinguish between good and evil. That's why we have been sharing the Word of God on His statutes for so long now. It's because our knowledge of the statutes of God is too weak and shallow, and therefore we need to examine them in much more depth and in detail. When we really think about it, we would realize what a wonderful blessing it is that God has given us such statutes. If God had not given us His statutes, if He had not established the Law for us, and if He had not taught us clearly how we ought to live to be saved, then our lives would have been utterly ruined. Words cannot describe just how blessed God's statutes are.

We ought to thank the Lord always for giving us His statutes and teaching us the right way to lead our lives. If we had come up with our own rules, we would have accomplished nothing. But thankfully, the Lord has personally set the rules for us. It is all by the grace of God that He has set His statutes to govern us, teaching us how we ought to live, how we ought to believe, and how we ought to receive the remission of sins. And by this grace, God has saved us according to these statutes. So I ask you all to keep God's statues and practice them, just as God commanded us to do so. Even though we have many shortcomings, Jesus Christ already bore all our sins. Therefore, despite our shortcomings, if we follow the God-established statutes and do everything with one heart united with the Church, the Body of God, then God will surely reveal Himself to us, bless us, and guide us all. Precisely because we are God's people, we must keep His statutes in our lives. ✉

HAVE YOU TRULY BEEN BORN AGAIN OF WATER AND THE SPIRIT?

PAUL C. JONG

Among many Christian books written about being born again, this is the first book of our time to preach the gospel of the water and the Spirit in strict accordance with the Scriptures. Man can't enter the Kingdom of Heaven without being born again of water and the Spirit. To be born again means that a sinner is saved from all his lifelong sins by believing in the baptism of Jesus and His blood of the Cross. Let's believe in the gospel of the water and the Spirit and enter the Kingdom of Heaven as the righteous who have no sin.

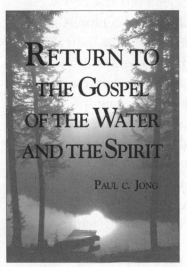

RETURN TO THE GOSPEL OF THE WATER AND THE SPIRIT

PAUL C. JONG

Let's return to the gospel of the water and the Spirit. Theology and doctrines themselves can't save us. However, many Christians still follow them, and consequently have not been born again yet. This book clearly tells us what mistakes theology and doctrines have made and how to believe in Jesus in the most proper way.

The Fail-safe Way for You to Receive the Holy Spirit

In Christianity, the most significantly discussed issue is salvation from sins and the indwelling of the Holy Spirit. However, few people have the exact knowledge of these two topics. Nevertheless, in reality people say that they believe in Jesus Christ while they are ignorant of true redemption and the Holy Spirit.

Do you know the true gospel that makes you receive the Holy Spirit? If you want to ask God for the indwelling of the Holy Spirit, then you must first know the gospel of the water and the Spirit and have faith in it. This book will certainly lead all Christians worldwide to receive the Holy Spirit through the remission of all their sins.

Our LORD Who Becomes the Righteousness of God (I) & (II)

The teachings in these books will satisfy the thirst in your heart. Today's Christians continue to live while not knowing the true solution to the personal sins that they are committing daily. Do you know what God's righteousness is? The author hopes that you will ask yourself this question and believe in God's righteousness, which is dealt with in detail in these books.

The Doctrines of Predestination, Justification, and Incremental Sanctification are the major Christian doctrines, which brought only confusion and emptiness into the souls of believers. But, dear Christians, now is the time when you must continue in the Truth which you have learned and been assured of.

These books will provide your soul with a great understanding and lead it to peace. The author wants you to possess the blessing of knowing God's righteousness.

IS THE AGE OF THE ANTICHRIST, MARTYRDOM, RAPTURE AND THE MILLENNIAL KINGDOM COMING? (I)

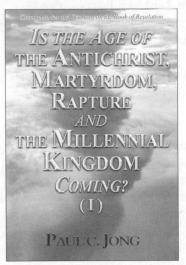

After the 9/11 terrorist attacks, traffic to "www.raptureready.com," an Internet site providing information on the end times, is reported to have increased to over 8 million hits, and according to a joint survey by CNN and TIME, over 59% of the Americans now believe in apocalyptic eschatology.

Responding to such demands of the time, the author provides a clear exposition of the key themes of the Book of Revelation, including the coming Antichrist, the martyrdom of the saints and their rapture, the Millennial Kingdom, and the New Heaven and Earth-all in the context of the whole Scripture and under the guidance of the Holy Spirit.

This book provides verse-by-verse commentaries on the Book of Revelation supplemented by the author's inspired sermons. Anyone who reads this book will come to grasp all the plans that God has in store for this world.

IS THE AGE OF THE ANTICHRIST, MARTYRDOM, RAPTURE AND THE MILLENNIAL KINGDOM COMING? (II)

Most Christians today believe in the theory of pre-tribulation rapture. Because they believe in this false doctrine teaching them that they would be lifted before the coming of the Great Tribulation of seven years, they are leading idle religious lives steeped in complacency.

But the rapture of the saints will occur only after the plagues of the seven trumpets run their course until the sixth plague is all poured-that is, the rapture will happen after the Antichrist emerges amidst global chaos and the born-again saints are martyred, and when the seventh trumpet is blown. It is at this time that Jesus would descend from Heaven, and the resurrection and rapture of the born-again saints would occur (1 Thessalonians 4:16-17).

The righteous who were born again by believing in "the gospel of the water and the Spirit" will be resurrected and take part in the Rapture, and thus become heirs to the Millennial Kingdom and the eternal Kingdom of Heaven, but the sinners who were unable to participate in this first resurrection will face the great punishment of the seven bowls poured by God and be cast into the eternal fire of hell.

The TABERNACLE: A Detailed Portrait of Jesus Christ (I)

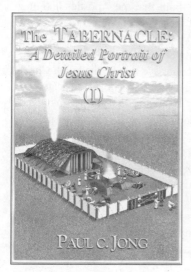

How can we find out the truth hidden in the Tabernacle? Only by knowing the gospel of the water and the Spirit, the real substance of the Tabernacle, can we correctly understand and know the answer to this question.

In fact, the blue, purple, and scarlet thread and the fine woven linen manifested in the gate of the Tabernacle's court show us the works of Jesus Christ in the New Testament's time that have saved the mankind. In this way, the Old Testament's Word of the Tabernacle and the Word of the New Testament are closely and definitely related to each other, like fine woven linen. But, unfortunately, this truth has been hidden for a long time to every truth seeker in Christianity.

Coming to this earth, Jesus Christ was baptized by John and shed His blood on the Cross. Without understanding and believing in the gospel of the water and the Spirit, none of us can ever find out the truth revealed in the Tabernacle. We must now learn this truth of the Tabernacle and believe in it. We all need to realize and believe in the truth manifested in the blue, purple, and scarlet thread and the fine woven linen of the gate of the Tabernacle's court.

The TABERNACLE: A Detailed Portrait of Jesus Christ (II)

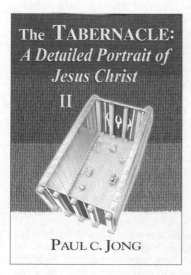

As God had commanded Moses to build the Tabernacle in the Old Testament, in the New Testament, God wants us to also build a Sanctuary in each of our hearts so that He may dwell in us. The material of faith with which we can build this Sanctuary in our hearts is the Word of the gospel of the water and the Spirit. With this gospel of the water and the Spirit, we must wash away all our sins and be cleansed. By telling us to build Him a Sanctuary, God is telling us to empty our hearts and believe in the gospel of the water and the Spirit. We must all cleanse our hearts by believing in the gospel of the water and the Spirit.

When we cleanse away all the sins of our hearts by believing in this gospel Truth, God then comes to dwell in them. It is by believing in this true gospel that you can build the holy Temples in your hearts. It is highly likely that until now, at least some of you have probably been offering your prayers of repentance to cleanse your hearts, trying to build the Temples by yourselves. But now is the time for you to abandon this false faith and be transformed by the renewing of your minds by believing in the gospel of the water and the Spirit.

The Elementary Principles of CHRIST

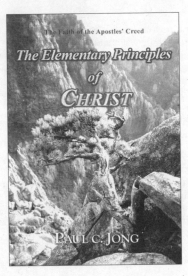

We must have the faith that the Apostles had and believe as they did, for their faith and beliefs came from the Holy Spirit. The Apostles believed in Jesus Christ, His Father, and the Holy Spirit as their God.

The Apostle Paul confessed that he died with Christ and was brought to new life with Him. He became an instrument of God by believing that he was baptized into Jesus Christ (Galatians 3:27). In God's gospel are found the baptism that Jesus received, the blood that He shed on the Cross, and the gift of the Holy Spirit that He has bestowed on everyone who believes in this true gospel of the water and the Spirit.

Do you know and believe in this original gospel? This is the very gospel that the Apostles had also believed. We, too, must therefore all believe in the gospel of the water and the Spirit.

The Gospel of Matthew (I), (II), (III), (IV), (V), (VI)

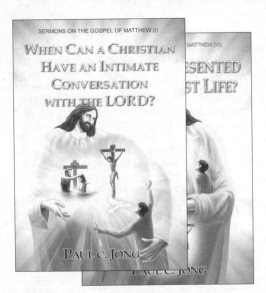

There are countless new Christians throughout the world, who have just been born again by believing in the gospel of the water and the Spirit that we have been spreading. We are indeed yearning to feed on the bread of life to them. But it is difficult for them to have fellowship with us in the true gospel, for they are all far away from us.

Therefore, to meet the spiritual needs of these people of Jesus Christ, the King of kings, The author proclaims that those who have received the remission of their sins by believing in the Word of Jesus Christ, must feed on His pure Word in order to defend their faith and sustain their spiritual lives. The sermons in these books have been prepared as new bread of life that will nourish the born-again to edify their spiritual growth.

Through His Church and servants, God will continue to provide you with this bread of life. May God's blessings be on all those who have been born again of water and the Spirit, who desires to have true spiritual fellowship with us in Jesus Christ.

The First Epistle of John (I) & (II)

He who believes that Jesus, who is God and the Savior, came by the gospel of the water and the Spirit to deliver all sinners from their sins, is saved from all his sins, and becomes a child of God the Father.

The First Epistle of John states that Jesus, who is God, came to us by the gospel of the water and the Spirit, and that He is the Son of God the Father. The Book, in other words, mostly emphasizes that Jesus is God (1 John 5:20), and concretely testifies the gospel of the water and the Spirit in chapter 5.

We must not hesitate to believe that Jesus Christ is God and to follow Him.

Sermons on Galatians: From Physical Circumcision to the Doctrine of Repentance (I) & (II)

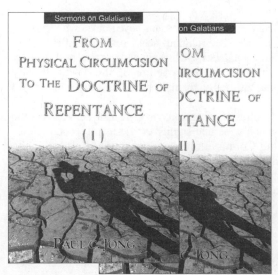

Today's Christianity has turned into merely a world religion. Most Christians nowadays live in a situation of being sinners because they haven't been born again by spiritual faith. It is because they have only relied on Christian doctrines without being aware of the gospel of the water and the Spirit until now.

Therefore, now is the time for you to know the spiritual fallacies of the circumcisionists and keep distance from such faith. You have to know the contradictoriness of the prayers of repentance. Now is the time for you to stand firmer than ever on the gospel of the water and the Spirit.

If you haven't believed in this true gospel so far, you have to believe in our Savior who came to us by the gospel of the water and the Spirit even now. Now, you have to be complete Christians with the faith of believing in the gospel Truth of the water and the Spirit.

The Love of God Revealed through Jesus,
The Only Begotten Son (I), (II), (III)

It is written, "No one has seen God at any time. The only begotten Son, who is in the bosom of the Father, He has declared Him" (John 1:18).

How perfectly did Jesus reveal the love of God to us! How perfectly did Jesus deliver us! What perfect Truth of salvation is the gospel of the water and the Spirit! We have never regretted receiving our salvation through our faith in Jesus, who came by water and blood (1 John 5:6).

Now, we have become His sinless people. Whoever believes in the gospel of the water and the Spirit can receive the eternal remission of sins and earn eternal life.

Eat My Flesh And Drink My Blood

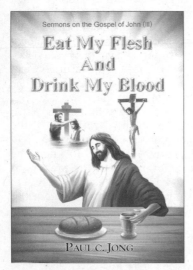

Until now, most Christians have not known the Truth, but only inherited religious acts. From the gospel to Holy Communion, today's Christianity maintains its orthodoxy not through the knowledge of the Truth, but by emphasizing only formal procedures and consecrated rites.

As a result, when today's Christians come across the bread and wine that signify the flesh and blood of Jesus during Communion, they are thankful only for the sacrifice of His blood, and they can't help but remain completely ignorant of the fact that Christ took upon Himself all their sins once and for all by being baptized by John the Baptist.

Therefore, I admonish all Christians throughout the whole world to learn, even from now on, what the flesh and blood of Jesus mean within the gospel of the water and the Spirit, to believe in it, and to thereby receive their salvation and also partake in Holy Communion with the right faith.

The Relationship Between the Ministry of JESUS and That of JOHN the BAPTIST Recorded in the Four Gospels

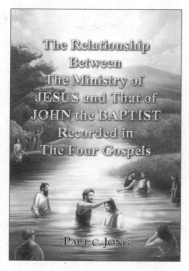

Do you perhaps think that it doesn't matter whether there needs to be the ministry of John the Baptist or not? You must believe according to the written Word of God. We must understand and believe in the ministry of John the Baptist within the frame of the ministry of Jesus Christ. John the Baptist in the New Testament was the prophet Elijah promised to be sent down to this earth according to the Book of Malachi chapter 4, verses 4-5. As the prophet Elijah to come, John the Baptist was born six months before Jesus, and he was the one who passed on the sins of this world at once by giving Jesus the baptism at the Jordan River at the age of thirty. Thus, we must become the recipients of God's blessing by knowing the ministry of John the Baptist and accepting the ministry of Jesus Christ.

THE WILL OF THE HOLY TRINITY FOR HUMAN BEINGS

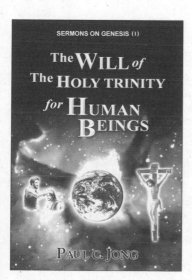

Through the Book of Genesis, God wants us to realize His good intentions toward us. Where is God's will for us revealed? It is revealed in the gospel Truth of the water and the Spirit that God accomplished through Jesus Christ. We must come into this good intention of God by faith, manifested in the gospel of the water and the Spirit. To do so, when we consider God's Word, we need to cast aside our existing carnal thoughts we have had, and believe in God's Word exactly as it is. All of us must throw away our mistaken knowledge accumulated until now, and open our spiritual eyes by placing our faith in the righteousness of God.

The Fall of Man and the Perfect Salvation of God

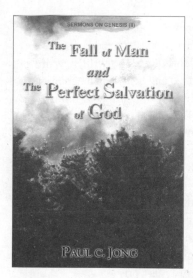

In the Book of Genesis, the purpose for which God created us is contained. When architects design a building or artists draw a painting, they first conceive the work that would be completed in their minds before they actually begin working on their project. Just like this, our God also had our salvation of mankind in His mind even before He created the heavens and the earth, and He made Adam and Eve with this purpose in mind. And God needed to explain to us the domain of Heaven, which is not seen by our eyes of the flesh, by drawing an analogy to the domain of the earth that we can all see and understand.

Even before the foundation of the world, God wanted to save mankind perfectly by giving the gospel of the water and the Spirit to everyone's heart. So although all human beings were made out of dust, they must learn and know the gospel Truth of the water and the Spirit to benefit their own souls. If people continue to live without knowing the dominion of Heaven, they will lose not only the things of the earth, but also everything that belongs to Heaven.

Heretics, Who Followed the Sins of Jeroboam (I) & (II)

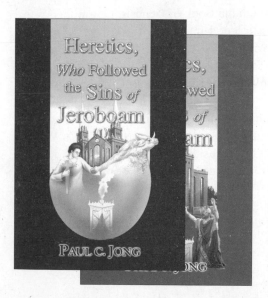

Christians today do not know what the gospel Truth of the water and the Spirit that the Lord has made and given us is. Thus, they continue to believe in the doctrines of Christianity and not the gospel of the water and the Spirit. For that reason, the fact of the matter is that despite their claim of having faith in Jesus, they continue to believe in and follow golden calves.

We must discern those that worship golden calves as God within Christianity. And by coming back before God of the Truth, we must offer the sacrifices of righteousness to God. The sacrifice that God receives with rejoice is the sacrifice of righteousness that people offer by faith after having received the remission of sin by having faith in the gospel of the water and the Spirit. Before God, you must seriously think about whether or not you are offering the sacrifice of God-given righteousness by the faith of believing in the gospel of the water and the Spirit.

The Lord's Prayer : Misinterpretations and Truth

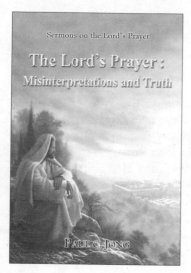

In order to interpret the Lord's Prayer correctly, we must first correctly understand the gospel of the water and the Spirit, which was spoken to us by the Lord. We have Truth in us when we not only know and understand the gospel of the water and the Spirit but also believe it with our hearts. The true gospel, which we believe in, has led us so far, so that we can lead truly faithful lives that the Lord wants from us in the Lord's Prayer.

Exegesis on the Book of ROMANS (I)

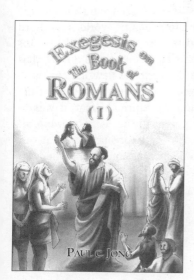

The righteousness of God is transparent. God's righteousness cannot be substituted by anything. That is because His righteousness is different from the righteousness of man. We need to know what God's righteousness is, and we need to believe in it.

God's righteousness is fundamentally different from human righteousness. The righteousness of mankind is like a filthy rag, but the righteousness of God is like a brilliant pearl shining forever. God's righteousness is the Truth that is absolutely needed by every sinner, transcending all ages.

HAVE YOU MET JESUS WITH THE GOSPEL OF THE WATER AND THE SPIRIT?

It is written, "No one has seen God at any time. The only begotten Son, who is in the bosom of the Father, He has declared Him" (John 1:18).

How perfectly did Jesus reveal the love of God to us! How perfectly did Jesus deliver us! What perfect Truth of salvation is the gospel of the water and the Spirit! We have never regretted receiving our salvation through our faith in Jesus, who came by water and blood (1 John 5:6).

Now, we have become His sinless people. Whoever believes in the gospel of the water and the Spirit can receive the eternal remission of sins and earn eternal life.

Sermons on the Gospel of Luke (I), (II), (III), (IV), (V), (VI), (VII)

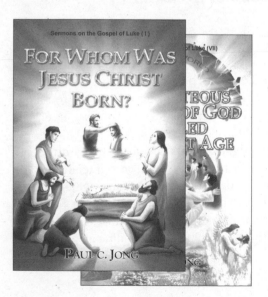

It is Jesus Christ who moves the entire history of this world. Our Lord came to this earth to save all humans from the sins of the world, and He has become the bread of new life for those of us who believe in the gospel of the water and the Spirit. In fact, it was to give this new life to us, who were all destined to hell for our sins that our Lord came looking for you and me.

No More Chaos, Void or Darkness Now (I) & (II)

Although we may be powerless and because the Word of God has power, when the Word falls to the ground it bears fruit without fail. Further, because the Word of God is alive we can see for ourselves that it is the same today and tomorrow, and forever unchanging. Unlike the words of man, God's Word never changes, for it is ever faithful. When God speaks, He fulfills exactly according to His Words.

For the Word of God has power, so when God said, "Let there be light," there was light, and when He said, "Let there be a greater light and a lesser light," it was fulfilled just as He had commanded.

THE DIFFERENCE BETWEEN ABEL'S FAITH AND CAIN'S FAITH

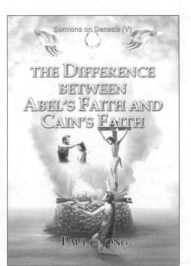

Whenever we stand before the presence of God to glorify Him, we should not approach Him through some religious rituals, but instead we have to approach Him by trusting in what He has done for us and thanking Him for His love. Only then does God accept our worship and pour the Holy Spirit on us abundantly.

FOR THE LOST SHEEP (I) & (II)

What God wants to do is to make us into His children by making us born again through the gospel of the water and the Spirit.

We humans are born as God's creations first, but if we receive the remission of sins by believing in the gospel of the water and the Spirit, we are born again as the children of God. This means that, after the Lord came and remitted all our sins, we who were blind could now obtain our sight.

WISDOM OF THE PRIMITIVE GOSPEL

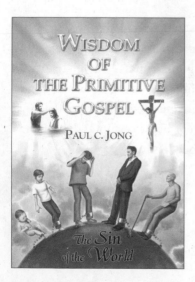

The primitive gospel is the Truth of salvation that's absolutely indispensable to everyone. Transcending all denominations, this primitive gospel will clearly teach every Christian how God's blessings could be bestowed on them. This true gospel will now fill your heart with God's overflowing love. And it will be the most precious gift to all your loved ones.

BE A GOSPEL WITNESS WHO SAVES
THE HUMAN RACE FROM DESTRUCTION

Mankind, who had eaten the fruit of the knowledge of good and evil, came to have the different standard for good and evil from God's. Then, which is correct, God's Word or our judgment? Our standard is always relative and selfish. Therefore we should cast away our own ideas and simply trust and follow God's Word focusing on "What does the Word of God say?" Ignoring God's Word and seeking self-righteousness is Cain's faith and religious belief. Abel put his faith in the Word of God he heard from his father, Adam, and offered the firstborn of his flock and of their fat. But self-conceited Cain brought an offering of the fruit of the ground to the Lord. God accepted Abel's offering but refused Cain's offering. It is God's lesson that faith in man-made religions cannot bring salvation.

THOSE WHO POSSESS ABRAHAM'S FAITH

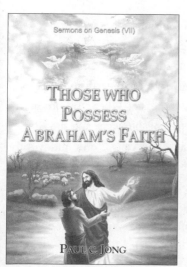

There are two kinds of righteousness in this world which are constantly in conflict and struggle with each another; these are the righteousness of God and the righteousness of man. Although God's righteousness faces many obstacles, it always prevails over the righteousness of man and leads us to the victorious way. That's because the Word of God is almighty. Because God's almighty power is with us, we are able to taste His blessings, for the Word of God has the power to reach our hearts, thoughts and souls, and brings all His blessings to us.

WHAT SHOULD WE STRIVE TO BELIEVE AND PREACH?

The Gospel of Mark testifies that Jesus Christ is the Son of God and God Himself. And it also testifies that He is our Savior. So we can see the writer of the Gospel of Mark bearing witness of Jesus forcefully, testifying that He is the very God and our Savior. This is why I would like to bear witness of this Jesus Christ who is manifested in the Gospel of Mark as much as possible based on the gospel of the water and the Spirit. What is obvious is that the core Truth of Christianity is found in the gospel of the water and the Spirit. Jesus said to Nicodemus, "Most assuredly, I say to you, unless one is born of water and the Spirit, he cannot enter the kingdom of God" (John 3:5).

FROM THIS CORRUPTED WORLD TO HEAVEN ABOVE

We must open our spiritual eyes and clearly see the wonders and beauty of this world. This is possible only when we escape from darkness through the Lord and live out our faith with the conviction that we have no sin. When you are born again through the gospel of the water and the Spirit and open your spiritual eyes, your life in this world will be more enjoyable than anyone else's life. So you must escape from darkness and dwell in the light, taking and enjoying everything the Lord has given you in your life, for the Word of God says, *"Let the hearts of those rejoice who seek the LORD!" (Psalm 105:3).*

THE BLESSING OF FAITH RECEIVED WITH THE HEART

This special day of amnesty, when the remission of sins and the blessings of faith are received by believing in the gospel of the water and the Spirit with the heart, is found in no country in this world, but it is the greatest holiday that can be celebrated together with people from any country in the world. Today is the day you can receive the remission of sins, and it is the only common holiday celebrated together with God's people from all over the world.

The TABERNACLE (III): A Prefiguration of The Gospel of The Water and the Spirit

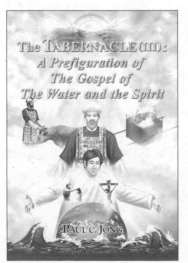

All Christians should stand firm in the faith of the gospel of the water and the Spirit. They will then understand the gospel of the water and the Spirit through the revelations which are manifested in the Tabernacle system as written in the Old Testament. They also can be sure of having received the remission of sins by faith. If you have as yet not possessed such faith, you need to strive to get it as soon as possible.

You should receive the remission of sins first if you want the Holy Spirit to abide in your heart. To do so, you need to put your faith in the righteousness of God fulfilled by the Lord. This is the only way the Holy Spirit can dwell in your heart.

WHAT GOD IS SAYING TO US THROUGH THE EPISTLE TO THE EPHESIANS

Today God has founded His Church on the faith of the believers in the gospel of the water and the Spirit. God's Church is the gathering of those who have been saved by believing in the gospel of the water and the Spirit. Therefore, if your hearts now have faith in the gospel of the water and the Spirit, you can then lead the true life of faith. Such a life of faith is possible only in God's Church. Furthermore, only such faith qualifies us to live forever in the Kingdom of the Lord. Through this faith we must receive the love of salvation and all the spiritual blessings of Heaven from God the Father, Jesus Christ and the Holy Spirit.

HOW CAN YOU STRENGTHEN YOUR FAITH?

Every sinner must now believe in the genuine gospel. The God-given gospel of salvation is the gospel of the water and the Spirit that is manifested in the righteousness of God. The writer of the Book of Hebrews is trying to correct your misguided faith. Therefore, our faith needs to be deep rooted in the foundation of the gospel of the water and the Spirit. Those who are standing sure-footed on this absolute gospel Truth abide most certainly in the faith in the righteousness of Jesus Christ.

SERMONS FOR THOSE WHO HAVE BECOME OUR COWORKERS (I), (II), (III), (IV)

This book is a collection of sermons that have been written to direct our fellow coworkers and saints and to show them how to lead a life as a true servant of God. For this reason, these books are entitled *"Sermons for Those Who Have Become Our Coworkers."*

The author earnestly desires to share fellowship with coworkers within the faith, those who believe wholeheartedly in the righteousness of Christ, excluding personal interests. He does really desire this because he has met them by faith in the Lord's righteousness and they are also preaching it now.

ARE YOU NOW LIVING AS THE OBJECT OF GOD'S AFFECTION?

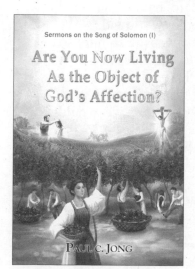

If you want to experience the Lord's love in your life always, listen closely to His voice. If you want to be loved by the Lord in your ministry, accept the God-given gospel of the water and the Spirit into your heart and then carry out the Lord's work. The Lord loves us precisely because we believe in and serve the gospel of the water and the Spirit. Our Lord cannot help but love whoever believes in His gospel of the water and the Spirit and serves Him faithfully to spread this gospel all over the world.

Paul C. Jong's Christian books have been translated into 76 major languages at this point: Afrikaans, Albanian, Arabic, Asante, Bengali, Bulgarian, Burmese, Cebuano, Chichewa, Chin, Chinese, Croatian, Czech, Danish, Dioula, Dutch, English, Fongbe, French, Georgian, German, Greek, Gujarati, Hebrew, Hindi, Hungarian, Indonesian, Iranian, Italian, Japanese, Javanese, Kannada, Khmer, Kirghiz, Kirundi, Kissi, Latvian, Luganda, Luo, Madi, Malagasy, Malayalam, Marathi, Mindat, Mizo, Mongolian, Nepali, Oriya, Polish, Portuguese, Punjabi, Romanian, Russian, Serbian, Shona, Slovak, Slovene, Spanish, Swahili, Swedish, Tagalog, Taiwanese, Tamil, Telugu, Thai, Turkish, Ukrainian, Urdu, Vietnamese, and Zou. They are also available now through our free e-book service.

E-book is digital book designed for you to feel a printed book on screen. You can read it easily on your PC monitor in your native language after downloading the viewer software and a text file. Feel free to visit our web site at http://www.nlmission.com or http://www.bjnewlife.org to download our e-books, and you will get the most remarkable Christian e-books absolutely for free.

And, would you like to take part in having our free Christian books known to more people worldwide? We would be very thankful if you link your website to ours so that many people get an opportunity to meet Jesus Christ through our inspired Christian books. Please visit our site at http://www.bjnewlife.org/english/about/take_banners.php to take our banners to your website. In addition, we would also be very grateful if you introduce our website to the webmasters around you for adding our link.

The New Life Mission
Contact: John Shin, General Secretary
E-mail: newlife@bjnewlife.org

Memo

Worldwide websites of

 The New Life Mission

Please find your vernacular websites below.
You can download Christian e-books and request Christian books for free.
Feel free to visit our websites below right now!

A
www.nlmafghanistan.com
www.nlmafrikaans.com
www.nlmalbania.com
www.nlmamharic.com
www.nlmangola.com
www.nlmarabemirates.com
www.nlmarabic.com
www.nlmargentina.com
www.nlmarmenia.com
www.nlmaruba.com
www.nlmaustralia.com
www.nlmaustria.com

B
www.nlmbahamas.com
www.nlmbahrain.com
www.nlmbangladesh.com
www.nlmbelarus.com
www.nlmbelgium.com
www.nlmbengali.com
www.nlmbenin.com
www.nlmbhutan.com
www.nlmbolivia.com
www.nlmbotswana.com
www.nlmbrasil.com
www.nlmbriton.com
www.nlmbrunei.com
www.nlmbulgalia.com
www.nlmburkinafaso.com
www.nlmburundi.com

C
www.nlmcameroon.com
www.nlmcanada.com
www.nlmcebuano.com
www.nlmchichewa.com
www.nlmchile.com
www.nlmchin.com

www.nlmchina.com
www.nlmcolombia.com
www.nlmcongo.com
www.nlmcostarica.com
www.nlmcotedivoire.com
www.nlmcroatia.com
www.nlmczech.com

D
www.nlmdenmark.com
www.nlmdioula.com
www.nlmdominica.com
www.nlmdrcongo.com
www.nlmdutch.com

E
www.nlmecuador.com
www.nlmegypt.com
www.nlmelsalvador.com
www.nlmequatorialguinea.com
www.nlmethiopia.com

F
www.nlmfinland.com
www.nlmfrance.com
www.nlmfrench.com

G
www.nlmgabon.com
www.nlmgeorgian.com
www.nlmgerman.com
www.nlmgermany.com
www.nlmghana.com
www.nlmgreek.com
www.nlmgrenada.com
www.nlmguatemala.com
www.nlmgujarati.com

H
www.nlmhaiti.com
www.nlmhindi.com
www.nlmholland.com
www.nlmhonduras.com
www.nlmhungary.com

Turn over

Worldwide websites of
 The New Life Mission

I
www.nlm-india.com
www.nlmindonesia.com
www.nlmiran.com
www.nlmiraq.com
www.nlmisrael.com
www.nlmitaly.com

J
www.nlmjamaica.com
www.nlmjapan.com
www.nlmjavanese.com

K
www.nlmkannada.com
www.nlmkazakhstan.com
www.nlmkenya.com
www.nlmkhmer.com
www.nlmkinyarwanda.com
www.nlmkirghiz.com
www.nlmkirundi.com
www.nlmkorea.com

L
www.nlmlatvia.com
www.nlmluganda.com
www.nlmluo.com

M
www.nlmmadi.com
www.nlmmalagasy.com
www.nlmmalayalam.com
www.nlmmalaysia.com
www.nlmmarathi.com
www.nlmmauritius.com
www.nlmmexico.com
www.nlmmindat.com
www.nlmmizo.com
www.nlmmoldova.com
www.nlmmongolia.com
www.nlmmyanmar.com

N
www.nlmnepal.com
www.nlmnewzealand.com
www.nlmnigeria.com
www.nlmnorthkorea.com
www.nlmnorway.com

P
www.nlmpakistan.com
www.nlmpanama.com
www.nlmperu.com
www.nlmphilippines.com
www.nlmpoland.com

www.nlmportugal.com
www.nlmportuguese.com
www.nlmprcongo.com

Q
www.nlmqatar.com

R
www.nlmromania.com
www.nlmrussia.com
www.nlmrwanda.com

S
www.nlmsaudiarabia.com
www.nlmserbian.com
www.nlmshona.com
www.nlmsingapore.com
www.nlmslovakia.com
www.nlmslovene.com
www.nlmsolomon.com
www.nlmsouthafrica.com
www.nlmspain.com
www.nlmspanish.com
www.nlmsrilanka.com
www.nlmsuriname.com
www.nlmswahili.com
www.nlmswaziland.com
www.nlmsweden.com
www.nlmswiss.com

T
www.nlmtagalog.com
www.nlmtaiwan.com
www.nlmtamil.com
www.nlmtanzania.com
www.nlmtelugu.com
www.nlmthailand.com
www.nlmtogo.com
www.nlmtonga.com
www.nlmturkey.com

U
www.nlmuganda.com
www.nlmukraine.com
www.nlmurdu.com
www.nlmusa.com

V
www.nlmvenezuela.com
www.nlmvietnam.com

Z
www.nlmzambia.com
www.nlmzimbabwe.com
www.nlmzou.com